D1566255

Sister Republics

Sister Republics

THE ORIGINS OF FRENCH
AND AMERICAN REPUBLICANISM

PATRICE HIGONNET

HARVARD UNIVERSITY PRESS
CAMBRIDGE, MASSACHUSETTS
LONDON, ENGLAND
1988

This book is printed on acid-free paper, and its binding materials
have been chosen for strength and durability.

Library of Congress Cataloging-in-Publication Data

Higonnet, Patrice L. R.
  Sister republics: the origins of French and American
  republicanism / Patrice Higonnet.
    p.   cm.
  Bibliography: p.
  Includes index.
  ISBN 0-674-80982-3 (alk. paper)
    1. United States—Politics and government—Revolution, 1775–1783.
2. United States—History—Revolution, 1775–1783—Social aspects.
3. France—Politics and government—Revolution, 1789–1799.
4. France—History—Revolution, 1789–1799—Social aspects. 5. Republicanism—United States—History—18th century. 6. Republicanism—France—History—18th century. 7. Individualism—Social
aspects—United States—History—18th century. 8. Individualism—
Social aspects—France—History—18th century.   I. Title.
E210.H64   1988   88-880
973.3′1—dc19   CIP

For Margaret Randolph Cardwell and Guy Adams Cardwell

and to the living memory of their revolutionary kinsman
Thomas Jefferson, visionary architect of America's
democratic and promised liberty

Contents

Sister Republics

Every emancipation is a restoration of the human world and of human relationships to man himself.

Marx, *On the Jewish Question*

Republicanism in France and America

THE FRENCH AND AMERICAN REVOLUTIONS have often been juxtaposed. Many of the same people figured in both events, either as actors or as witnesses: the Marquis de Lafayette; Thomas Paine, who wrote *Common Sense* in 1776 and was a deputy to the French Convention in 1792; Gouverneur Morris (no admirer of Tom Paine), who was America's patrician representative in Paris during the Terror; Thomas Jefferson, the most Parisian of the Virginian philosophes; Joel Barlow, a Connecticut "wit," land speculator, and would-be epic poet; the Comte de Saint-Simon, a future utopian socialist, who fought in America's War of Independence; and his fellow officer Count Fersen, an elegant Swedish aristocrat who despised American democracy and, as the lover of Marie Antoinette, organized the unsuccessful flight of the French king to Varennes in 1791. Other, less picturesque aspects have also drawn scholars to compare the two revolutions. The two events embodied many similar principles, to the annoyance of many Americans. John Quincy Adams thought himself on safe ground when he wrote of a conservative pamphlet which he had translated from the German in 1800 that it rescued the American Revolution "from the disgraceful imputation of having proceeded from the same principles as the French."[1] Adams's indignation seems inappropriate. Both revolutions stood for popular sovereignty, nationalism, the rights of man, no taxation without representation, Republicanism, and suspicion of established religion. Many Frenchmen were convinced that

America's achievement was wholly relevant to their own ambitions. Many of the terms and formulations they used were borrowed from America's recent past. Several French institutions and concepts had American precedents, including the Convention, the Committee of Public Safety, federalism, a written constitution, political clubs, paper money, loyalty oaths, and the Declaration of the Rights of Man.

At the same time, of course, the two revolutions, originally so similar, did unfold in strikingly different ways. True, each revolution had a propensity for intolerant moralizing: in a letter written from Paris in 1787, Jefferson concluded that "the tree of liberty must be refreshed from time to time with the blood of patriots and tyrants." Bertrand Barère likewise argued at the trial of Louis XVI in January 1793 that "the tree of liberty can only grow if watered by the blood of kings." But the implications of the two statements were utterly different; in America not a single person—not even King George—was executed for political crimes between 1776 and 1783, whereas the execution of Louis XVI on the Place de la Révolution (now the Place de la Concorde) prefigured the demise not only of his supporters but of his most confirmed enemies during the various phases of the Great Terror of late 1793 and 1794.

THE CENTRAL METHODOLOGICAL PRINCIPLE of this book is that the bewildering events of the two revolutions can be similarly stylized. First, both were the birth throes of new political systems designed to express the importance of individualism in social life. Second, the trajectories of the two events—the one successful, the other not—represent the realization in politics of prerevolutionary social and cultural circumstances. The coherence, or, as it happened, the varying incoherences, of the ways in which the prerevolutionary rights of the one and the many were structured in each society go a long way toward explaining the particular form of revolutionary politics. To emphasize continuities of this kind is not to claim that men are powerless to shape their political destinies: men have free will. But it is also said that the sins of fathers are often visited on the children.

The first theme (individualism) is easier to follow than the second. From 1789 to 1791 French legislators made individualism the new pivot of social and economic life. Guilds, "combinations," corporate entities, and associations of all kinds were declared illegal. In business or in politics each individual, each man especially, was to stand alone. No institutions of any kind, social or political, could be allowed to separate the citizen from the nation. The state withdrew from society. Even the right of Jacobin clubs to offer collective petitions to the French National Assembly was brought into question, as was the legality of the clubs themselves. Economic relations were "depoliticized." Some people might sell their labor; others would want to buy it. The liberal state would enforce these agreements, but it would not venture "beyond the four corners" of such contracts. It would have nothing to say about the nature of private dealings. "Caveat emptor" became the first principle of social life.

But four years later, in Robespierre's dictatorial Republic of Virtue, these policies were in many respects reversed: individualism was narrowly restrained, especially in the political domain. The role of the state was dramatically broadened. Wages and prices were set by law. Foreign trade and the production of weapons were nationalized. Grain and many raw materials were requisitioned. Peasants were forced to sell their produce for paper money. Due process and the rule of law were suspended. These drastic steps not only looked back to the worst aspects of arbitrary, monarchic rule, but they also foreshadowed modern totalitarianism.

The American Revolution followed an inverse trajectory. In 1776, in the name of a commonly held right that was inalienable, historical, and perhaps also natural, a united and virtuous people favored by Providence denounced the corruption of a foreign monarch. But a mere decade later, in 1787, American republicanism was suddenly recast in a more individualist and pluralist form. The legacy of America's recent past was not denied: the sovereignty of the one and indivisible American people was in fact reasserted. Americans remained convinced that theirs was an exemplary and fraternal state: "The preservation of the holy fire is confided to us by the world," wrote Jefferson in 1810, "and the sparks which will emanate from it will ever serve to rekindle it in other quarters of the globe." But at the same time a federal political system of checks and balances was instituted that differed strikingly from the government of the revolutionary confederacy.

The American case for the separation of powers was argued in a new and altogether different way. Before 1776 colonial Americans had assumed that the best way to preserve liberty was by balancing the sovereign powers of commons, lords, and king as history had shown to be desirable. After 1776 the founders of the new Republic set out to preserve the liberty of each citizen by scientifically balancing within the single sovereignty of the nation the varying responsibilities of many different institutions: senators (two from each state, regardless of size), congressmen elected in proportion of population, a president elected by the whole people but through an electoral college organized by states, a cabinet appointed by the president with senatorial consent, and judges similarly chosen—all of them responsible to an indivisible people. In this new and variegated institutional context, soon to be modified by a bill of rights, the institutional space of social pluralism and of the individual was broadly defined. By contrast, in revolutionary France the all-encompassing General Will of a unitary state might or might not overlap with the majority's will. The two revolutions, then, developed as mirror opposites: the centrality of individualism that triumphed in the one was badly shaken in the other.

The second theme of this book is that these varying political developments were in no small part implied by the antecedent social histories of the two nations. Although many of Britain's American colonies had been originally designed as prescriptive communities— as highly structured societies where individual endeavor was closely supervised or distrusted—they were soon restructured economically and socially along more individualistic lines. Colonial Americans ruthlessly turned to private profit. But before independence the social individualism of the colonies could not find expression in politics. Even during the Revolution, Americans were convinced that civic virtue mattered far more than self-interest. The distant subjects of King George acted in one way socially; but they thought of themselves politically in another way—as English restorationists reaching for a "golden past." Their political sensibility was still determined by an inherited mode of thinking that was even then being updated by their English cousins. Until America became a nation, colonial Anglo-Americans were unable to bring forth a political culture of their own. But between 1776 and 1787 Americans did move forward with stunning speed to forge a new political consciousness that resolved the tensions of their historical experience and reconciled their inherited ideological, religious, or communitarian nostalgias with the practical realities of American social life. That sustaining compromise remains today in transmuted form, the foundation of both America's civil religion and its pragmatic (and forever unfulfilled) republican and Jeffersonian liberal idealism. This mixed doctrine came into being during colonial times when free wheeling capitalism was grafted to the transcendental definition of self and the religiously rooted memory of Americans as a free and chosen people.

Prerevolutionary France was a social and ideological inversion of the thirteen colonies. While on the western shores of the Atlantic a capitalist society spoke through a communitarian rhetoric of virtue, in France the reverse was true. Though strongly attached to an anti-individualist corporate ethos, many members of the French propertied elite of liberal nobles and rich non-nobles mistakenly thought of themselves as Enlightenment liberals. And while American society was fundamentally individualistic in its social forms—for example, in its acceptance of capitalistic practice—even though it remained communitarian in its "superstructural" political forms, the enlightened subjects of the French king turned that relationship upside down. Theoretically won over to individualistic values, they nevertheless remained corporatist in their hearts.

The reason for this imbalance between French fact and fiction was the decline of the traditional institutions of French corporate life. On the eve of the Revolution the monarchy, the church, the courts, and most of the economic and social *corps,* or corporations, that structured French urban and rural life were on the verge of collapse. In the ensuing void, the French apologists of possessive, or propertied individualism were uniquely situated to secure an "ideologized" audience, both propertied and popular. But their initial success, though made more palatable by the universalist ideology in which the defense of their possessive program was set in 1789, could not be sustained.

The new individualistic convictions of the French did not run deep: individualism was not a generally accepted principle of social action in France. In 1789 both rich and poor were far more hostile to the idea of possessive individualism than has ordinarily been supposed. The institutional apparatus of corporatism had decayed, but the longing for collectively sanctioned norms was still strong. The prerevolutionary commitment of the French to a politicized ideology of Promethean individualism was shallow, even if French men and women, taken one by one, feared the anti-individualist arbitrariness of the state and despised the oppressive power of their more privileged neighbors. This discontinuity between the proper-tied elite's explicit desire to institutionalize individualism and the masses' implicit desire to limit the economic effects of individualism played a crucial role in the French Revolution.

In reorganizing French social and political institutions between 1789 and 1791, the successful revolutionary deputies of the new National Assembly—most of them bourgeois, many of them liberal nobles, and nearly all of them propertied—followed the principle of individualism more closely than had ever been done in any society. This first, ill-fated political arrangement soon collapsed: a relentless progression runs from the unbending institutionalization of the rights of the one by the liberal, propertied Feuillants (1789–1791) to the countervailing reassertions (after 1792) of the rights of the many by antiliberal dissenters of all kinds, some of them ultraconservative and others communistic.

On the right, at first fumblingly and then more coherently after 1800, traditionalist reactionaries rejected capitalistic individualism as a cultural value. They proclaimed instead the integrative, philo-monarchic virtues of hierarchic ruralism, patriarchal familialism, and Catholic organicism. On the far left at much the same time (from 1791–92 to 1796), the urban crowds, the celebrated plebeian sansculottes and their spokesmen, many of whom were women, also rejected economic individualism together with its political equivalent—parliamentary liberalism. They drifted instead toward a more socially deterministic and politically constraining creed of communitarian property and politics. This leftist counterethic re-mained inchoate at first, but it was conceptualized in 1795–96 by Gracchus Babeuf, the first modern dictatorial and revolutionary communist, much admired in later times by Marx and Lenin.

No less significant was the evolution of the mainstream, bour-geois republicans who wrested control of the French state from the

Feuillants in late 1791. From late in 1792 to 1794, during two of the most important years in the political history of Western society, the paradoxical reaction of the most articulate wing of the revolutionary and propertied French elite—the Jacobins—to the breakdown of the individualist revolution was to strike an even *more* daring bargain with "le peuple." From late 1791 to late 1793, at least, these bourgeois radicals, drugged by their own universalistic words, strove to resolve the dysfunctions of their political world view by aggravating its initial imbalance. They hoped that propertied and unpropertied alike would hold together as citizens of a fraternal and ideologically radical Republic that nonetheless respected inherited differences of wealth. The bourgeois Jacobins taken one by one did not give up on possessive individualism (they were keen purchasers, for example, of former church lands); but collectively they managed to combine their desire for other people's property and labor with an increasingly meaningless communitarian rhetoric. Much of their success derived from the expression of their private greed in an ideological context of universalist egalitarianism, a mix that found echoes in the unconscious atavisms of the new nation, many of whose citizens were frustrated anti-individualists.

This second, contradictory, Jacobin arrangement was bound to collapse as well. In 1791–92 the poor had rejected the Feuillants' assertion of propertied individualism as a central political and social value; in 1793 they moved forward once again. In response, the shrinking phalanx of Jacobins who followed Robespierre stuck to their guns and in 1793–94 asserted an ever more "virtuous" and tyrannical political equality that satisfied the communitarian nostalgia for fraternal forms. But this was their undoing. When in the late summer and early fall of 1793 the sansculottes, availing themselves of the opening given them by the Jacobins' universalistic ideology, made still more demanding material claims on the propertied elite, the revolutionary bourgeoisie realized how dangerous their rhetoric had become. By the summer of 1794, the impracticality of Robespierre's bridging solution had become plain even to its most faithful advocates: his rhetoric had become unacceptable both to the sansculottes, whose poverty had eroded their good will, and to the propertied Jacobins, whose fear of the poor had increased. Then too, the terrorist aspect of Jacobinism was repellent; although violence was endemic in eighteenth-century France, the bloodletting of the Great Terror in the late spring and summer of 1794 horrified everyone, including most Jacobins, who, taken individually, were decent members of the middle classes. In July a bewildered and incorruptible Robespierre was overthrown in a palace coup staged by sleazy parliamentary conspirators, with the assent of a national Convention whose faithful representative Robespierre had been for the past two years.

After 1795, during the period of the Directory, the contradictory ideals of French Jacobinism unraveled further, and by 1799 revolutionary French politics could no longer be managed by anyone. In America, the Constitution of 1787 was universally accepted, and the tension between communitarian rhetoric and individualistic fact was resolved. In France, the troublesome ambiguities of the pre-revolutionary and early revolutionary periods, which had proved to be irreconcilable, found a new outlet in either collectivist Babouvism or antiliberal and Catholic royalism. Beset with enemies and distrusted by its own supporters, French republicanism fell apart. Whereas Robespierre had been violently overthrown in 1794, like the monarchy in 1792, in 1799 the republican regime simply collapsed. Bonaparte's suspension of politics on 18 Brumaire was arranged by the leaders of the Directory themselves and was accepted with relief by nearly everyone, from former republican terrorists, such as Fouché, to propertied liberals such as Benjamin Constant, and Catholic traditionalists, such as Chateaubriand.

In 1789 General George Washington, more widely respected in America than General Bonaparte ever was in France, chose to become a modern Cincinnatus—America's first constitutional president. In 1804 the Corsican upstart, the man on horseback whose rise to power Burke had predicted in 1790, appeared as a romanized emperor, one of the greatest political mountebanks of all times, Napoleon I.

Alexis de Tocqueville was right in saying that the result of the French Revolution was to strengthen the French state; but his explanation of why that consolidation occurred is incomplete. In Tocqueville's view, Napoleon's rise to power was caused by Frenchmen's "un-English" inability to rule themselves. This sensible institutional reading does not go far enough. The catastrophic failure of the Revolution did indeed give faltering bureaucratic centralism a new lease on life in France. Nonetheless, the failure of the Revolution had more to do with the increasingly contradictory world view of the Jacobin elite than with the French nation's lack of political experience before 1789. It was the breakdown of the revolutionary synthesis of virtuous universalism and possessive, materialist individualism, rather than the inherited configuration of governmental structures, that led to the Napoleonic authoritarian recasting of the French state.

In any case, the failure of French revolutionary republicanism in 1799 was complete, and it had a critical effect not just on subsequent French political history but also on French social structures. First, the political failure of the Revolution set limits on the social message of French middle-class republicanism. In the words of Dr. Johnson, the prospect of hanging wonderfully concentrates the minds of men. This was the effect that the events of 1794 had on the French propertied elite, who wrongly supposed that they had come close to hanging. The nineteenth-century definition of individualism became even more strict than it had been in the eighteenth century: a great distance separates even the old Jefferson from the young Guizot. As Marc Richir has quipped, it was not the French bourgeoisie that made the French Revolution; it was the failure of the Revolution which made the French bourgeoisie. A wide gulf divides the avuncular and open-minded prerevolutionary elite from the avaricious and philistine bourgeoisie of the nineteenth century, which even such socially privileged writers as Constant, Stendhal, Baudelaire, and Flaubert instinctively hated.

Second, by a process of reaction the French Revolution helped create a new French working class. The same practical failure of the compensatory, rhetorical Jacobin ideal explains much of modern *popular* class consciousness in France. On the right and center of the political spectrum, fear of the plebs hardened many bourgeois republican hearts in the nineteenth century. On the far left, the June days of 1848 and the slaughter of May 1871 served as catalysts for the crystallization in France, as in no other country, of modern socialist, communist, and anarchist theories of permanent revolution and class war.

In America, the radical Whig and secularized Puritan communitarian sensibility of prerevolutionary times survived (however feebly) in an age of high capitalism because it was transformed. Its legacy is still an important part of the hopeful American world view—at once Jeffersonian, democratic, genuinely liberal, and individualistic.

In France, a comparable if differently accented compromise was destroyed. The failure of its revolution narrowed the scope of its republican tradition. It generated a hostile class consciousness on the left and exacerbated traditionalist resistance on the right. For nearly two hundred years after 1793, French bourgeois republicans struggled on two fronts, as social conservatives against the poor and as progressive ideologues against the right. That double legacy is more blunted today than it has ever been; but it has affected the whole breadth of modern French history. The antirepublican Vichy regime of Marshal Pétain, for example, with its deep and disgracing complicity in Nazi and French fascist schemes of racial extermination, cannot be explained without reference to the lasting hatred of the French Revolution, which had no counterpart in America. As Karl Marx puts it, men make their history, but they do not make it as they please: "The traditions of all the dead generations," he wrote, "weigh like a nightmare on the brains of the living."[2]

I

Forced Community and Transcendental Individualism in America's First Colonies

Louis Hartz, in a self-deprecating description of his magisterial book *The Liberal Tradition in America,* explained that its organizing principle had been "the storybook truth about American history: that our nation was settled by men who fled from the feudal and clerical oppressions of the Old World." American political culture, he thought, has at its center "this fixed, dogmatic liberalism of a liberal way of life."[1] America has neither a feudal past nor a socialist tradition: "The hidden origin of socialist thought everywhere in the West is to be found in the Feudal ethos. The ancien régime inspires Rousseau; both inspire Marx." Some pieces of our national history, Hartz readily admitted, do not fit that mold; but these divergences (like Puritanism) were for Hartz no more than "the liabilities of any large generalization, danger points but not insuperable barriers."[2] John Locke is, as it were, America's patron saint. Indeed, Locke's thought, Hartz wrote, is "so basic that we have not recognized his significance."[3] It was Hartz's brilliant achievement to delineate Locke's critical influence.

My own "large generalization" is of a different order. It does grant that in its practice colonial American society had by 1700 been restructured around the principle of rampant individualism, just as Hartz has argued. But my interpretation also posits that the American colonies were conceived in a different, often more communitarian, spirit, one that, though transmuted over the years, continues to infuse Americans' perception of their society and of its cultural or political purpose.

EACH COLONIAL SETTLEMENT presents a variant of that anti-individualist regard for the public good. The precise purposes of the settlers and their backers were always different. But a broad pattern of communitarian or at least collective endeavor is everywhere visible.

This driving concern for organized action was a rule of thumb because the English, like other Europeans, thought it to be a practical necessity. America was far away: it took weeks or months to cross the ocean, which until the end of the eighteenth century was all but impassable during the winter months. The eastern seaboard of North America, today the center of world culture, was then no more than the furthermost rim of western Europe.

With the advantage of hindsight, we can see that in 1560, when Englishmen began to think of overseas settlement in earnest, Europe had already begun its long march from parochial and state-sponsored economic growth toward world domination and modern social forms—which can be conveniently subsumed under the rubrics of industrial capitalism and secular rationality. We can see also that by 1600 the maritime powers of Western Europe (Portugal, Spain, France, Holland, and Britain) were well on their way to achieving imperial suzerainty in the global economic system. Spain's victory over the Turkish fleet at Lepanto in 1578 initiated the long sequence of Christian victories that continued through the successful defense of Vienna against the Turks in 1683 to the breakup of the Ottoman Empire in 1918. Portugal's naval supremacy in the Indian Ocean presaged the conquest of India in the late eighteenth century and the European powers' domination over China from the Opium War of 1839 up to the Communist revolution of 1948.

In 1600, however, what Europeans saw when they looked westward were the hardships and risks of transatlantic voyages and the need for social cooperation. The difficulties of creating and sustaining a settlement three thousand miles from a home base seemed materially overwhelming, and with good cause: from Roanoke to the abortive French Protestant settlements in Brazil, the American Atlantic coastline was studded with colonial failures. The edge of technological superiority that Europeans could bring to bear on native peoples was narrow and fortuitous. In the Americas, disease was the whites' best weapon. Europeans were not medically able to withstand contagions endemic to Africa until the late nineteenth century; but in North America it was the native Americans who succumbed to European diseases such as smallpox, typhoid, tuberculosis, and diphtheria. (When the Pilgrims and Puritans arrived in the 1620s and 1630s, for example, the tribes who lived in what would soon be called New England had just been decimated by an epidemic.) Without the immunities that they had gained through centuries of unsanitary urban life, Europeans could not have conquered the Americas when they did.

The lamentable story of the Jamestown colony, founded in 1607 and dissolved in 1624, best illustrates the frailty of early English settlements. It also reveals the first organizing principles of early colonial social life and the cultural response engendered by colonial failure.

Incapable of growing enough food on a site where the water supply was badly polluted, the Jamestown colony soon faced both starvation and disease. In fact, some settlers did starve, and a few of them became cannibals. Others followed their natural bent toward banditry. They tried first to demand and then to steal food from the Indians, whose ability to grow crops outstripped their own. Reprisals soon followed. In 1622, 347 of the colonists were killed in a surprise raid. Life during these "starving times" was intolerable. Between 1618 and 1624 Jamestown's population did not rise above 1500 although 3700 migrants went there. The persistence of the colonists in the face of such difficulties gives us some insight into the misery of the poor in Britain, where about one-third of the population were propertyless wanderers, as well as into the character of the colonists.

The first reaction of the shareholders of the English Jamestown company (a private corporation that, typically, had financed the venture without state help and whose owners were personally liable for any debts the company might incur) was to tighten discipline. For the next decade Jamestown was run not just as a community but as a martial colony, each settler holding military rank. Settlers did not live in private homes but in barracks. Work was obligatory;

private property was restrained; and the Anglican state religion went unchallenged. Organized effort was meant to make up for technological weakness.

These efforts were supported by the previous experience of British colonial undertakings. The strict anti-individualism of the Jamestown colony had a practical precedent in Ireland, which had been militarily subdued and organized shortly before, and which had been described as a "blueprint for America." Early Virginian municipal incorporations, for example, were modeled on the Ulster "plantations" where royal officialdom provided the nucleus of further settlement.[4]

Most striking, however, in the organization of the British North American settlements was the implicit cultural assumption that British colonies *ought* to be organized as highly structured communities. The private motivation of ambitious fund raisers and participants alike could hardly have been more individualistic. Their earnest and invariable hope was to turn a quick profit at the expense of defenseless natives. Nonetheless, their cultural assumptions concerning the nature of the public good were cast in another mold. The colonial mind set of the English in 1600 was in this respect quite similar to that of the French or the Spanish; all felt that structured and communitarian action rather than individualism was the right note to strike abroad. It is revealing that the English planners of seventeenth-century settlements persisted in their anti-individualist cultural assumption long after individualism had triumphed as a social value in Britain's earliest colonies, and at home as well. Georgia, founded quite late (1732), was still set in a collective mode that was mercantilist, philanthropic, slaveless, and state-directed. The rights of Georgia's Indians were to be respected by the supervised and "honest convicts" who would be deported there.

Most bizarre in this respect was the sponsorship by John Locke, an arch-individualist at home, of feudalism as an appropriate social framework for the projected settlement in the Carolinas. The vestigial power of corporate longing is underlined by the backward-looking and involuted nature of Locke's project, with its hierarchic ranking of margraves and caciques, all of whom were to be members of a "Council of Nobles." This deistical empiricist had, it seems, two measures: one for the rest of the world, and one for colonial America. In his *Treatise on Civil Government* of 1690, a bible for liberals on two continents, which was translated into French in 1724, Locke had reflected on what the state of nature might have been: "In the beginning, all the world was America." Modern Americans, still savages of a kind, remained in exceptional need of structured administration.

Individualism, however, soon proved to be the better solution to the problems of the American colonists. In the middle and southern colonies, the neofeudal values of the founders were honored mostly in the breach, except where constraints were very light, as in Pennsylvania, where the quitrent due to William Penn and his successors was little more than nominal. Only in New England did community as a social ideal prove to be ideologically and culturally durable, and even there a dramatic and poignant struggle took place between community-oriented values and antinomian individualism.

Seventeenth-century American Puritans, although in many ways individualist innovators, thought of themselves as communitarian-minded traditionalists. The Puritans were earnest, moral, and often propertied men and women whose religious faith enabled them, first, to wrench themselves as individuals out of a familiar culture, and second, to restrain momentarily the scope of individualism as a cultural value in their new society. Puritan solidarity has aptly been described as "an anachronistic [and] tribalist instinct."[5] It longed nostalgically for older social forms, for a golden and selfless past.

In its spirit, Puritan society in America was intensely communitarian. It was conceived as a set of interlocking and binding entities, both spiritual and physical: "Wee must be knit together in the worke as one man," said Winthrop aboard the *Arbella* in 1630, "always haveing before our eyes our Commission and Community in the worke, our Community as members of the same body, soe shall we keepe the unitie of the spirit in the bond of peace." Puritans identified the central malaise of the human condition as man's self-seeking will: "The very names of Self and Own," wrote one of them, "should sound in the watchful Christian's ear as very terrible, wakening words, that are next to the names of sin and Satan";[6] and in the next century Jonathan Edwards was still avidly searching for earthly and moral means of self-denial, because "great instances of mortification . . . are deep wounds, given to the body of sin." In seventeenth-century New England, damnation and social disorder were thought to be the necessary consequence of private willfulness: "For if each man may do what is good in his owne eyes," Thomas Hooker explained in 1648, "so that none may crosse him or controll him by any power; there must of necessity follow the distraction and desolation of the whole." The aim of the Holy Commonwealth, explained Richard Baxter, was to punish vice and reward virtue.[7] Each sinner carried within himself or herself the salvation of the whole, but the sinner might also think that his or her single fault would with the devil's help bring everyone down in general disgrace: as Tryal Pore repentantly put it, "By this sin, I have not only donne what I can to pull down judgment from the Lord on myself, but also on the place where I live." Because he feared the inclination of his own heart, the Puritan willingly—or so ran the theory—submitted his will to that of his more saintly neighbors. In the words of the convenant of 1667 of the First Church in Beverly, the New Englander agreed "to submitt to the order, discipline and government of Christ in this his Church . . . and to the brotherly watch of fellow members."[8] Mankind's capacity for self-deception was nearly boundless. Christians needed to subordinate themselves to God and others, the two being in some sense coterminous in a Society of Saints. Believers were required to trust one another, because they could not trust themselves.

Of the necessary institutions of communitarian fellowship (or constraint) in early New England, the first was the Puritan family. Unlike early Virginia or French Canada, which attracted young, restless, and unmarried men, the Great Migration of the 1630s to Massachusetts Bay (like the German migration of the next century) was made up of families. Single migrants to Boston were sometimes denied permission to remain. Married men who refused to arrange for the migration to New England of their families ran the risk of being sent back home. Initially, "solitary living" was within varying limits forbidden by law in all the New England colonies, and in Connecticut (in theory at least) until 1750. Young men, and young women especially, were expected to form new families when they left their parents' homestead. It was families that were expected to carry forward and enforce the message of the Puritan covenant. Puritan thought and action did not envisage that drastic separation of the private (that is to say, the familial and the feminine) from the public (the active and the masculine) which became characteristic of modern liberal or "bourgeois" culture during the middle decades of the nineteenth century. As Benjamin Wadsworth tellingly asserted, without family care the labor of Magistrates and "Ministers for the Reformation and propagating of religion is likely to be in a great measure unsuccessful. It's much to be feared (that) young persons won't much mind what's said by the Ministers in publick, if they are not instructed at home, nor will they much regard good Laws made by civil Authority, if they are not well counsel'd and governed at home."[9]

The Puritan family was a chosen theater of self-criticism. Confessions and conversions were familial and public events. The family was an instrument of rigid socialization: dutiful and self-righteous Puritan parents studiously spied out in their children early manifestations of intolerable willfulness. Lurid descriptions have come down to us of the struggles of will between Puritan sons and fathers. Sexuality was strictly watched and strictly repressed in adolescents. Though intensely respectable Puritan gentlemen might write sexually explicit letters to their wives, sexuality outside the familial unit was anathema. (As late as 1807, an unmarried mother was fined in Plymouth for not being married.) Masturbation, a subcategory of "lewd, lascivious, wanton behavior," was a legal offense punished by whipping.[10] (In France, by contrast, this form of "onanism," although theologically culpable, was never grounds for civil punishment by the courts.)[11] Other forms of extrafamilial sexual irregularity were drastically punished as well. Thomas Granger of Duxbury "being about 16 or 17 years of age," was executed in 1642 for "buggery," defined in this instance as a sexual act involving animals. His death, remarked Governor Bradford of Plymouth colony, was "a very sad spectakle."[12]

Early New England families and households were also durable economic units. The difficulties that faced single parents made remarriage a practical if relatively infrequent necessity since New England, unlike the Chesapeake area, or Europe for that matter, was an unusually healthy place. Life expectancy in this part of

North America was long. Death in childbirth or childhood was relatively rare. It was unusual for New England wills to involve heirs who were not kin to the deceased. The physical vitality of its members contributed to the moral vitality of the Puritan family.

The next circle of public good was the town, which was small enough to allow constant and reciprocal observation: the average population of a New England town was under four hundred in 1650, and little more than eleven hundred in most places even in 1770. With the passage of time, the limits of the town often came to overlap those of the extended family: mid-eighteenth-century Southampton, Massachusetts, comprised eighteen Pomeroy families, eleven Clarks, eighteen Searls, six Strongs, and thirteen Clapps. The Puritans' belief that "a family [is] a little commonwealth, and a commonwealth is a greate family" could often be construed quite literally. Revealingly, it was the town authorities who stood in loco parentis to orphaned minors.

Everywhere in New England (and especially in Connecticut and Rhode Island) the town was a fundamental judicial and political matrix—one that the original settlers were most eager to maintain because their religious enemies, the Stuart monarchs, were working hard to curtail local privilege. In the Bay colony, only residents could serve as delegates of a town to the provincial General Court at Boston. The local town meeting appointed the minister and set the terms of his contract. Towns also regulated the morals of their inhabitants formally as well as informally: from 1675 to the 1720s (traces of the institution were still extant in the 1750s), the task of maintaining social discipline, first in Massachusetts and later in some other New England colonies as well, was often assigned to "tythingmen," whose task was "dilligently [to] inspect" ten families and to watch for "all Saboath breakers and disorderly tipsters."[13] Unnecessary Sunday travel was still a punishable offense in Worcester in 1800.

Towns were also religious congregations. The first churches (or meetinghouses) were fortified buildings, set in the center of the settlement and laid out according to a particular design. The interiors were not elongated spaces dominated by a distant altar, but were square in shape and focused on the pulpit of the minister, who was both pedagogue and scholar. Although Puritan rites of passage (weddings especially) were private rather than public events, much of public life revolved around interminable Sunday services, where the disposition of pews and benches reflected the order of the local hierarchy. Puritan life, in the words of Perry Miller (the founding father of modern American Puritan studies), "was centered upon a corporate and communal ceremony, upon the oral delivery of a lecture."[14]

Towns had important economic functions. For a decade or so, settlers were required by law to live within half a mile of a meetinghouse. At first, in places such as Sudbury, the agricultural cycle of planting and harvesting was regulated in part by communal decision. Grants of land to individuals were made by the towns, which had been given this power by the General Court.[15] Towns at first used their power to deny the admission or "confluence of many ill and doubtfull persons." The criteria of allocation varied according to different principles: need, merit, or rank. In the day-to-day business of life, towns also enjoyed a high degree of political and financial autonomy. Taxes were apportioned by the General Court not to individuals but to the towns. Poor relief was also a local responsibility; hence the expulsions or "warnings-out" of the non-indigenous poor. Towns were also required by law to maintain elementary schools, an important function in the Bible-reading commonwealth.

Above the family and the town was another instrument of community, the province. De facto, the provincial capital was the fountainhead of authority in Massachusetts. For reasons that are not clear, the charter granted to the Puritans by the king in 1629 did not require the shareholders of the Massachusetts Bay Company to reside in London, as was ordinarily the case. The parameters of provincial economic and cultural life were set in Boston, as were the definitions of religious doctrine. It was a provincial fiat that brought Harvard College into being in 1636; and the "philosophic" community of the province rested on the common educational experience of Puritan ministers in that first American college. The right education was intended to guarantee provincial ideological conformity, and for many decades it did work to that end. Many important social rituals in Massachusetts were provincewide, such as fast days (which were occasions of public and collective reflection), election days, militia training days, and, in a different way, the Harvard Commencement.

Important also to an understanding of the New England Puritan communitarian world view are two informal institutions: the Puritans' shared conception of New England politics and their sense of religious mission.

The Puritan state was conceived as the visible, divinely blessed expression of the settlers' common will and God's stated purpose. It presupposed the harmonious cohabitation of the ruler and the ruled. Politics was an extension of religious conformity. In both Massachusetts and New Haven, only the truly orthodox "visible saints" were allowed to vote. Political institutions and the decisions they produced were by nature "such as are commanded and ordained by God." Precisely what that injunction meant was often unclear, but it implied the rulers' general recognition of the "rights" and wishes of the assembled people. In the New England view, "the people [were] not for the Rulers, but the Rulers for the people, to minister to their welfare." The need for periodic provincewide elections was assumed. Taxation also presupposed advice, if not consent. At the same time, however, it was assumed that the ruled community, as Governor Winthrop explained in 1645, should "quietly and cheerfully submit unto that authority which is set over you, in all the administrations of it, for your good." In this holistic context, it may be added, the formalistic distinctions between the judiciary and the executive were of no more interest than the precise conditions of the right to vote.

The state was not in the Church, and yet it was in some sense of the Church. The civil magistrates interpreted God's will. The minister of God comforted the governors, who in turn sought the advice of the ministers. This was a political arrangement that obviously presupposed the existence of consensus and the absence of divisive cleavages between rich and poor, men and women, parents and children, the ruler and the ruled. In their consensual theorizing Puritan thinkers were hardly atypical; William Penn in his political fantasizing made the same assumption: "[We] composed the frame of government," he wrote, "to the great end of all government—to support power in reverence with the people, and to secure the people from the abuse of power."[16]

The strongest communitarian force in Massachusetts Bay hinged, of course, on the Puritans' particular sense of religious apartness. Theirs was not a "missionary creed" but it was decidedly exemplary. New England was—as an independent America would again become in the following century—"a Commonwealth erected in a wildernesse," a second Israel: "The Lord will be our God," wrote Governor Winthrop, "and delight to dwell among us." As one of the elect put it in the deeply immodest tone that comes to men who see their fate in epic terms, "God sifted a whole nation to bring choice grain into the wilderness." Sacvan Bercovitch has shown that Christology was the mode in which Puritan literators framed the lives of their mythologized heroes; similarly, the story of biblical Israel was the model for New England as a whole. Theirs was emphatically to be "a citty on the hill." When they left Great Britain, the Puritans did not think that they had abandoned Protestantism in its darkest hour. They were mindful of the Thirty Years War, which was setting Catholics and Protestants at each other's throats in Germany and throughout the rest of Europe, oftentimes to the advantage of popish superstition. "The Lord hath . . . sent this People to . . . this Wilderness," wrote one of the first settlers, "to proclaime to all Nations the neere approach of the most wonderful workes that ever the Sonnes of men saw."[17]

The Church did not coerce membership: indeed, it specifically excluded those who were not worthy of belonging to it. Nonetheless, the social and political life of the colony presupposed a general and "voluntary" participation in established religious life. Exceptions could not be entertained. Three Quakers were hung in Boston in 1651 for their antinomianism. The Puritans were first and foremost a community of saints which had been touched by divine grace. They were united as a people to God in a Church: "When we enter into Church covenant," wrote one of them, "we bind ourselves to God, and to our Brethren, to walke with God and one another, according to the rules of divine politie." Not surprisingly, Puritan pastors thought it their duty closely to supervise their flocks: "A pastor that can see sin prevailing among his people," wrote Cotton Mather in 1704, "but is afraid of reproving it, lest he lose his Gain from his Quarter, he may call himself a Shepherd, but God calls him a Dumb Dog."

Seemingly divisive social hierarchies were included in God's order only because they were the necessary gradations that articulated
a single cosmic whole. Sumptuary laws and the uneven distribution
of town lands—more being given to the rich than to the poor—
were for the Puritans conserving rather than excluding statements.
The ties were strong that bound all early New Englanders to one
another and to God: "We do *all* commit our cause unto the Lord,"
wrote John Higginson, "in the *same way* as we do *every one* commit
unto him the Salvation of our Soules."[18]

The Puritans had a fixed, premodern cosmology, a syncretic and
nostalgic doctrine that tried to make sense of many divergent Western traditions. They were heirs of Augustine and the early Christian
Church, but they also embraced many pre-Christian, Stoic principles. Puritanism attempted to reconcile reason and affection, logic
and rhetoric, the natural and supernatural, classical and modern
physics, philosophy and theology. Functionally, as we now know,
Puritanism was the prologue to rationalistic individualism. But
before 1660 its consciously stated goals were altogether different.
The Puritans thought of themselves as a single people. They believed in the need for controls of all kinds. They thought, as Aquinas
had, that goods should be sold at their "just price": "A man may not
sell above the current price and as another would give for it, if he
had occasion to use it," wrote John Cotton in his *Abstract of the
Laws of New England (Moses His Judicials)*.

MASSACHUSETTS PROVINCE was a limiting communitarian
case, but in one way or another—institutionally, culturally, or
economically—all of Britain's North American colonies were conceived as collective endeavors. Invariably this original communitarianism could not be sustained. The transition from that first
mode of social and cultural life to more individualistic arrangements
is most interesting in New England, but it is most obvious in the
Chesapeake colonies.

The character of the first immigrants to settle the Chesapeake area
was in itself a necessary and sufficient cause for decay. Many of the
original settlers of Virginia had been stylish and well-connected
men. Disappointed in their expectation of gold and swift profit,
soon these first migrants either left or, more commonly, simply

perished. Of the 104 settlers who arrived in Jamestown in mid-1607, only about 40 were still there in January 1608. Their successors were for the most part undisciplined and even desperate people, many of whom came to Virginia as indentured servants. Of the approximately 140,000 seventeenth-century migrants to the Chesapeake area, only about one-third had managed to finance their own trips, and nearly all of the unmarried women came as servants.[19] These people wanted little more than to better themselves, which in the seventeenth century they ordinarily did, especially after the 1670s when the mortality rate dropped steeply.

Because many of the migrants were unfree and the climate was unhealthy, the Chesapeake area was conducive neither ideologically nor physically to communitarian family life. Although the Virginia Company took care to export women to America after 1619, the sex ratio in the Chesapeake and southern colonies remained unbalanced for a century. Bachelors were common; spinsters were rare, and so were durable families. (The average duration of a marriage was about seven years.) The creation in the Chesapeake colonies of a new institution, the Orphans' Court, reflects this familial chaos. It proved very difficult to transpose traditional English ways to the middle and southern colonies. Although familial values were a critical part of the Puritan way, that was not so in early colonial Virginia. Primogeniture never did mean much there, as became obvious when this feudal pattern of inheritance was abolished in revolutionary times.

Economics, compounded by geography, was another irresistible centrifugal force, especially in the southern provinces. Tobacco, first exported in 1617, was the mainstay of Virginia. In the absence of metallic specie, Virginian settlers and proprietors alike favored an export-oriented, income-producing, staple economy over an autarkic subsistence economy. Colonies were expected to pay their way and to turn a profit, and it soon became obvious that only tobacco growing could provide that advantage. Even laborers spurned other tasks: in 1623 it was already being said of other kinds of work that "nothinge is done in anie one of them but all is vanished into smoke."[20] The military "Lawes" of 1622 were repealed; the company created a system of headrights, private plantations, and hundreds, whose owners turned to the energetic cultivation of the new crop. Within twenty years, one million pounds of tobacco were being exported annually from Virginia, and by 1670 more than fifteen million pounds. The cultivation of this crop was labor-intensive. It also impoverished the soil rapidly, and planters had to move on every three or four years. Booms and busts succeeded each other in dizzying succession, as often happens in economies that are both capitalist and monocultural. Planters were constantly on the move looking for cheap land. Virginians soon created the cult of the "big house," but in actuality their familial seats were peripatetic.

Social individualism had a geographic rationale as well. Of necessity, Virginians lived far apart from one another: land along the ocean shore of tidewater Virginia was (as its name implies) low-lying, and the coast line was jagged. Meandering waterways were numerous, but roads were few. The typical ambition of a Virginian, wrote Robert Beverley at the end of the seventeenth century, was "of being Lord of a vast, tho' unimproved Territory with the Advantage of many rivers which afforded a commodious Road of shipping at every Man's Door [but was destructive of] any Rule and Order." Settlers' lands were so widely spaced that outside of Georgia (a latecomer in any case), the county rather than the township was the institutional matrix of southern life. The white Virginian's ability to handle a gun, much admired by European visitors, further complicated the business of government: "How miserable that man is," mourned Sir William Berkeley, "that Governes a People wher six parts of seaven at least are Poore, Endebted, Discontented, and Armed." Parishes were so vast that regular church attendance was impossible. Virginian ministers were poorly trained, poorly paid, and few in number. Lay readers were common; in 1662 only one in five of the province's parishes had a resident cleric. The keeping of birth and death records became in Virginia the purview of the courts rather than of the church, an arrangement that would only be adopted in France in 1789.

In this social and economic free-for-all, the strong did well and the weak tolerably so; the very weak were gradually enslaved. The first blacks were brought to Virginia in 1619, though they may not have become slaves until 1640. On Virginia's "eastern shore," free blacks were competitive participants in the life of the colony. The labor contracts of white indentured servants may even have served as a pattern for the subsequent enslavement of blacks. In 1670 there were fewer than one thousand of these Afro-Virginians, but after that their number steadily rose as their situation worsened. By 1691 it had became illegal for masters simply to free their slaves, in the unlikely event that they wanted to do so. The condition of destitute white immigrants was likewise altered in the 1660s to the advantage of the resident landlords, but the thirst for gain in that domain had its limits: the harshness of colonial conditions slowed down the flow of voluntary arrivals from Britain. Unfettered by corporatist tradition or by a sense of noblesse oblige, greedy planters in this early colonial period treated all their servants, black and white, as harshly as they could. In principle, indentured whites could appeal to the courts; in practice, this right meant very little.

Native Americans suffered even more than the blacks who were enslaved. Disputes soon arose between land-hungry immigrants and the natives, who persisted in thinking that the land was theirs. In 1622 they struck back, an event that was likened later to the Irish revolt of 1641, which resulted in massive expropriation and the sale into slavery of 30,000 Irish men and women. The more successful Virginian planters, who owned land already, and the governor, who ruled with them, were admittedly reluctant to provoke the Indians into costly war. But this self-interested pacifism was anathema to the new, smaller planters: in 1676, under Bacon's leadership, they rebelled. The Indians, whose ability to fight back had been essentially broken in 1644, were driven still further into the hinterland.

Other southern and middle Atlantic colonies followed a similar or even stronger pattern of economic individualism. In 1628 Lord Baltimore had acquired rights over his proprietary colony from the English monarch that resembled those granted to proprietors in Spanish America. His colonists would, he thought, be tenants, not farmers, and subject to his seigneurial justice. By 1640, after the Virginian headright system had been introduced into Maryland, this dream had faded, and in 1650 the quarrel over property rights between the Protestant settlers and the Catholic proprietor resulted in victory for the settlers.

The demise of William Penn's proposed agricultural villages was also rapid. "I had in my view," he wrote in 1685, "Society, Assistance, Busy Commerce, Instruction of Youth, Government of Peoples manners, Conveniency of Religious Assembling, Encouragement of Mechanicks, distinct and beaten Roads," a program that was to be realized within "Townships or Villages, each of which contains 5,000 acres . . . and at least ten Families . . . Our Townships lie square; generally the Village in the Center . . . for near neighborhood."[21] Within twenty years of its foundation, the colony had little relation to Penn's earlier vision, and the proprietor's political rights soon vanished. In 1701 Penn was obliged to accept a revised charter in which power was divided between the British monarch and a unicameral colonial legislature.

The disintegration of communitarianism in New England was more gradual and far more subtle than in the middle or southern colonies. In some critical respects the community-minded ethos of the Puritans' great migration never died: in fact, its spiritual legacy has survived in secularized form to our own day in the specifically American forms of social and political culture.

To assign such importance to the survival in modern America of the culture and religion of colonial New England (sometimes called the New England way) may seem paradoxical in view of the recent work that has been done by historians of other colonial areas, particularly New York and the Chesapeake. My insistence on the primacy of Puritanism could also be criticized as a throwback to the hegemony of the New England or Harvard school of colonial history, which originated in 1839 with Jared Sparks's pioneering lectures on the American Revolution. To persist in looking at America's entire colonial history through the prism of New England culture is—for some—to underwrite once again a partial vision of America's history and to reify once again the paradoxical conjunction in the nineteenth century of northeastern industrial power and the literary talent of Harvard-trained intellectuals, many of whom were hostile to modern industrial and social forms.

In spite of these objections, America's intellectual history during the seventeenth and eighteenth centuries does justify an insistence on the importance of the New England way before 1800. Although New England's ideological forms (which were religious in the seventeenth century and became secular during the Georgian Age), were derived from English models, they were more developed and had achieved a greater specificity, which may be called American, than the ideological or cultural statements of the other colonies.

The widespread understanding of Puritanism among the New England colonists was attributable in part to the high rate of literacy there, thanks to the well-developed network of schools and to colleges whose governing boards were based in the community rather than in the institutions themselves. The New England ministry was numerous and intellectually aggressive: in 1650 Massachusetts counted more than one minister for every five hundred people, nearly ten times the ratio of contemporary Virginia. A century later nearly all of New England's lawyers had been trained locally, unlike the situation in South Carolina, where every member of the bar was English-trained. The eighteenth-century descendants of the early Puritans may not have been so devout as their forebears, but they were culturally unified. After independence, Philadelphia was more prosperous than Boston, but it was the Bostonians' understanding of British politics and of what Americans had achieved in their revolutionary struggle that prevailed. The weakness of other colonial intellectual forms, more ephemeral and more imitative of British aesthetic patterns (in the South especially) made it difficult for other Americans to resist the secularized New England vision of God's chosen people, with its definition of the place of individuals in matters sacred and profane.

It might even be argued that in one sense Boston was to America what Paris was to France. Just as the administrative void created by the French kings outside their capital meant that Paris would prevail in the postrevolutionary administration and politics of France, so did the domination of Puritan culture in colonial New England ensure its influence on the affairs of the new nation. The political history of late-eighteenth-century America is hard to decipher without an appreciation of New England's special place in the ideological history of the colonies, just as the history of the French Revolution, and of modern France generally, is impossible to grasp without an understanding of Parisian sensibilities and Parisian social history.

TO THE SEVENTEENTH-CENTURY MIND, which obviously could know nothing of the coming transmogrification of the New England way and its impact on modern America's sense of self, what mattered was the decline of Puritan communitarian spirituality. Indeed, the unfolding in the late seventeenth and eighteenth century of Puritanism's inner contradictions, together with its prefiguration of a modern individualist ethos, is probably the most important ideological phenomenon of prerevolutionary America. The struggle in the New England mind between jointly transcendental and antinomian individualism and an equally pervasive spirit of social and religious solidarity was comparable to the decline of traditionalism in prerevolutionary urban and corporate France.

Seventeenth-century Puritanism, as a doctrine of social communitarianism, carried within itself the seeds of its own partial destruction. In one sense, the Puritans' central doctrine, Augustinian predestination (from St. Augustine, the fifth-century church father), was devastatingly anti-individualistic. In its strict Calvinistic mode, Puritan Augustinianism held that individuals were powerless to save themselves. Man's fate had been set by God's will at the very moment of his creation. But all was not lost for the individual, because the Puritan divines, those ratiocinating engineers of the soul, were able to transform Calvin's unqualified pessimism into a more satisfying aporia. In their writings, the central paradox of divine grace was that "the Lord must work in me that which I must do on my own."[22] Congregationalism emphasized the humanity of Christ as the son of God, a relationship that did not degrade Christ but ennobled man. The Puritan spoke directly to God, and, unlike the French Catholic Augustinians or Jansenists of the same era, the New Englander fully expected to be answered.

Freedom of conscience—of a sort—was also part of the Puritan world view. To be sure, the Puritans assumed that only one path, their own, led to God; but they agreed also, in the words of Thomas Hooker, that "faith is not forced." Heartfelt, sincere, informed, and free conversion, ordinarily sanctioned by a public "relation," or sort of confession, was in the New World that exclusive path to salvation. In Catholic Europe, visual effects—like the blue, green, and pink pastel shades so typical of baroque and Jesuitical architecture—aimed to seduce. The bare, white-walled Congregational church incited the believer to calm reflection. So great was the Puritan emphasis on the self that the role of the Protestant church itself was implicitly brought into question, especially by Roger Williams. New Englanders agreed that their Puritan ministers, the learned and wise graduates of Cambridge University or Harvard College, could best explicate the Bible. But the minister did not stand between man or woman and God. God's grace was not in his gift. In the New Haven colony, created under Hooker's guidance by migrants from Massachusetts and possibly the most rigorous of the Bible commonwealths, the learned Ezekiel Cheever refused in the 1640s to condemn the excommunicated Anne Yale Eaton, daughter of a bishop and wife of the governor. To empower the elders, he explained, would be to silence the brethren: it would "impeach their true liberty and [make] them afraid to speak when they apprehend they have a just cause."[23] One can see why the churchgoing Puritans detested the anarchistic Quakers and Baptists, who were so repellently close and yet so manifestly heretical, nearly as much as they did the wholly alien Roman Catholics.

In the end, Puritanism did not allow mankind to get much help from tradition. It took away the "pillow of custom" and demanded that the individual confront existence directly on all sides. It never set itself within the comforting limits of a finite, earthly cosmos, like the self-contained physical universe that would soon be conjectured by the French philosophes. Puritanism was a drastically dynamic doctrine, which propelled the Christian, essentially unaided, toward many goals both sacred and profane, both charted and inscrutable.

Many Puritan institutions reflected in their structure this same tension between the desire to impose tribal norms and the assertion that every Christian is an island. Like Calvinism itself, New England family life was constrained but also liberating. In some respects, at least, it was so even for women, if their situation is considered in the context of seventeenth-century Christendom. Puritans had a novel view of sexuality. It contrasted with the perspective of medieval Christian Europe, which had identified sexuality with a debased view of women and had linked reasoned morality with masculine privilege. The Puritans were less severe, and the sensuality of the marriage bed seemed to them not merely legitimate but positively blessed. In fact, Governor Winthrop's Victorian descendants found it necessary to delete from their edition of his letters the compliments he had addressed to his wife. Catholic theologians had thundered about heterosexual immorality but had calculatingly ignored the problem of masturbation. The Puritans reversed this issue, and the divines' stern condemnation of sexual onanism coexisted with a broader view of matrimonial sexual pleasure.

The rules that governed marriage were also relatively flexible. Divorce, though very infrequent, was in New England a legal possibility, as it was in Calvinist Scotland where, unique in Europe, adultery by either partner had been since 1560 grounds for the dissolution of marriage. Historians have identified twenty-seven instances of divorce in Massachusetts between 1639 and 1692. In New England, as a rule, neither young men nor young women were to marry against their will, and in 1707 Fitz John Winthrop concluded that "it has been the way and custome of the country for young folkes to choose, and where there is noe visible exception everybody approves it." Wife-beating was an offense. The rights of women as witnesses were broadened. Widows received propertied settlements as a matter of course. The fate of women in New England was not without its darker side, however. As a rule, condemned dissenters or witches were females. The domination of wives by husbands was part and parcel of a hierarchic, divinely sanctioned world order. Moralized constraint is a difficult cross to bear, as can be seen in some of Anne Bradstreet's poetry, which is quietly expressive of her feminine discontent. But the balance of the New England family was more favorably tilted toward the second sex and toward individualism generally than in France and perhaps also in Britain. As a result, family cohesion waned in the New World. The unenforceable laws of Connecticut and Massachusetts that provided the death penalty for filial disobedience were a sure sign of growing disorder. It could be argued also that the great importance the Puritans attached to formal schooling reflected their lack of faith in the family as a pedagogic institution.

Puritan law was similarly ambiguous in placing the rights of the community above those of the individual. Until the 1660s the instinct of the lawmakers of the Bible Commonwealth was to defend collective norms. Lawyers were almost unknown, and trial by jury was unusual. Actual practice, however, soon drifted toward the rationalization and humanization of English procedure: the good of the one should ideally overlap the good of all; but if that could not be achieved, the rights of plaintiffs were not to be sacrificed. By 1637, claims against self-incrimination had already been made before the Massachusetts General Court; and legislation against compulsory self-incrimination was included in the Body of Liberties of 1641 and renewed in the Lawes and Liberties of 1647, a modernized legal compendium that drew—prophetically—on both biblical lore and English common law.

Ultimately, Puritan politics was based on consent, and the doctrines of Governor Winthrop can be seen as a kind of occidental Confucianism that sought to conciliate individual choice with communitarian traditions of propriety. Although the defense of the faith was the first concern of the Puritan state, private political consciences could not be coerced, and to some a certain kind of pluralism seemed logical. "Civil weapons," explained Roger Williams (no impartial witness), "are improper in this business and are never able to reach the soul."

Massachusetts was perhaps a theocratic state, but of a peculiar and unstable kind. The influence of the clergy was made compatible with a broad definition of private rights and political liberty: "These three things," wrote a minister in 1636 to Lord Saye and Sele, an English aristocrat who wisely decided not to settle in the Bay colony, "do mutually and strongly maintain one another . . . authority in magistrates, liberty in people, purity in church."[24] New England communitarianism made room for individual conscience and for many other fundamental principles of modern (that is, nineteenth-century) bourgeois life as well. Puritans were readers of the printed word and their theology was extremely rationalistic. Sermons were laborious concatenations of logically connected, reasonable arguments. In retrospect, the Ramist system of logic followed by the Puritans (from Petrus or Pierre Ramus, a French Calvinist thinker murdered on Saint Bartholomew's Day in 1572) was closer to the primitive Thomistic rationalism (from Thomas Aquinas) it aimed to supplant than to modern, more rational, seventeenth-century Cartesian logic. But Ramism, whatever its defects, made rationality a fundamental principle of intellectual and cultural order. Perfect rationality was, for the Puritans, one of God's essential attributes. In the mind of Deity was a coherent, orderly, rational plan, the matrix of earthly creation. Reason, said the seventeenth-century William Hubbard, is "our most faithful and best Councellor." Far from supplanting faith, reason bolstered it: "The most religious," explained one divine, "are the most truly, and nobly, rational."[25]

Puritan "theologians" were neither ascetic nor mystical but practical-minded people. Their metaphoric imagination, though vivid, was bookish. (Twenty booksellers set up shop in Boston from 1669 to 1690, and the first American copyright law was designed to protect their interests rather than those of the writers whose works they sold.) Thomas Hooker, famous for his learning and a close reader of Ramus, but delicate in his constitution, was said to stand during the wintertime in close relation to both God and his fireplace. The Puritans' concern for prophecies and omens (such as that of the mouse that passed over the New Testament but nibbled at the Book of Common Prayer) were echoes of premodern times but signs also of their modern belief that the world made reasonable sense. Thanks to the Bible and the ministry, God's will on earth could be deciphered, understood, and obeyed. Though predestination was their main tenet, the temptation of Arminianism, which related salvation to good works and practical achievement, was strongly felt in Massachusetts Bay, especially among the more prosperous coastal merchants. The celebrated Protestant work ethic was noticeable in Boston, where it was thought a sin to let one's talents go to waste. Work was good, spending and ostentation bad. Even catastrophes had their use: they reminded the sinner of God's might and of the need to give further evidence of one's salvation through piety and more work. "Heavenly Merchandise," as Samuel Willard wrote in 1685 of the conversion experience, was also by its earthly effect a very desirable commodity.

The central aspect of Puritan theology, the theme of the covenant, was both a prefiguration and an unwitting parody of modern liberal legal principles. A covenant, explained Samuel Willard, was "a deliberate thing wherein there is a Counsel and a Consent between Rational and free Agents,"[26] and Puritan culture was replete with such agreements. The first of these contracts bound man's fate to God's will. This was the Covenant of Grace, by which God agreed to be a just and good God to mankind, just as mankind agreed to be "perfect with [him]." No Puritan, including those who had experienced conversion, could be sure of being covered by the invisible print of this surprising contract; but an awareness of the assured existence of the Covenant of Grace worked in Boston to limit the Calvinist emphasis on God's right to withhold his gift of grace. The Puritans were "ambidextrous theologians": what the right hand took away, the left hand could ingeniously retrieve.

Invariably, and quite conveniently, Puritans skipped from one covenant to the next. To the horror of other Protestants, including such fellow Calvinists as the English Presbyterians, the New England Puritans postulated the existence of many such agreements. God, for example, had "Covenanted with Christ that if he would pay the full price for the redemption of believers, they would be discharged. Christ has paid the price; God must be unjust, or else hee must set free from all iniquitie." Membership in the church and in politics was conceptualized in similar terms. In the language of this theocratic calculus, original sin became a kind of debt owed by mankind to God; salvation was the typically American end of many a successful horse trade.

The short-run purpose of a theology of covenants was to bind the believer to the church, the community, the state, and to a neo-medieval cosmology. But its long-range effect was to institutionalize contract, rationality, and individualism as the axes of New England culture. Perry Miller aptly noted that "federal" covenant theology, as he called it, led to passages that anticipated Locke's treatises. By its content, Puritan contractual theory did have its point of reference in the past. By its method, however, it foreshadowed the cardinal principles of Victorian bourgeois life, of liberal, utilitarian, and individualistic achievement. Just as the Mathers had united sixteenth-century Calvinism to the cultural modernism of their own time by blending Ramism and Augustinianism, so, much later, Jonathan Edwards brought together Lockean empiricist epistemology and the Calvinist doctrine of predestination. The argumentative style of federal theology was at once agile in its method and, from the Puritan point of view, problematical in its conclusions.

The fissures in these early compromises did not take long to appear. Anne Hutchinson's defiant antinomianism with its rejection of clerical guidance and supremacy (a stand which, incidentally, struck a responsive chord among her merchant friends), as well as her emphasis on the personal and the affective and her disinterest in learning, dated to 1638 or before. Moreover, all of these attitudes were implicit in the doctrine of the men who condemned her out of hand.

Puritan culture rested on two destabilizing aporias. The first was that mankind must strive ceaselessly to please God, whose gift of grace could never be explained. The other was that even a true Christian would care deeply about a material social context which he or she was also required to ignore. Though ostensibly pious, communitarian, and even tribal, Puritanism strained from the first toward a wholly different end. Behind every saintly, transcendent-minded Puritan stood, as many social historians have observed, a shrewd and cunning Yankee. The partition between religious responsibility and secular individualism proved far more porous than Puritan theologians had imagined. This characteristic of Puritan New England contrasted sharply with the ideologically more consistent contemporary French culture, which, especially in its Jansenist and Augustinian form, dissociated the rights of the one from the rights of the many. In France the relevance of good works to the salvation of the Augustinian faithful was denied, as was the exemplary nature of any social forms. In late seventeenth-century New England, however, the two sets of values—individualistic and communitarian—were always entwined and always changing. Inexorably, the uncertain, shifting balance between the two tilted toward individual rights at the expense of the joint prerogatives of the family, the church, the town, and the province.

Not surprisingly, the disintegration of the cake of custom that accompanied the unfolding of individualistic values in Puritan life and culture was for the very devout a traumatic experience. Beginning in the late 1640s, New England divines sensed that their city on the hill was not so true to communitarian theocracy as they would have liked. Jeremiad and declension became the set topoi of the New England sermon: "O sacred bond whilst inviolably preserved," wailed Governor Bradford in 1650. "How sweet and precious were the fruits that flowed from the same! But when this fidelity decayed, then their ruin approached. O that these ancient members had not yet died or been dissipated, or else that this holy care and constant faithfulness had still lived." In America, a restorative myth of the country's golden past came into being before the country had any past to speak of, or had even become an independent nation.

Nor were the stresses of New England public life thought by the faithful to be part of some distant process. New England's historical dilemmas were consciously reflected in many private lives. The celebrated Salem witchcraft trials of 1692 had a pronounced social dimension. These ghastly proceedings—soon to be disavowed by the colony's elite—often ranged the local, impoverished, rural, self-styled inquisitors against their prosperous, urbanized, and more worldly victims. Even more important, all the participants, condemned and condemning, had internalized the assumptions—and problems—of Puritan religiosity. New England families were riddled with tensions, both psychological and sexual, between the publicly upheld principles of self-sacrificing communitarianism and the equally sanctioned private goals of self-fulfillment.

Indeed, the claims that could be made on behalf of the Puritans' sense of a private self were all the more demanding because their self-seeking was often couched in transcendental terms. Puritans could suppose that they were furthering the common good by realizing their own deepest yearning for independence. A more negative (or a more materialistic and competitive) definition of the self would have obliged devout Puritans to see involvement in the world as a threat. But a complex Puritan eschatalogy made it possible to accept as ideologically correct many solutions whose long-run material and social consequence was to pull Puritan culture apart. As Cotton Mather explained in another context, it is the "men that are most Ensnared [who] are least sensible of their Snares."

BECAUSE THE FIRST cause of society's drift toward more individuated forms in the Chesapeake colonies was economic and social rather than religious, the history of those middle and southern provinces is less relevant to the argument of this book than the history of Massachusetts. But even in what was to become the Bay State the failure of a collectively run economy soon became evident. Although the Puritans despised capitalism, they seemed fated to further its cause as no other society had ever done.

The first Puritans held trade in low esteem. Merchants who shamelessly maximized their profits risked public humiliation. To their surprise, the first settlers, who thought of agriculture as their sanctioned vocation, found that some money was to be made in fur and fishing; but the colony regulated these unavoidable activities as best it could.

In the 1640s the first economic adjustment took place when the defeat of Charles I and the victory of religious dissent in England dried up emigration to New England. Moreover, of the 21,000 people who had gone there in the 1630s, as many as one-sixth may have returned to Britain. The local economy, which had depended on the sale of necessities at a high price to new and monied migrants, was badly hit. The price of a cow in Boston fell suddenly from twenty pounds to five.

In its second phase of economic development, the colony tried to make up its losses by encouraging the production of manufactured goods designed to be locally consumed. In 1641 the authorities in both Massachusetts and Connecticut agreed to subsidize textile manufacturing. In that same year, the Saugus iron works were officially launched under the supervision of Governor Winthrop's son, and by 1648 they were yielding one ton of metal a day. In 1652, however, this state-subsidized enterprise went bankrupt; by 1678 it had shut down.[27] Local textiles, whose production would have obviated importation from the outside world, did no better.

In the third phase, economic salvation came from a source that would have distressed the pious founders of the Bay colony, many of whom were gentlemen landlords or lawyers, graduates of Cambridge University. Though they supported individualism in religion and politics, they did not admire the economic individualism of merchants. And yet it was trade, and trade of the most modern kind, that insured the growth of New England. In 1643 five New England trading vessels set off across the seas. The first triangular voyage took place in 1646, sailing from New England to Africa and returning by way of the Caribbean, where Spain's grasp on the islands had loosened, leaving them ripe for plunder. By 1647 Rhode Island farmers were breeding horses for export to Barbados, where they were used to run the sugar mills; in the 1670s ship's supplies were being exported to Britain and fish and grain to the Caribbean.

It was the common practice "of those that had any store of Cattel," wrote a New Englander about his neighbors in 1654, "to sell every year a Cow or two, which cloath'd their backs, fil'd their bellies with more variety than the Country of itself afforded, and put gold and silver in their purses beside." In the early 1770s, one third of Boston's adult males were part owners of some merchant vessel.

Per-capita income rose quickly between 1650 and 1680. Because the institutions of international banking and commerce were undeveloped, trade was often carried out through personal or even familial networks of Englishmen at home and abroad or by newer migrants, Huguenots and Jews, with contacts overseas. But these arrangements proved lucrative enough.

By the 1680's individualism had become the cornerstone of New England's economic life, just as it lay at the heart of New England culture. In March 1635 the General Court had authorized nine men representing the nine towns in Massachusetts Bay to board incoming ships, decide on a "just price," "acquainte their partners therewith," and resell the cargoes at a 5 percent profit, "and not above."[28] Five months later this profit-limiting law was repealed. In 1679–80 a reformist synod deplored in its church members "an insatiable desire after Land, and worldly Accommodations, yea, so as to forsake Churches and Ordinances, and to live like Heathen, only that so they might have elbow-room enough in the world. Farms and merchandising have been preferred before things of God."

Experiments in communal agriculture were soon abandoned, first in Watertown in 1655 and later in Sudbury and Andover. Feudal forms of land tenure were specifically rejected in the Body of Liberties: "All our lands and heritage shall be free from all fines and licenses upon Alienation, and from all harriotts, wardships, Liveries, Primerseisins, yeare day and wast, Escheates and forfeitures." Even Puritan ministers bought and sold. Between 1680 and 1740, one divine out of every twenty resigned in a huff over pay. The size of their stipends was the subject of hot discussions that were only marginally more seemly than the annual Virginian tugs of war between ministers and parish vestries concerning the value of glebe lands and tobacco payments. The shape and size of New England townships reflected this new individualist outlook. Nuclear villages broke up. Some colonies, including Rhode Island and Plymouth, had allowed isolated homesteads from the beginning, and other areas soon followed. An early surveyor of one such township observed that "the people of this Towne have of late placed their dwellings so much distanced the one from the other, that they are like to divide into two Churches."[29] Uncultivated land which had initially belonged to the towns gradually fell into the hands of well-connected private persons. By the end of the century, the merchants who dominated Boston socially had become adept speculators in land as well.

THE POLITICAL STRUCTURES of the American colonies, especially those in New England, followed a similar drift toward open-ended solutions. Until the American Revolution, the three cardinal principles of modern politics—popular sovereignty, direct representation, and universal suffrage—existed only inchoately. It was widely believed in late-seventeenth-century America that some form of parliamentary representation was the natural or at least the inherited right of Englishmen; that power should be shared between the crown and politically representative assemblies; and that freemen should have a direct role in choosing some of their political representatives. English traditions that emphasized the immanence of common law and judicial independence strengthened these "democratic" foreshadowings.

Cultural predispositions to more open structures of government were most visible in the New England colonies. A cascade of decisions decentralized the original governmental system. In Massachusetts the definition of a politically enfranchised freeman was immediately expanded to include not just the original shareholders of the company but all male churchgoers. In 1632 these electors acquired the right to vote for both the governor and the deputy governor. In 1634 the General Court ordered that town representatives be "deputed by the freemen of [the] severall plantacions, to deale in their behalfe in the publique affayres of the commonwealth" and to approve the levying of taxation.[30]

Because political enfranchisement had depended on church membership since 1631, it followed, as John Cotton explained in 1636 to Lord Saye and Sele, that belonging to some particular social estate, however lofty, could not affect the enfranchisement of Puritan church members. Of the sixty-nine householders who lived in Roxbury between 1638 and 1640, forty-nine were church members and voters. The Body of Liberties of 1641 was not only a defense of individual rights and of freehold property but also an attack on monopolies, the highly unpopular "patents of sale" that the English crown had fostered, ostensibly to ensure economic growth but actually to further political patronage and royal domination. Trial by jury soon became the rule in Boston and a very popular institution, since American juries throughout the colonial period both enforced and created law. In Massachusetts, the ability to coerce at any institutional level was shadowy. Local constables were elected officials (often chosen against their will), who were reluctant to use, much less abuse, their power. It was also relevant to the growth of open political forms that the rights of towns, controlled by the freemen, grew in Massachusetts at the expense of those of the county, which were favored by more influential residents such as Governor Winthrop, who assumed that bigger political units would be the preserve of bigger men like himself.

Provincial institutions were weak and local autonomy strong—as appeared during the Salem witch trials of 1692, which were judicially local affairs. The building of roads, the erection of public buildings, poor relief, the selection of ministers, the management of schools, and the requests of hamlets for greater autonomy were all settled locally, often by secret ballot. Township governance in New England was not uniform from place to place, but by European standards it was always open in structure. Even the power of the Church was institutionally curtailed in the colony as a whole. Many of the richer Puritans, including Governor Winthrop, had been socially eminent in Britain and were not used to deferring to ministers. They carried these habits of civil supremacy from Old to New England, and were doubtless encouraged to do so by the climate of British politics, which from 1610 to 1640 revolved around the activities of the established Church.

The ability in New England of the Church to exclude some from membership shrank from year to year. Requirements for full membership were soon relaxed, and the Cambridge Platform of 1648 delicately reminded the ministry: "Severity of examination is to be avoyded."[31] The euphemistically named Halfway Covenant of 1662 weakened further the criteria for the admission of the children of the faithful to the community. The churches were pledged in effect not to look into the genuineness of religious feeling. Evangelicalism yielded to piety as the norm of ecclesiastical propriety. Ministers had to make do with "decourous semblances." In Massachusetts, Anglicans and Quakers had become by 1720 established and tolerated minorities. In 1721, Increase Mather and his son agreed to participate in the ordination of a Baptist minister. As Perry Miller observed, religion was essentially defined by "the inner consciousness of the individual."

Although the drift in New England toward more open forms of government had internal causes, such as the principles of Puritanism and the pioneer temperament of the settlers, the form of local institutions also had exogenous roots deriving from the colonies' relationship to England.

"Salutary neglect" was for decades England's fundamental colonial policy. The role of the British state in sixteenth-century imperial affairs had been consistently weak by Spanish or even French standards, and it remained so afterward: the years between the death of Queen Elizabeth in 1603 and the Glorious Revolution of 1688 marked the formative period of American colonization and an epoch of political and cultural upheaval in Britain. England's rulers had too many other things on their minds to do much more than legalize private colonial ventures. For Americans the benefits of distance and indifference were great. Though governors appointed by the crown did eventually become the rule—and many of these were military men—all of the original North American colonies began as charter companies, some of them with elected governors. In the 1640s and 1650s the New England colonies, after drafting an agreement for military and judicial cooperation wherein they styled themselves the "United Colonies of New England," were virtually an independent nation. Within the colonies, moreover, legislative assemblies immediately asserted their right to exist. The powers of governors, whether appointed by crown or proprietor, were whittled down. In Pennsylvania, for example, Penn's right to appoint a governor and veto laws was drastically curtailed in 1701. In Virginia, it was the governors themselves who helped to bring into being an elected lower House of Burgesses.

The rules of the game did tilt somewhat in Britain's favor in the last decade of the seventeenth century. A series of convulsions shook the colonies from the Carolinas and Maryland to New York and Massachusetts. Some of these upheavals, including Bacon's rebellion in Virginia in 1676, reflected domestic strains. Others followed the first concerted efforts by James II to impose a more direct British rule, especially in New England—a policy that went down very badly in Boston, where political indignation was compounded by Governor Andros's questioning of land titles and freehold property.

The rule of Andros did not last very long in Massachusetts (he was unceremoniously packed off to Britain as soon as news of the Glorious Revolution arrived in Boston early in 1689), but when the smoke cleared in the late 1690s, conditions had nonetheless changed in Britain's favor. The colonies' imperial ties were everywhere strengthened, as was Britain's right to regulate the patterns of trade and policy. Royal governors (like Andros, who was made governor of Virginia in 1692) were freer to distribute patronage. But everywhere their power was restrained: first, by judges and assemblies in the provinces; second, by the local authorities. In Massachusetts the crown decided in 1688 that governors would henceforth be appointed, but in 1693 the General Court passed a residence requirement for officeholders. The new political and cultural forms created by New Englanders contrasted strikingly with the old imperial forms found in the colonies of the other European Powers.

THE MOST CHARACTERISTIC aspect of American particularism, however, was neither political nor economic but social, the "non-transplantation" to America of two fundamental European economic institutions: the urban guild and the peasant commune that structured rural life.

The absence in America of professional corporations (whose role in France was immense) has not aroused much historical interest: a dog that does not bark is ordinarily ignored. This disinterest is regrettable because the issue is of considerable importance. In view of the Puritans' social goal in America—which was not to create but to recreate—their inability to reproduce these critical institutions is surprising. Moreover, in the next century, especially during the formative decades of the 1770s and 1780s, the political possibility of changing the prevailing caste system to a class system would have been greatly enhanced by the existence of urban guilds.

In France, the breakdown of the individualist-universalist compromise of 1789—of the French propertied elite's belief that a narrowly defined social individualism could be reconciled with a politically sweeping, universalist statement—can be partly attributed to the cultural legacies after 1789 of such ancient and formal corporate institutions as the guilds. For centuries prescriptive corporations and estates (or castes) had been a central feature of French culture, and the assertion of possessive individualism elicited strong reactions of class solidarity. Babouvian socialism was a modern graft on an ancient trunk.

The working-class consciousness of nineteenth-century France resulted partly from the need to adapt traditional corporate sensibilities to the exigencies of modern economic and industrial life. This syncretic pattern was not peculiar to the French. The history of the modern British working class shows a progression from the "Moral Economy of the Crowd" to a pattern of class confrontation. In revolutionary America, of course, this kind of confrontation did not occur.

Isolated efforts to create craft guilds did take place in the colonies, however. In the 1640s the General Court of Massachusetts created a chartered company to supervise shipbuilding. In 1648 a shoemakers' guild was authorized in Boston at the request of the shoemakers themselves, who claimed the need to exclude from their market the poor-quality shoes being manufactured in inland towns. This act elicited a strong protest. The country cobblers pointed out that their Boston rivals did not make superior shoes. In any case, the would-be guild members had not belonged to "such a body in o'r [our] Native Country."[32] Then why create one here? At the end of three years, the guild experiment was not renewed. In New York, only one mention of a weaver's guild, in Westchester, appears in the records. Pennsylvania's last effort in this area was made in 1721.

There were at least two reasons for the failure of guilds in America. First, colonial artisans probably reasoned that they would do better economically and perhaps socially in a free market where they could move about and sell their labor as they wished. Second, since wages in America were high and general starvation unknown, the mechanisms of mutual aid that guilds offered the poor in Europe may have seemed less important. And third, in a similar if inverted way propertied colonials and the public authorities may have concluded that the desirable control of quality which guilds might afford would be offset by undesirable coalitions demanding higher wages.

The idea of state intervention in economic life was not offensive: acts of governmental interference designed to stimulate production were numerous in colonial America and would become commonplace during and after the American Revolution. American provincial governments in the seventeenth and eighteenth centuries also tried very hard to increase the price of the staple crops that were sold abroad. But collectivist political and economic activities of this kind had nothing to do with the maintenance of social or corporate solidarity. The motivation behind them was to lower wages and maximize the use of available labor: offenses that were punished in Britain by debtors' prisons were transformed in America into convictions to involuntary labor. In 1692 a Maryland act provided that white women marrying Negroes would become servants for seven years; their husbands, if free, would be indentured for life.[33] Any excuse was a good one to force people to work; but even here, American officials hovered uneasily between a desire to enforce the rights of masters over servants and a desire to attract more workers from Europe with the lure of higher wages. The motivation of coercive colonial regulation was quite different from the spirit of the more static, market-regulating customs that survived in France and Britain until the end of the eighteenth century. Lucre rather than social order was the first concern.

Typically, the one corporatist institution that did resurface in America was soon transformed in its purpose. Apprenticeship was common in the New World and often hard to bear, as the teenage Benjamin Franklin found in his brother's Boston printing shop. The purpose of apprenticeship in America was educational (to train artisans) and exploitative (to secure cheap child labor), not, as it usually was in Europe, the legal requirement for practicing a given trade. In 1675 some ships' carpenters who had ridden an interloper out on a rail because he had worked in a yard without having completed his apprenticeship were fined by the Massachusetts General Court. The carpenters argued that "they understood that such things were usually in England,"[34] but the judge was indifferent to their plea.

Most American artisans and certainly most colonial consumers appear not to have wanted guilds: although it had become customary in seventeenth-century England for masters not to sell the labor contracts of their apprentices without guild approval, it was in America accepted as a matter of course—and seemingly by all the involved parties—that the contracts of even white indentured servants could be sold at will.

Not only were guilds and peasant communes not transplanted to America, but the traditional cultural fabric in which the rules of European social and economic corporatism were informally embedded was also missing. In France before 1789 corporate bodies had their roots in a web of ceremonies, parades, pilgrimages, feast days, fairs, charivaris, riots, and other public manifestations. All over Western Europe social institutions had in addition acquired a ludic dimension: the entrance of the French monarch into a city was the occasion for a fete, as was the king's acceptance of the keys of a city from the local notables; the popular rejoicing that followed these solemn occasions symbolized the organic nature of society and politics. Similarly, the celebration of a peasant marriage might become a village holiday. Horizontal solidarities of this kind found a vertical analogue in the theory of the king's two bodies. In France, kingship never lapsed: "I am dying," said Louis XIV to his courtiers, "but the State never dies." All of life, past and present, formed a single whole as did society's constituent parts.

This feeling of cultural continuity reinforced in the minds of French artisans a sense of social involvement, perhaps even of social responsibility. But seventeenth- and eighteenth-century migrants to America brought precious little of this culture with them. The innumerable customs and rites that were associated in France (or Britain) with particular places, hamlets, or villages were not transportable, nor was the larger context of traditional culture. Witchcraft was the exception which confirmed that rule, but even that practice was in New England highly intellectualized. For the Puritans, sorcery was no longer the expression of mysterious forces. It was learnedly redefined as the reverse of Christian charity, or even as the breaking of man's covenant with God. Isolated instances of American alchemic practices have come down to us, as well as occasional references to books of magic and astrology. Nonetheless, by the first decades of the eighteenth century such cases had become mere curiosities. After 1692 Massachusetts courts no longer recognized spectral evidence as proof positive. Sailors, who remained more faithful to ancient lore than others, were thought to be unusually superstitious. In 1730 a New Jersey Presbyterian synod formally condemned astrological practices.

European traditional and popular culture had not been conceived in abstraction as Puritanism had. It grew over time, partly as a reflection of high culture but also around particular events, places, saints, heroes, and institutions, such as the guilds. Popular culture, along with the secular organization of labor, had been part of an organic whole. It proved impossible to recreate this pattern in the wilds of America and in the uncongenial cultural climate of rationalistic individualism. As the first settlers in Jamestown discovered, the pragmatic necessities of pioneering life suggested new social rankings that did not have much to do with European habits. Guilds presupposed the existence of accepted, interlocking norms and ways of doing things; life in America brought all of these old ways into question.

BY THE END of the seventeenth century the material and political conditions of Britain's North American colonies—the New England, middle, and southern colonies—were far more convergent and consistent than had been true earlier in the century, when New England and the Chesapeake area had differed widely. Communitarian experiment had everywhere yielded to material stability set in a context of individualistic, and therefore transient, social forms.

The appalling death rate of the Chesapeake colonies had leveled off. The conjunction of economic well-being with longevity and fecundity made possible a more settled family life. The settlers who arrived in the Chesapeake in the 1660s to produce Virginia's First Families differed from their predecessors in many ways; moreover, they usually survived. Individualism, although rampant, was anchored in ranked, extended families. To choose a case at random, the marriage in Middlesex County, Virginia, in 1671 of Doodes Minor, whose father had arrived from Holland some decades before, brought together guests and cousins who individually held hundreds of acres of land and who all belonged to five related families. These ties were somewhat exceptional at that time, but by 1724 more than half of that same county's families were linked to at least five other families.[35] American society did not cease to change, but it did so in a more orderly way.

By 1700 the basic features of the American colonial economy had appeared. Blacks had been reduced to servitude, and communitarian restraints on individual endeavor were honored mostly in the breach. In 1639 the General Court of Massachusetts had censured Robert Keayne for selling his goods too dear (which he "did with tears acknowledge and bewail his covetous and corrupt heart"). In 1707 Samuel Lillie of Boston owned shares in no less than 108 ships, and he was soon to flee to Britain, a ruined man, his public life a prime example of the vicissitudes of nascent American capitalism. Stock manipulation was by no means unknown in Europe at the time: Dutch tulips, South Sea shares, and in France, Law's financial and colonial schemes. In America, speculation, though less explosive, was more general and sustained.

The myth of the divinely sanctioned community remained very strong in America, as did the idea of a more communitarian, moralistic, and golden past. Indeed, nostalgias of this kind would soon become a cardinal principle of American political culture. But even before 1700 the connection between myth and social reality was tenuous. By 1700 the practice of community was understood in America to be little more than a means of enforcing right-thinking individualism, or even less than that: New England towns that had no more land to distribute to their inhabitants were prone to sue neighboring communities in the hope of securing additional territorial spoils. This application of the communitarian spirit hardly reflected the founders' intent.

THE FIRST PURITANS had hoped to create a model society that would inspire the nations of Protestant and northern Europe. In the 1630s the inhabitants of the Massachusetts Bay colony, however frail it was physically, regarded their society as a cosmopolitan and ideological beacon for the world. Cromwell's ambassador to the Hague, George Downing (who gave the name to London's Downing Street), a patron of Samuel Pepys, was the nephew of Governor Winthrop and a Harvard graduate. But by the 1690s Harvard had become an obscure provincial academy, just as Massachusetts was and would remain an ideological backwater until the Great Awakening and the political crises of the 1760s. Fitz-John Winthrop, a grandson of the governor, who served as Connecticut's agent in London in the 1690s, was quite homesick: "I think it very long till I am with you," he wrote to his brother, "noething [is] more pleasing than our owne Country."

By then what had begun as a visionary community of saints had been transformed into a stable, orderly, provincial Yankee colony of shrewd and seemingly narrow-minded farmers and petty merchants. Embedded in that provincial spirit, however, was a transcendental will that would not be denied.

2

The Decay of Traditionalist Corporatism in Seventeenth-Century France

THE HISTORY OF seventeenth- and eighteenth-century France centers on the gradual decline of its traditional and (in theory) ordered social and political hierarchies. The story has two parts. The first describes the decline of its hierarchies. The second tells of the compensatory but incomplete rise of rationality and of a highly particular, negativist individualism as the new principles of cultural and social action. The unbridgeable contradictions between these two principles led to the collapse of the ancien régime.

The transition from the earlier to the more "modern" mode in France was unusually long and difficult. From the second half of the seventeenth century on, both sets of values, modern and inherited, coexisted uneasily in France—in the provinces, *pays* (regions), towns, guilds, and estates.

Ambiguity was the first characteristic of the Old Regime—a term that became popular in 1790 to describe monarchic France as it had been since the reign of Louis XIII (who had died in 1643) and his first minister, the Cardinal de Richelieu. Unlike colonial America, which nearly from the first was wholeheartedly committed to individual achievement as a central social value, late monarchic France seesawed between individual prowess and traditionalist conformity, between rationality and the acceptance of the status quo.

French cleavages ran very deep. Individualism had a growing impact on the French elites, some of them nobles and others bourgeois, of whom some were working as bureaucrats for the state and others were doing their best to thwart monarchic rule. The great mass of French men and women, however, accepted the lessons of the past as a guide in the present struggle. While the conscious mind of French elites was increasingly turned toward a more individualistic future, the deep, chthonic instincts of the culture were still sustained by a broad range of formal and informal economic and social communities whose collective requirements took precedence over the desires of individual Frenchmen and Frenchwomen.

THE FIRST CORPORATE institution in French life was the family. The ideal type of corporate familial life was the extended family, which ranged diachronically from grandparents to grandchildren and synchronically with sisters and brothers, aunts and uncles, some of whom might themselves be married. All of these family members lived in principle, under a single roof, called in the south the *mas* or *manse* and in other places the *meix* or *masure*. (The English words "manse" and "mansion" share with these terms a common origin, forcefully expressing their cultural power.)

In actuality, such extended families were few, in northern France especially (they were most common in central France); more important, however, the size of households was not sociologically critical. Most French families in the seventeenth century were rather small, smaller certainly than those of New England at the time. But not too much should be made of this numerical divergence. Smallness was a physical fact with no connotations as to solidarity. It is, in any case, an illusion to suppose that extended families are by nature more organic and less tolerant of individual quirks than nuclear families. As a matter of fact, the larger families of the French elites were often innovative associations whose first aim was the conquest of wealth and power, whereas the smaller families of ordinary Frenchmen before 1789 were often the bastions of tradition. Families in France were small because they were physically rather than morally fissiparous.

Disease, death, and need—rather than social principle—were the first causes of family size, which was essentially a function of arbitrary circumstance rather than of fixed and principled volition. The likes and dislikes and the ambitions of the women and men making up the families were not at issue. Personal autonomy was not yet relevant. At the top of the age pyramid, older children in rural France were routinely sent out to work for neighboring families. Many children never lived to work at all. Perhaps a quarter of all newborns died before they reached the age of one, and another quarter died before reaching adulthood. Birthrates were very high, three times higher than today; but death rates were also high, even in normal times, since most people were chronically undernourished; and every twenty or thirty years some larger catastrophe brought on a dramatic and perhaps decimating *mortalité*. Plagues were a frequent bane. (The last major instance of this type of disease in France occurred in 1720 and the last cholera epidemic in 1849.)

French peasant families were essential cogs in a theoretically settled social order. In spite of their small size and fragility, these units were regarded as organic wholes. Many contemporaries understood this quite well and for that reason relied instinctively on familial images to justify the organicity of the monarchic structure, a metaphoric state of affairs which made the dependent, personal situation of women in the family a political rather than a private choice.

The economic life of most peasants was geared not to the call of the market or to the chance for individual betterment but to subsistence agriculture as a means of meeting the claims of the landlord, the *seigneur*, and the state, and of maintaining familial unity. Seventeenth-century administrators and intellectuals (a word that came into use only in the 1890s) might conceive of France as a vast and single "political economy," but members of peasant households lived out their lives in the context of "domestic economies," small human units that were materially as self-contained as the times and taxes would allow. Peasants who had money to invest bought land if they had many children, or bought animals if they did not. Their choice was rational, but their rationality was not of a primarily economic kind. The authority of the father was great. Children's individual right to inherit equally was ordinarily sanctioned by custom, especially in northern France; but fathers were by law entitled to imprison their wayward children and sometimes did so. Although peasant and artisanal marriages were economic rather than affective partnerships, infidelity was rare. Young women were unusually chaste: only one Frenchwoman in ten was pregnant at marriage. (In colonial Pennsylvania, one Quaker woman in five gave birth within nine months of her marriage.) Rural rates for illegitimate births, though rising, were extremely low, sometimes as low as 1 percent.

Families were the basic social unit of public life. Taxes were set not on individuals but on hearths. Families were vital economic entities. The landless wandered within their province from place to place, but landowning peasants had it in their mind's eye to relive their fathers' and mothers' lives on inherited family farms. Many children were cared for by their grandparents while their parents worked in the fields. Artisanal trades were also inherited, and peasants often were themselves part-time artisans who had picked up their skills at home. Couperins and Rameaus succeeded each other from generation to generation, as did lawyers, jurists, soldiers, and royal officials. Bishop Bossuet, a famous and censorious churchman at the court of Versailles, a lawyer's son, worked hard to have one of his grandnephews succeed him as Bishop of Meaux. Marriages united children from families that belonged to the same trade: in the Beaujolais region, members of vintners' families married into vintners' families nine out of ten times. In Paris, more than eight out of ten woodworkers' sons married woodworkers' daughters, whose professional and marketing skills dovetailed neatly with their own. Women married three or four years later than in America, a situation that delayed private sexual gratification but insured better familial balance. Because they did not qualify as suitable economic matches, many young, poor women, perhaps as many as a third in some places, remained unmarried, a social state that was much more common in France than in prerevolutionary America.

ABOVE THE FAMILY, in the countryside, were the village communities. Rural topography and village layout no more determined the social structure of French villages than size directed the social orientation of French families. Some villages were divided into hamlets and others into isolated homesteads. Still other villages—in eastern France for example—were strung out along a line. But this varying topography was not of great importance. Southern villages that were physically drawn in on themselves often had fewer communitarian structures than western villages which were sometimes so diffuse as to exist, geographically, only in name.

The same relationship of fact and spirit applied to agricultural technique: on the face of it, France seemed divided into the communitarian open-field system of the North and the more individuated small plots and *bocage,* or hedge country, of the West and South. South of the Loire, moreover, land was fragmented into innumerable small holdings, in sharp contrast to the vast wheat-growing areas or "champion" fields of northern France, where after harvesttime land was thrown open, without regard to property rights, to any animals that any villager might own—cows and sheep ordinarily, rather than hogs, then as now an American favorite.

But differences between agricultural techniques, like the differences between the layouts of villages or the sizes of families, were not so critical as at first appeared. The sense of village community was also strong (or so the politics of the peasantry in revolutionary times would suggest) in areas of western France, where privatized land was the rule. The critical factors were not strictly material or geographical. Market orientation mattered more than the size of plots: vintners who owned small plots were far more involved in the market than the richer inhabitants of the northern champion fields.

Inherited distinctions of tenure and land division (though they have attracted the attention of many historians) mattered principally when they were made to overlap with other and newer concerns. For example, French peasants, by European standards at least, owned a great deal of land: nearly 40 percent of the nation's surface belonged to them (and 10 percent of that in turn belonged to rural communities.) These percentages are critical to an understanding of the place of the French peasantry in revolutionary politics and in the politics of the nineteenth century as well. In retrospect, however, the basic fact of French rural life appears to have been that many peasants, however much land they owned and however their villages and plots were shaped, used their property in a negativist way, to protect themselves from modern economic life rather than to participate in it.

Where geography and economic modernization overlapped, as in eighteenth-century England, the differences between the sizes and shapes of farms did make a great historical difference: in England the distinction between open-field and hedge country was increasingly critical because newly hedged land was purposefully "enclosed," that is, wholly privatized and made commercially productive. In seventeenth-century France, by contrast, communitarian habits transcended supposed differences in agrarian technology: most peasants were basically family-oriented, whether or not they opened their fields after harvest for communal grazing, or whether they were rich or poor. The strength of the French peasant communities did vary from province to province, from closed- to open-field country, but less from technological determinism than as a reflection of secular pressures, both state and seigneurial.

The cohesion of French villages depended not just on the use of land, therefore, but on other positive functions, which remained more numerous than was often supposed either at the time of the Revolution or in the nineteenth century. Tocqueville especially underestimated their importance. Though French villages were not as a rule meaningful political entities, they did matter in many ways: local syndics might decide on the times for planting and harvesting. Taxes and fines were often apportioned by the state not to individuals but to the villages, whose elders or consuls were left to collect them from each inhabitant as they could. Villages were legal units that might sue individuals, other villages, or even their feudal lords.

At times, though by no means always, villages were also feudal and seigneurial units, subject to economic or judicial dues which, in northern France especially, could still be of financial consequence. For a number of reasons, however, *seigneuries* were much less important than they had been: their legal function, for example, was drastically curtailed by the inroads of the centralizing state. Seigneurs were often absenteeowners. Some of them were bourgeois landlords of doubtful prestige. Many seigneuries had been subdivided nearly unto death.

Even though the village did not matter much as feudal unit, its religious functions were important. Symbolically, the modern administrative division of France follows the boundaries of former parishes rather than those of the former seigneuries. When Sieyès in 1789 tried to define what France was, he began by excluding nobles and by including parishes: "Where shall we find the nation? We shall find it where it actually is: in the forty thousand parishes which encompass the whole of our territory."[1]

In western France and in many other parts of the country, parish meetings could overlap with village assemblies, which were often tilted to represent the interest of the richer peasants. It was there that village elders would set the cycles of rural life and decide the dates of harvest or planting. Sunday church services brought together the village as a whole in a church consecrated to some patron saint whose name, in hundreds of instances (more than in any other European country) was also the name of the village itself. Parish vestries were entitled to own property, which they used for poor relief and education. The Catholic priests had many important cultural tasks; but they also served as political intermediaries between the parishioners and the state, and vice versa, for priests were required on Sunday to read official royal pronouncements from the pulpit. Ordinarily appointed by the regional bishop, country priests, especially in the eighteenth century, often came from the richer peasantry of the region. In those parts of France where the population had been forcibly converted from Protestantism to Catholicism or had never been thoroughly depaganized, priests were the natural doctrinal enemies of their flocks. More practical disputes were also not unknown. Ordinarily, however, the parish priest was a respected local figure and the living symbol of the village as a community. In many instances, local priests no longer collected the local tithes, which were paid instead to outsiders. But this usurpation of the curés' rights was widely resented, partly because the peasants were then obliged to make supplementary payments to the church, and partly because they assumed that their tithes should go to to the local priests.

THE COMMUNAL LIFE of French cities in the seventeenth and early eighteenth centuries was more complex than that of the villages. In theory, French cities, which included about 15 percent of the population, enjoyed some form of corporate self-government. They were privileged entities vis-à-vis the countryside and enjoyed "liberties," as well as many kinds of fiscal exemptions. In actuality, most city dwellers had no say in local self-government and did not identify with it. The villages of rural, roadless France were more autonomous than urban France, if only because of their inaccessibility. The cities were much more closely watched by the state, and over the centuries urban freedoms were gradually eroded. With the rise after 1650 of the French absolutist state, municipal rights in many parts of France were quite narrowly defined. Even local elites (not just the poor) were estranged from local government. Although cities theoretically were legal entities, owned property, and might be charged with policing themselves, their political autonomy under Louis XIV was virtually nonexistent. Even municipal police powers fell into the hands of the royal courts and then, during the second half of the seventeenth century, into those of appointed royal officials, the so-called lieutenants of police. Local militias were disbanded. In 1692 municipal offices, which had been elective, were put up for sale: the centralizing crown benefited twice from this change—by pocketing the money, and by creating a political void which the purchasers of offices, who had no local following, could not fill.

Nonetheless, the communitarian element of French urban life remained strong: it was not focused on local government, as it often was in New England, but it did have two powerful magnetic centers: tangible professional associations, and the intangible quality of daily life.

Urban districts, even in very large cities like Paris, were like small villages where everyone knew everyone else. Just as most peasants in isolated townships hung together because epidemics and crop failures affected rich and poor, if in different degrees, so were city dwellers intensely aware of one another's physical existence. In part because of constraining medieval walls that ordinarily survived into the nineteenth century, the population density (and insalubrity) of French cities was very high. People lived cheek by jowl along darkened streets, huddled inside unbelievably crowded apartments. In the mid-eighteenth century, three-quarters of Parisian families lived in a single room; before that date, conditions may have been even worse. Cities and their constituent "quartiers," or neighborhoods, were living things, rabbit warrens, laid out on lines sanctioned by immemorial custom. Public monuments, churches, hospitals, schools, and university buildings were objects of great civic pride. Parisians were particularly fond of their city hall, an unusually handsome building put up in the sixteenth century close to the Place de Grève, the site of gruesome public executions and of a citywide labor market before 1789, which after that became the state for much revolutionary drama. Urban sociability was in large part structured either around formal institutions that had a geographical dimension, like the parish or the church vestry or the militia; or around informal institutions like cafés, which also had a set, local clientele. It was impossible to live in a French city, especially Paris, without having a powerful sense of place.

Critical also to the awareness of community were institutions that focused on specific trades: indeed, it was the professional guilds or corporations—which were never recreated in America—that gave the particular texture to French urban life. City dwellers were everywhere organized in *corps*, which grouped together the practitioners of some profession (butchers, bakers, candlestick makers, and so on) or even of "subprofessions" (such as the spur makers' guild). These urban corporations (as they came to be known in France in 1750 in imitation of British practice) were clearly defined legal, social, and political units. Every organization was sanctioned by a written legal document, and admission to each of them was highly ritualized.

The corps were strong and their function often overlapped with that of other institutions. In the large cities, corps participated in the political rituals of monarchic visits and in vestigial municipal elections. Each one of them was placed under the protection of some patron saint. By the mechanism of apprenticeship, the corps had an educational function. They served as burial societies and provided some help for widows and orphans. Membership in a corps was often a familial treasure passed on from generation to generation. Even skilled journeymen sometimes found it difficult to gain access to the corps of their trade; the best way for one of them to do so was to marry either his employer's daughter or his widow. From the point of view of the state, the corps were a convenient way to control labor and production, but from the perspective of the laborers the corps' first purpose was to protect workers from competition. What the two perspectives had in common was an esssential distrust of individual economic impulse.

Local corps reproduced the broader societal values that prevailed in the culture: they were hierarchically organized. The older, experienced members enforced work discipline and "quality control." In municipal festivities, corps paraded in order of dignity and social status.

The most prestigious corporations were those closest to the church and the state. Notaries, lawyers, and clerks all had their set place on the ladder of prestige. Even state functionaries thought of their agencies as prestigious corporations of a kind, and each governmental agency had a strongly defined esprit de corps. Jurisdictional quarrels, which were the joy of learned, experienced lawyers, were the bane of indignant clients who had to pay the fees. In the more mundane world of artisanal life, some corps had clear precedence: Parisian tanners who lived in unsalubrious proximity to the rue Mouffetard were much despised by their more highly skilled and richer brethren, the locksmiths, goldsmiths, or jewelers who lived next to the Cathedral of Notre-Dame on the Ile de la Cité. Members of the professions who did not work with their hands looked down on those who did, just as the skilled despised the less skilled: goldsmiths did not think much of locksmiths. In some ways, the ancien régime was a *cascade de mépris,* a continuous chain of disdain.

The number of guilds varied considerably from place to place: Lyons had few; Poitiers, a much smaller place, had forty-two. Some occupational groups, such as grain merchants or millers, were purposely not organized into corps. This was also true, if for different reasons, of some cities, for example, Clermont, and of some parts of Paris, such as the Faubourg Saint-Antoine, whose furniture makers figured prominently during the Revolution. Police controls regulated to some extent those artisanal professions that did not regulate themselves.

The need for association was powerfully felt by the poor, who were linked not only in groups fostered by the state but by illegal associations also. Many urban dwellers also belonged to intermittently legal *confréries* (their rough rural analogues were *chambrées*), whose function was more plainly sociable. Illegal but also tolerated by the authorities were national associations of workers, taken craft by craft. Except in Paris, where these artisanal associations, or *compagnonnages,* were unimportant, young men who had completed their training as apprentices would join the Gavots, or Dévorants, or the Enfants du Père Soubise, and travel from town to town on an extensive *Tour de France* that might last many years. In every large city, the *compagnons* would find in the local "maison-mère" employment, food, shelter, and the companionship of other Gavots or Dévorants, some of them in the same craft and others not.

Although the social geography of urban France, like that of rural

France, was varied, the basic pattern was roughly the same everywhere. Even those city dwellers who did not belong to guilds constructed their lives around the principles of loyalty and exclusion which the guilds had made familiar. The ethos of the corps was pervasive even where its formal organization lapsed. Frenchmen felt that an ordered society should not consist of isolated, comparable individuals with abstract loyalties, but of collective entities of very unequal rank, all of them in theory harmoniously linked to one another. The culture of the working poor was highly structured. The ensuing social fabric had obvious political significance because a sudden or life-threatening rise in prices—like any other sudden change in the rules of life—easily engendered community-based and riotous protest.

So pervasive was this sense of variegated corporate solidarity that the economic underclass of urban drifters is best described negatively, as people who did *not* belong to a corps. This human flotsam and jetsam was, in premodern France, always numerous; and its numbers swelled suddenly in hard times, when the price of bread shot up or when seasonal employment dropped off. In both town and country, tens of thousands of people were constantly wandering from place to place: beggars, former soldiers, camp followers, destitute peasants, unemployed artisans, actors, musicians, village idiots, orphans, vagrants, criminals, monks, peddlers, prostitutes, and pilgrims, all of them moving ceaselessly from village to village in search of handouts, or in very hard times from small villages to the larger cities, where such public charity as might be had was parsimoniously given out, usually by the church. It is a revealing sign of the hold of the corporate ethic on the minds of the French that these vagabonds often traveled or lived in bands that were parodic versions of the corps. Typically also, French officials persisted in thinking their unending and unavoidable migrations to be unnatural. From time to time, fearful and useless edicts were proclaimed, threatening with dire punishment all who had no fixed abode. French officialdom labored long to codify, typologize, and occasionally institutionalize these drifters. The bureaucratic taxonomy of beggary was highly developed.

Professional corporations—like families—were thought to be part of a larger system, a Great Social Chain of Being that covered society as a whole. Corps were the subcategories of an interlocking set of estates, of broad and organically related groups that were defined by birth or function. "Every [estate]," wrote the noble apologist, the chevalier d'Arcq, in 1756, "has its separate function . . . and all of them constitute together a kind of body [corps] which moves under the authority of laws and the power of the Prince. The functions of each of the corps have as their object the general interest, and this general interest lies at the point where the three estates meet."[2] Estates and corporations were alike in nature, and so much so that the Catholic Church, which was the First Estate of the realm, was also a professional corporation whose legal status, unlike that of the estates as such, was punctiliously codified by the concordat, or agreement, drawn up in 1515 by king and pope.

The boundaries of the nobility or Second Estate were much less clear than those of the clergy. In Britain, the rights of nobles had been spelled out in law by 1650, but only because they had already been drastically narrowed by the crown. French nobles occupied a broader and vaguer field. Theoretically, they were defined by their birth (more precisely, by their father's rather than their mother's). Few French noble families, however, could trace their lineage back before 1400. In 1789 perhaps as many as nine out of ten French nobles belonged to families that had been raised to their new status within the past two centuries.

Nobles in the seventeenth century stood apart, nevertheless, as a reasonably distinct social entity, and they enjoyed many fiscal exemptions. Although some of them paid as many taxes as nonnobles did, and although all of them paid some tax, their fiscal situation was of a distinctive kind. In the main their corporate status was informally defined by their social prestige; but they had formal privileges, some of them real, others purely honorary. They wore swords and had the right to put up weather vanes on their country houses. Only the seigneur (the lord of the manor) could own a dung-producing dovecote. In 1700 aristocracy was already less clear as a fact than as a concept, but it remained a recognizable category.

AT THE DEATH of Louis XIV in 1715 this network of interlocking communities, formal and informal—even though often honored in the breach, since pitched battles between the members of different corporations were quite common—was thought by nearly everyone in France to be completely natural. The mental map of the world of seventeenth-century Frenchmen was made up of vertical and horizontal complementarities that echoed their view of a socially harmonious world. Christ, who was God and man, had died voluntarily, at once abandoned and all-powerful. The Virgin was both a virgin and a mother. The distinction between private and public was much less sharply drawn than in later times, and sexual types were conceived in seventeenth-century France as complementary. In nineteenth-century bourgeois society, men were thought naturally rapacious, fated to public and material life. Women then were not their complements but their opposites: irrational, undersexed, hysterical, frail, cultured, homebound, faithful, and spiritual—angels in the house, though of a somewhat neurotic kind. Seventeenth-century popular culture emphasized instead the interweaving of sex roles. Both men and women had bipartite bodies, reflective and potentially angelic at the top, sexual and digestive in their lower parts, linked by spells and magic to a larger Manichaean cosmos where God and the Devil were in constant rivalry. Women were thought to be even more highly sexed than men. Work roles were sexually differentiated in both town and country—to such a degree that marriages were first and foremost laboring partnerships in the economy of the home; but everyone worked. Witches, whose corporation was a satanic one, were inverted, destructive, selfish women, their place in the mythology of the times reminiscent of that of lesbians in the age of Baudelaire. Celibacy outside the church was, for all but the very rich and the very poor, an almost insuperable economic challenge.

The traditional principle of complementarity was evident in the relationship of old and young; in the nature of popular rejoicings, which often blended order and disorder in sophisticated stagings of managed chaos; and in the ways that crimes were both punished and perceived. Criminals were assumed to be personally malevolent. At times they were also thought, like all deviants, to have been the victims of some particularly unfortunate environment or heredity: the Bible did say that the sins of the fathers would be visited upon the children for three generations. Before the Enlightenment, however, these moral issues, which bore on the criminal's personal responsibility as an individual for his crime, were of marginal penological and social interest. What mattered in seventeenth-century France was less the criminal himself, or the causes that had made him what he was, than the criminal's debt to society. As in seventeenth-century Massachusetts, executions were public spectacles, and murderers walking or riding to their death were expected to repent and exhort the crowd to good behavior. Occasionally, a crowd might surge forward to release the culprit; more often, the bemused spectators intoned hymns to comfort the repentant sinner on his or her way to another world.

Two of the most striking aspects of socialization in the affective, organic complementarity typical of premodern France were the irrelevance of schools and the collapse of public and private educational concerns. In nineteenth-century bourgeois life, schools were in theory public, neutral institutions whose aim was to transmit knowledge to all children rather than to develop them morally. During the ancien régime, however, instruction and education overlapped, and most children in town or country did not attend any school for any length of time. Children learned both at home (or in the street) and in the school. One made up for the other in a context of easy duality: in mountain districts, for example, where schools were rare but winter evenings were long, children had high rates of literacy. For a number of reasons, one of which was the sordidness of private housing, street life was both intense and educational. Although ordinary people could not read, they were often read to. The cautionary tales of open-air theaters, mimes, shows, and fairs were a normal part of the urban scene. Moralizing theaters, ambulatory in the provinces and fixed in the larger cities, had large audiences, half a million per year in mid-eighteenth-century Paris.

Generally speaking, groups mattered more than individuals. Love and hatred were differently understood. Despite modern and self-congratulatory views on this matter, parents in "prebourgeois" France did love their offspring, although they had less cause to mourn their deaths for they knew that a child's baptized innocence guaranteed it a place on the right hand of the Father. Children were loved in a different way, and perhaps more generously than they are today, less as projections of the parent and more as archetypal figures, as representations of the child Jesus, and as members of a larger group.

These attitudes contrasted strongly with both nineteenth-century antibourgeois romanticism, which thrived on irreconcilable contradiction (between the great criminal and his victim, the genius and the bourgeois, the revolutionary and the reactionary) and the nineteenth-century bourgeois world view, which admired atomized if ordered individualities and was fascinated by horrid deviants of all kinds. Seventeenth-century French men and women lived, learned, worked, fought, and danced in groups. The title of Rousseau's *Rêveries d'un promeneur solitaire* was both programmatic and innovative.

French society and culture before 1700 were still structured around concepts of reconciliation and forced consensus. In 1685 Louis XIV's revocation of the Protestants' Edict of Toleration was understood by that devout if self-indulgent monarch in terms not of persecution but of enforced harmony. The heroes of the seventeenth-century dramatist Corneille strained to prove themselves worthy of feudal values; and the honor of Racine's characters, though more moralized and metaphysical, was even more demanding. French men and women of all ranks entered and left life not alone, but in company. Neither death nor birth was a private event. At Versailles, in the next century, dozens of courtiers and servants, some of them standing on top of dressers, witnessed the birth of Marie-Antoinette's three children. Less eminent women were more secluded, but even they gave birth surrounded by family and women friends, since childbirth was a high point not just of female anguish but of feminine sociability.

Death, like birth, was accompanied by elaborate ritual. High mortality rates meant that death in premodern France came early and often. Young men and women died of disease, hunger, or accidents. One woman in every twenty died in labor, as contrasted with one in 6,366 in America today. To ease man's fear of death, prerevolutionary France made of dying an elaborate and socialized art form. Tracts on the subject circulated with a frequency comparable only to manuals on sex in our own times: one million of these mortuary pamphlets, together with 150,000 prints of dying men and women, were sold in eighteenth-century France. One Parisian home in two displayed some kind of mortuary scene. This extreme interest in death, which testifies also to the emotivity of the culture, led to complex communitarian staging. The habit of making wills that regulated the circumstances of one's departure for a better world was widely observed. Less than half of French adults, however poor, died intestate. Death-bed and public confessions of repentance were expected of saints and sinners, kings and peasants. It was less from seemly hypocrisy than from a desire to do the right thing that Louis XIV in his last days expressed regret for his extravagant expenditures on wars and palaces and implored the forgiveness of his subjects and of the Mother Church. By custom, passersby who saw a priest taking the sacrament of extreme unction to a dying parishioner were entitled to follow him to the death chamber. Funerals were replete with appropriate ceremonies, vestments, gifts, and meals. They sometimes brought together as many as a hundred people, some of them beggars whose presence in the midst of an extended and propertied family was a reminder of all men's equality in death and of man's membership in a Christian and mortal race.

The ubiquitous principles of social harmony and inclusion implied an active and enforced exclusion of deviants and eccentrics instead of the resigned toleration exhibited in our own times. A profession or a corps could be defined by reference to those whom it left out as well as by those whom it brought in. "Ways of seeing" are also, of their nature, ways of nonseeing. Heretics, however discreet they might be, were from the very fact of their existence an offense. The line was thin between acceptable political dissent and death-deserving treason. Even when schooled under a single roof, boys and girls were brought up separately. For masters and their servants or the rich and the poor, close physical proximity went hand in hand with an obstinate assertion of symbolic differences in dress and manners. Witches were betrayers of religious and social commonality.

THE SOCIAL PRINCIPLES of inclusion and exclusion had clear political and religious extensions. The king was the father of his people. The French monarch was the apex of a feudal and universal pyramid of fealty and allegiance: in 1692 Louis XIV went out of his way to remind his vassals of this overriding suzerainty and of his own regal place as the unquestioned leader of a pyramidal society of interlocking feudal privilege and responsibility. The king of France also invoked, especially in judicial matters, the completely different and modern principle of imperium, based on Roman precedent, which his legal counselors over the centuries had worked very hard to revive. The essence of monarchic prestige in the seventeenth century still lay, nevertheless, in the king's paternal and Christian role—and to such a degree that the decline after 1760 of this political myth was a critical factor in the coming of the French Revolution. This was the image of a law-abiding monarch, suspicious of luxury or wealth, the architect of a divinely sanctioned world order, that was popularized by Bishop Fénelon in his highly popular *Les Aventures de Télémaque* (1699), a cautionary tale written to guide the footsteps of the heir to the French throne.

The king was the eldest son of the church. In diplomatic documents he was styled "his most Christian Majesty." He was a quasi-religious person, anointed in the Cathedral of Rheims with holy chrism brought by doves from heaven. He could cure the sick by his touch. Although the autonomy of the national Catholic Church directed by the king was differently interpreted by Gallicans at home and papalist ultramontanes beyond the Alps, the king was understood by everyone to have broad religious powers. Subject to Rome's approval, he appointed all the bishops and many abbots.

The French took political sovereignty to be divinely sanctioned, indivisible, and incarnate in the person of a sacred monarch-priest whose political existence was more real and tangible than society itself. Although the theory of the "king's two bodies" was not so developed in France as it had been in medieval Britain, the French in the seventeenth century still assumed that the nation as a whole was represented in the king's second and immortal body.[3] As Jean Bodin had explained in the sixteenth century, and the Gallican Bishop Bossuet repeated in 1682, a monarch's authority was deathless. An effigy of the live king preceded his dead body to burial at the Abbey of Saint-Denis, where heralds ended the ceremony with the cry, "Le roi est mort. Vive le roi!" For Anglo-Americans the modern British state had already lost its sacred character by 1688. This colonial and minimalist view of high politics implied that the British state might be easily ignored by Americans, once its utilitarian appeal was gone. But the perception of sovereignty by the French—though it might eventually be transferred to some other agency (such as a revolutionary and republican people, or the Jacobin clubs)—was so deep and pervasive that it colored their understanding of the universalist state.

The church, like the monarchy it buttressed, was a powerful cohesive force which probably owed less to the state than the monarchy did to religion. Assemblies of the French Church met every five years, ritually made a "voluntary" contribution to the expenses of the state, and underwrote the state's political decisions. Religious rites and social customs were also interwoven, and irreligion was less a voluntary choice than an unnatural deviance, rather as homosexuality was regarded by the bourgeoisie in the nineteenth century.

Clerical associations were an important vehicle of sociability in both town and country, for rich and poor. In the seventeenth century an extensive and growing network of convents and monasteries gave institutional expression, for women especially, to a cultural yearning for self-fulfillment within a communitarian framework of Christian charity. Pilgrimages and public celebrations on feast days came thick and fast, as did public incantations for better harvests and more clement weather. In the late eighteenth century thousands of Parisians, many of whom would soon become sansculottes, followed the statue of Sainte-Geneviève around the city in times of drought. Word of miraculous intercessions by local saints drew immediate, widespread attention. France counted 170,000 secular priests, monks, and nuns. Families were swift in arranging for the baptism of the newborn: in nine out of ten cases, only two days elapsed between birth and holy baptism. Parents were mindful not only of the incidence of death in infancy but also of limbo's uncertain merits and of hell's unnumbered terrors.

Since the Tridentine reforms of the sixteenth century, the church in France had taken its proselytizing duties very seriously. Municipal brothels were shut down. The instruction of the clergy, increasingly trained in seminaries, was closely watched, as was their morality. And the faithful were carefully supervised: in the earlier part of the seventeenth century, missions were sent to reinforce rural faith. Ninety percent of French men and women took communion at least once a year, as canon law required them to do at Easter. It was at church, under the guidance of the village priest, who identified his ministrations with those of Christ, that the assembled communities—rich and poor, nobles and peasants acquired their sense of self. Although individual street singers were very numerous, group singing depended on clerical sponsorship. The ringing of church bells, many of them named after female saints, elicited powerful cultural echoes, as the revolutionaries were well aware when they ordered them to be melted down in 1794.

The list of activities in which the church was *not* involved is shorter than that of those which it controlled or in which it participated. The parish church and the numerous voluntary associations which it sheltered were powerful instruments of sociability. Many fundamental social roles were played by churchmen. Priests kept records of births and deaths, dispensed charity, arbitrated disputes, and interceded for their parishioners with the authorities, whether of church or state. The curé either taught in the village school or chose and supervised those who taught. In one way or another the church monopolized higher education as well. To guarantee church domination of university teaching, after 1707 French students were forbidden to study abroad. By its blessing of animals and crops, the church supervised production, and by its strictures it regulated reproduction also: to make infanticide more difficult, women were required by law to register their pregnancies with the church. The local priest licensed midwives. He also kept track of local mores through the ritual of confession.

Religion was the visible organizing principle of French cultural life. For the subjects of Louis XIV, God and the supernatural were omnipresent. Granted prayer was like magic. Life was a gift of God; and death, especially collective death in times of plague or war, a divine punishment. Doctors, and especially surgeons, were held in poor esteem, first because the application of their pseudoscience, satirized by Molière in the seventeenth century, was far more likely to worsen than to improve the condition of their patients; and second because it was man's fate to be powerless before God's wrath. The people and their clerical shepherds might differ on how men and women should try to steer their bark: priests emphasized the power of God; folk lore looked to the pantheistic and Manichaean struggle of good and evil. Priests, magicians, and the people agreed, however, that mysterious and ritualized incantations, whether sacred or profane, were man's best recourse. Neither God nor the devil could help those daring individuals who tried to help themselves. Only tradition and divine or magical intercession could render the physical universe less uncertain. In the material world, accidents, plagues, and misfortunes of all kinds were just around the corner; but the universe of folk lore, like the universe of God, his saints, and the devil, was completely charted. Words, when carefully chosen, mattered more than things. Necromancers could predict and even set the future.

In seventeenth-century France, as in New England at the same time, religion was the glue of society and politics. Surprisingly, this was even more noticeable in the French provinces than in the Bay colony. In some respects, New England was a theocracy, which France was not and had never been. In actual fact, however, religion was more deeply embedded in France than it was in New England, not to speak of Pennsylvania or, worse yet, New York. Religion was everywhere in Massachusetts, but its connection with the state was one of juxtaposition rather than interpenetration. Theologically inclined divines worked from reason up to religion. They were not priests who started from hidden mysteries. Religious precepts which in Boston proved commercially or politically deleterious were rapidly disowned. The connection in France between natural and supernatural was more deeply felt, by working people at least, and in the eighteenth century it was more deeply resented by those who had successfully emancipated themselves from it. Private lives were perhaps more sheltered from religious inquisition in Puritan New England than they were in France. Every French church displayed learned inscriptions of naive ex-votos, public rewards to a patron saint for averted private, familial disasters. It is hard to imagine the likes of this in a New England meetinghouse.

French culture in the first half of the seventeenth century was affective and tradition-bound. Life was about immediate, face-to-face relationships that were much less filtered by a screen of ratiocination than in Puritan America. Sounds, sermons, songs, and hundreds of thousands of prints and pictures mattered more in France than either abstract reasoning or the printed word. Historians have rightly emphasized the importance in this earlier French culture of direct sensory experience and its accompanying unreasoned violence. It is difficult for those who live in a society where brutality has been sublimated into malice, personal or nationalistic, to recapture the omnipresence of physical brutality in France at the beginning of the ancien régime. In our twentieth-century world, violence and death (which is the ultimate form of nature's brutality) are carefully dissembled, but willful physicality in its positive and degenerative forms was in France a fact of daily life. Nature impinged everywhere. So did the weather—storms at sea, droughts, thunder, floods, and extremes of cold and heat. The favorite toys of children were animals.

Life was cast in a Hobbesian mode, short and often brutish. Seventeenth-century prisons, hospitals, madhouses, schools, convents, armies, navies, and institutions of all kinds relied on sustained, cruel, and unusual punishment as a means of governance. A person of modern sensibility transported in H. G. Wells's time machine would surely be shocked by the violent vulgarity of colonial America life; but he would be far more horrified by the brutality of social life in early modern France. An extreme sensitivity to the need for controlling others coincided there with a broad tolerance, in daily life, of filth and disgusting table and personal manners. Wives, children, domestics, prisoners, and animals were beaten as a matter of course, and animals were pitted against each other for public sport. While torture was the exception rather than the rule in America, and death for criminals was ordinarily by hanging, suspects in France were ordered by statute to be tortured, and criminals were broken on the wheel.

The sublimation of violence into fear and humiliation was the best that could be hoped for. Practical jokes and mockingly savage rites of collective social humiliation, the so-called charivaris, were common fare for the plebs. Catholic sermons dwelt lovingly on hell fire and on the perpetual torment of the damned. The striking stylizations of baroque art forms with their the violent contrasts and their arrested movements are expressive sublimations of the spirit of this age. The extreme refinement of forms of address or of movement, the stifling etiquette of court life, and the ritualization of social intercourse all expressed an extreme need for order and self-imposed control in situations of personal exchange. The seventeenth-century tragedies of Racine can be tangentially imagined as social fantasies, as life resolutely "aristocratized" and shorn of the innumerable threats and vulgarities which crowded in always on the men—and especially on the women—of his time.

Voltaire found the seventeenth century pleasingly greater than his own mid-eighteenth century because he saw it as an age of ordered and official grandeur, the Age of Louis XIV, of Versailles, of academies (especially the Académie Française, to which he belonged and which had been founded by Richelieu in 1635), as the age of Racine, of Corneille, and of rhyming alexandrine couplets. What impresses current historians about the *grand siècle*, however, is not its monarchic imprint but the surviving wholeness of a traditional medieval culture and society, so different from our own epoch, which is in many ways more ordered, open, and tolerant but also more atomized and incoherent.

THE PROCESS OF change toward rationally and more individuated social forms that began in seventeenth-century France was a matter of very gradual transition rather than revolution. Set between the world of high politics, which was subject to human passions, and the near immutability of natural circumstances (rainfall, temperature, crops), the intermediary cultural, social, and political forms evolved very slowly. By contrast, the American settlements, created de novo, rapidly introduced new modes of action, of social individualism in all its forms—economic, matrimonial, or religious. Change there was, however, in seventeenth-century France. Some of it took place within established cultural or institutional forms, and some of it was elaborated in direct opposition to them.

The Catholic Church was in 1650 far removed from what it had been one hundred years before. The Counter-Reformation of the sixteenth and seventeenth centuries transformed the French Church, which emerged both purified and bureaucratized. Although the decisions of the Council of Trent, which ended in 1563, were never accepted as such by the French state, its recommendations were not without effect. The hold of bishops on their dioceses was strengthened. Local superstitions and beliefs were wiped out or transmogrified: where the memory of pagan fertility rites was strong, churchmen took to blessing the marriage bed of newlyweds. The sexual mores of the one hundred thousand parish priests who regimented France were themselves more closely watched: the proportion of curés whose households were of a suspicious cast fell from one-fifth in the 1650s to one-twentieth in the 1720s. Priests were better trained, many of them in Parisian seminaries. By 1700 nearly all dioceses had at least one such educational institution. The church in the next century was to be weakened in a way by this self-discipline, which diminished its ability to respond to popular, millenarian impulses.

By the end of the seventeenth century, feudalism in France, like religion, had become culturally ambiguous. Its first principles, obviously, were hierarchic and prescriptive, but this self-consciously upheld, antiquated world view implied individual self-assertion, if only on certain terms and within an established code. Feudalistic individualism, though a negative and stylized force, could not be ignored. Corneille's heroes certainly knew that they should conform to set rules, but their task was nonetheless to choose from conflicting goals that could not be reconciled, even if all of them were culturally sanctioned.

French culture was deeply marked by this ancient and divided feudal cultural heritage that simultaneously emphasized individual elegance or style and placed a high premium on rhetorical convention and the stylized mastery of social savoir faire. The feudal ethos was one of the starting points for the modern cultural and political assertion of the French self. As has often been remarked, the liberal notion that a man's home is his castle was first argued by men whose homes *were* castles. Although most great nobles by 1680 had been domesticated by the crown and lived in the king's palace at Versailles, the ancient ethos of aristocratic independence and insolence became after 1700 the foundation of a revulsion against monarchic absolutism. That rejection was ephemeral, but it was institutionalized momentarily in a fleeting type of government called the Polysynodie during the regency that followed the death in 1715 of the Sun King. In addition, feudalism allowed some change because the bourgeoisie could achieve greater social respectability in the eyes of nobles and their own class by successfully imitating aristocratic modes and styles.

In late-seventeenth-century France the progress of ideological individualism and pragmatic rationality was not, however, achieved primarily from within, through the older, traditional values, but in direct if still limited opposition to them. France in the reign of Louis XIV counted a fair and growing number of religious dissidents or near dissidents, such as the Gallicans (who were religious nationalists), the Richerists (who argued for the rights of the lower clergy), and the mystical Quietists (who were close to the mainstream of the church). More significant still as a potential source of resistance were the Augustinian Jansenists, who were either heretical or close to it, and the Protestants, most of whom were Augustinians also.

Nearly a million Protestants lived in France. Many of them were individualistically minded Calvinists, some of them merchants who would emigrate to North America after 1685, when Louis XIV withdrew the Edict of Toleration that had afforded them precarious independence for nearly a century. (Gouverneur Morris, Paul Revere, John Jay, and Peter Faneuil, the founder in 1742 of Boston's Faneuil Hall, were the descendants of such Huguenot migrants.)

Completely different in inspiration but also difficult to absorb were the more daring habitués of some Parisian intellectual circles and salons, which were becoming important informal institutions. Atheistic libertines (including some women), though still elegant curiosities, were an interesting omen of the future cultural trajectory of the French elites.

Of these various dissident movements, inside and outside the church, the most significant was Jansenism—as appears from the importance which this world view had for both Pascal (who died in 1662) and Racine, respectively the most eloquent of all French philosophers and the greatest of all French playwrights. Jansenism was most expressive of the French bourgeoisie's new and latently anti-aristocratic—or at least antifeudal—world view. It may also have been the channel through which, in Paris especially, religious individualism reached down to the popular culture.

Like the New England Puritan Calvinists, French Jansenists were Augustinians who believed in predestination, and in divine grace as the solution to the crushing legacy of man's original sin. Yet their cultural stance emphasized the helpless solitude of mankind before an "absent" and hidden God, rather than man's compensatory ability to create. While Calvinism in its American and Puritan form hurled the puzzled believer into the world as it might become under Christian ministration, the French Jansenists drew in on themselves. For them man's depravity, expressed in the truth of original sin, was an overwhelming fact which could be understood but not transcended. Self-mortification was for the Jansenist an end in itself.

New England Puritans could not divine God's will, but their collective fate, they knew, was to be God's chosen people, to be, in Boston, a City on the Hill. By contrast, the first Jansenists were *solitaires*; their purest successors, at the Abbey Port-Royal (the Jansenist stronghold near Paris), rejected not merely worldly success but routine civil and clerical office as well. For them, no second Israel would mediate man's worldly fate and God's inscrutable will. In his Massachusetts election sermon of 1703, Solomon Stoddard explicitly drew the distinction between private vice and public good: "The Country is not Guilty of the Crimes of Particular Persons unless they make themselves guilty," he carefully explained; "if they countenance them, or connive at them, they make themselves guilty by participation: But when they are duely witnessed against, they bring no publick guilt." This view would have been unthinkable to the Jansenists, who envisaged public life not as the reverse but as the sum of private vices. In the tragedies of Racine, which were aesthetically the noblest stylization of their world view, there were no popular choruses, no guiding voices of the assembled people to warn or to explain. The gap that separated the sacred from the profane could not be bridged. Life in the world implied incessant compromise, and the *gloire* of Racine's heroes lay in their refusal of these worldly choices, in their unbending adherence to absolute values which drove them inexorably to disastrous refusal, even to the point of self-destruction.

In the seventeenth century the social and political effects of Jansenist doctrine were twofold. On the one hand, the new emphasis on the religious inner self weakened the French bourgeoisie's adherence both to absolute monarchy and to the revived, bastard feudalism which was encompassed by the administratively bureaucratized but socially deferential Old Regime. On the other hand, Jansenism weakened the French response to profitable and technological opportunity, a social development which certainly did not take place among New England's Calvinist merchants. Culturally, Jansenism was Janus-faced and, as such, closely suited to the social and cultural needs of many French lawyers who simultaneously held modernizing capitalism in low esteem and rejected traditional feudal and hierarchic obligation.

The relative importance of the Jansenists in influencing the development of French culture can be gauged by comparing them with both the Pilgrims and the Puritans. Like the Jansenists, the Plymouth Pilgrims were Separatists who believed—unlike their Puritan neighbors in Boston—that society as they knew it was beyond regeneration. The dominant church, thought both the Pilgrims and the French Jansenists, should be left to its own devices. In order to lead separate and more holy lives, the truly devout had no choice but to withdraw from society. Plymouth, unlike Boston but very much like Port-Royal, was a refuge from the world at large.

These three types of Augustinians differed, however, in that the Pilgrims were a simple people while the Jansenists and Puritans were intellectuals. Until Massachusetts absorbed their southern neighbors in 1691, no students from Plymouth attended Harvard College. The biblical tone of Governor Bradford's prose is not without its resolute grandeur, but it cannot be compared with the elegance and the terse, aristocratic grace of Racine's nearly contemporaneous verse. Essentially apolitical—neither of the world nor in the world—the Pilgrims, unlike the Puritans, did not prevail as a cultural model. Their selfless life became an American ideal, but it could not become an American example.

Plymouth was, even for Massachusetts, an anomaly; but Port-Royal was so important that Louis XIV soon ordered it razed to the ground. The place of Jansenism in the shaping of modern French culture was both critical and ambiguous. Though it remained in the seventeenth century the doctrine of a "middle-class" minority, the Jansenist origins of the modern French self are nonetheless deeply rooted. In the course of the eighteenth century, Jansenism appeared to wane in France, even as an informal institution: this seeming decline was not surprising since its visible tenets (especially its emphasis on the innate sinfulness of man) ran counter to the main arguments of the French Enlightenment. As a formal set of beliefs, Jansenism had practically vanished by 1789. And yet in retrospect, the inward-turning and somewhat lugubrious principles of that Christian doctrine were a more important formative force in French cultural life than the expansive, meliorist, and optimistic ideas of the Enlightenment. The Jansenist view of the past corroded the fabric of French traditionalism. Its emphasis on inner ideological coherence and its suspicion of day-to-day life in the world structured a solipsistic view of the self that molded many of the later characteristics of French life, including the propertied class's seeming indifference to tangible social problems; the propensity to ideologize reality; the preference for the kinds of capitalistic forms that distanced the producer from the consumer; and a noticeable incapacity for group action.

THE MOVE IN FRANCE from traditional corporate sensibilities to more modern individualist forms and to the cult of the private self was a checkered process, and its final result was strikingly different from the Promethean individualism of the American colonists. The French self sought protection from the world, rather than the right to shape it to its own ends. Relevant to the way in which the French defined the role of the individual in society was the negativist twist which the bureaucratic state gave to the excluded and increasingly powerless elites of the nation. As Tocqueville pointed out in his classic essay on the Old Regime, the corrosive action of the centralized state weakened not just the feudal system but the elites' capacity for self-government. The French aristocracy retained in the seventeenth century a fitful ability to rebel against monarchic fiat, but they lost an aptitude for consistent and positive action. The elites were more concerned with limiting the tax bite of the distant state than with using the state for their own ends. The result of centralized government in France was to distance not just the governed from the governing but families and individuals from one another. In a celebrated account of his visit to the house of a supposedly starving peasant who gradually revealed himself to be a well-stocked yeoman, Jean-Jacques Rousseau (in the next century) described the ingeniousness of Frenchmen in concealing their wealth from their observant neighbors, who might suddenly be pressed into service as tax collectors. The destructive effects of French administrative structures, it may be added, were felt all the more deeply because they coexisted with a deep suspicion of the law. The various legal systems—for laws differed widely from place to place—were like a mesh running through all private and public social and economic relations, including the relationship of guilds to one another. French men and women of all social ranks commonly assumed, as Mary Wollstonecraft would aptly put it in the next century in an account of French political foibles, that their courts and laws were "merely cobwebs to catch small flies."[4]

Few historians would venture to sort out precisely the causes of the development of individualism as a social value in seventeenth-century France. Two things are clear, however: the importance of that development; and the overall negativist coloration of individualism as it was defined and sustained from that time on. The state of social affairs in Ludovician France differentiated French cultural forms from those that were evolving in colonial America at the same time.

Methodological caution should also be applied to another dramatic cultural event in late-seventeenth-century France, namely, the shift of the boundary between the natural and supernatural. The causes of this shift are historically opaque—and from their nature will in all likelihood remain so—but the beginnings of this change in feeling may be readily perceived, although the description of the phenomenon as a whole is best left to a study of the eighteenth century. Suffice it to say that during the second half of the seventeenth century rationality gained wider currency among the elite as a principle of social action. Prosecutions for witchcraft dropped off in France during the third quarter of the seventeenth century. Sensibilities began to shift toward more individualistic and less theological responses: while the medieval literature on death had been overwhelmingly focused on agony and divine punishment, some seventeenth-century variants emphasized that a good life, reasonably conducted, was the best preparation for an easier death. Men and women would have to rely more on their own selves and less on the good will of the Lord. Medieval statuary had often portrayed a Virgin who carried the burdens of the world in the form of the dead Christ, or who sheltered priests, kings, and peas-

ants within the folds of her vast robes. Later statuary showed a
reclining, dying Christ, leaning on the Virgin, but more apart from
her than before.

DURING THE REIGNS of Louis XIII (1610–1643) and his son,
Louis XIV (1643–1715), an ambiguous compromise between an older
traditionalistic communitarianism and a more modern rationalistic
individualism became the hallmark of society. This mix was discernible in two critical areas: the economic life of the nation and its
political institutions.

France at the death of the Sun King in 1715 was still an overwhelmingly rural and economically static country. Every region was
particular to itself, but all of the variants were of the same basic
kind. Agricultural techniques and the organization of rural life in
1700 were as they had been for centuries. Peasant life was not
primarily turned toward the markets. Coins were few and their
value uncertain, partly because the monarch did not yet have a
monopoly of coinage. Even the urban bourgeois had a rentier
mentality rather than an entrepreneurial one: "It is a mean thing,"
wrote Claude Perrault (whose brother Charles reinvented the tale
of Little Red Hiding Hood), "to get anything whatever at too
cheap a price."[5] The collapse in the 1720s of both a royal bank
invented by a Scottish adventurer named Law and of the paper
currency his bank had issued furthered such suspicions. In the
business of finance, France fell a full century behind Britain—whose
Bank of England had been created in 1694 with the help of a
number of French Huguenot refugees.

And yet, although agriculture stagnated, economic structures
were beginning to change in the late seventeenth century. As would
soon be obvious, industry and trade were becoming more important. By 1700 textiles alone may have accounted for about 5 percent
of the national product. Millions of peasants were also part-time
artisans. By 1700 three canals had been built, one of them a major
effort (much admired by Locke when in exile in France during the
1670's), which linked the Mediterranean to the Atlantic Ocean.

The most suggestive changes in seventeenth-century French economic life, however, were those that affected the state's relationship
to industrial growth. The institutional shape of this change was

revealing. In Britain and the Netherlands economic change was carried out privately, the first role of the state being to make possible the development of private enterprise. In France, in accord with the mercantilist doctrine that held the volume of world trade to be fixed, the ministers of the crown—Colbert in particular—tried to improve the competitive situation of the nation as a whole. They attracted skilled foreigners to France by granting them monopolies and advantageous loans that would enable them to compete successfully. The state itself became a manufacturer of quality goods, such as those from the Saint-Gobain glass works, or the Gobelins tapestry works on the southern edge of Paris, or the manufactory for Savonnerie carpets, all of them still extant. These firms specialized in luxury goods for a small and captive market, but their limited industrial goals were vigorously pursued. Colbert, no friend of corporatist theory, did not hesitate to force workers into corporate organizations that would afford him some measure of control, blending modern and medieval conceptions of the economic good and exposing the growing ambiguity of French social forms.

The configuration of the French state reflected these ambiguities. The monarchy of Louis XIV took an economically modern view, one that was mercantilist and state-centered, as the political economists of the day said it should be. Colbert, again, tried to drive confréries and compagnonnages underground. In many other respects, however, the state was decidedly archaic, and Bourbon absolutism has often been described as the monarchic reformulation of an exhausted feudal order. The state often used rather than destroyed local aristocratic networks of patronage and dependence. Indeed, the means of government used by the monarchy were so contradictory that the political system was perhaps more ambiguous and more divided in its cultural inspiration than was any other French institution.

The French king had a divided role. As a feudal ruler he was, as most European monarchs had been for centuries, the suzerain of a countrywide pyramid of nobles, governors, marshals, seneschals, and bailiffs. Their offices had been created by the monarchy over the centuries, some of them before the reign of Philip Augustus (1165–1223), and had long since become largely hereditary or honorific.

The French king was at the same time a modern prince, the head of a bureaucratic system, which was in fact the first of its kind in the Western world. It is to the servants of the Bourbon state that we owe both the word "bureaucracy," from the word bureau (a desk, or the room in which a desk is put), and the more ominous term *commissaire,* an appointed agent of the state whose task it was to supplant the self-appointed *officier* who had either inherited or purchased his office. The gathering of statistics—those building blocks of modern statecraft—dates back to Colbert. Besides being a Christian monarch and a feudal figure, the king was also the head of a burgeoning bureaucracy, small in number (the ministry of foreign affairs at the end of the ancien régime contained less than a hundred permanent officials) but often honest and ordinarily efficacious. From the medieval curia the king's council—whose origins were said, wrongly, to reach back to Emperor Charlemagne in the ninth century, or, some thought, even before that time—had evolved into a network of interlocking councils whose members were appointed by the king and responsible to him only.

The most important of these councils was the Conseil d'Etat. Its youngest members, the *maîtres des requêtes,* were gifted young men, often related to one another by birth or marriage, who belonged to established bourgeois families, trained in the law, that were passing into the nobility. They thought highly of themselves, of the state, and of the monarch whom they served without question. After intensive training, the thirty or so councilors who had purchased their right to compete were promoted to more important posts. The most successful of them became either ambassadors or ministers to the king at home, perhaps after a stint as provincial intendants, that is to say, as representatives of the king in the provinces. (Brittany was the last province to be assigned an intendant, in 1689.) By the end of the seventeenth century the administration of the kingdom was in their hands and in those of their deputies, the *sub-délégués:* "You have neither Parlements . . . nor Estates, nor Governors," wrote financier John Law in the 1720s, "I might add neither king nor ministers, but thirty [men] . . . on whom depends the welfare or the misery of the provinces."[6] Law exaggerated somewhat: most intendants were eager to rule in ways that would not offend local worthies, and the secret of the French system's success lay in the unspoken and harmonious blending of institutions that were, in theory, quite incompatible. In the end, however, the appointed officials did do the king's bidding whether important locals liked it or not.

Other high officials stayed in Versailles or Paris, where many of them had been born and bred. They served in the many *conseils* that supervised royal finances or drafted laws or served as an administrative court, since the state was at once defendant and judge in all cases where its rights were being questioned. No system of government could have been more unlike the decentralized sharing of power in colonial Massachusetts, where a distant monarch left the real business of government to the representative General Court, to town meetings, and to elected town councils.

The French monarchic state was simultaneously the most antique and the most modern government of Europe. Most of the taxes it levied, such as the gabelle and the taille, were archaic and grotesquely distributed. But others, such as the *capitation,* were of a more modern kind, assigned in proportion to income and not according to social status.

Within this unusual, bicephalous state structure, the French judicial system more than any other branch of government expressed the contradictions of its double origin. In some ways, the two thousand or so members of the dozen law courts, or *parlements,* were commissaires. Their origin, like that of the conseil d'Etat, was in the royal curia. The king was the fountainhead of justice; and the *parlementaires* were in theory his appointed servants, just as the *conseillers* were. Justice was in principle a royal preserve, and the king did at times appoint new and special courts, to repress banditry, for example, or to examine nobles' claims to special status. Symbolically, every parlement, even in the eighteenth century, had a royal procurator appointed by the king.

In actuality, by the late seventeenth century the parlementaires were close to being noble-born officers. Though the parlements had indeed begun as bureaucratic agencies of a kind, they had gradually been transformed into traditionalist institutions. The parlementaires had begun as a type of commissaire and had become the reverse. The reason was the venality of offices: the kings, who were always short of money, first sold the right to become a parlementaire, and in 1604 compounded that mistake by institutionalizing the parlementaires' ability to turn their purchased function into a proprietary office which they might more easily pass on to their children. On the basis of this tolerated abuse, the parlementaire families grew in wealth and dignity. By 1650 they had reached the highest level of the Third Estate. Many of them were Jansenists. Soon they would pass into the Second Estate as a nobility of the robe, which was distinct from but very close to the classic nobility of the sword. In some parlements, robe and sword were intermingled before 1700. A good indication of the success of the parlementaires is the deep hatred of them that runs through the *Memoirs* of the Duc de Saint-Simon (1675–1755), one of the greatest snobs of modern times.

To summarize, during the second half of the seventeenth century French society and the French state were in a kind of precarious equilibrium. Though fundamentally a corporate society where the rights of the group took precedence over those of its members, France was irreversibly engaged in a process of social and institutional individuation.

The undecided nature of the French state had a close parallel in the social order: both the Bourbon state and the society it encompassed were mixtures of old and new. The unraveling of the ancien régime in the following century may therefore be conceptualized as a two-sided process. The individuation of society developed at an accelerated pace among the elites, but the state did not keep up with this cultural and social change. It gradually became more anachronistically inefficient, as well as less sympathetic to individual impulse. The Bourbon system of governance which in the seventeenth century mirrored the shape of a divided society had become a hindrance to society a hundred years later.

3

An Ideology of Virtue
in Eighteenth-Century America

AMERICAN COLONIAL SOCIETY in the eighteenth century was uniquely structured. By 1700 the colonies were no longer the gemeinschaft-like communities that their founders had envisaged. According to classical sociological theory, colonial society should then have become, in rapid order, first an individualistic, atomized society—a gesellschaft—and then a society made up of distinct, and warring, social classes. In American fact, as against European theory, neither of these two developments materialized.

Rampant American economic individualism "ought" to have engendered in the thirteen colonies the celebrated contradictions of capitalism, with a critical movement in social organization from caste to class. It is the argument of this book—vigorously denied by an impressive (but to my mind questionable) body of historical research—that this classic trajectory, observable in France and Britain at the end of the eighteenth and the beginning of the nineteenth century and in Germany after 1850, could not be seen in eighteenth-century America. Colonial life straddled all of these theoretical limits. The colonists retained in many respects an antiquated, communitarian world view: they did not lose their sense of belonging to a society, to provinces or towns that had a common purpose, shared religious traditions, and a common interest vis-à-vis the mother country. The fabric of their rural and of their urban life was still based on a sense of neighborliness that was probably infrequent even in the more traditional parts of rural France. Though Americans bought and sold, they managed in their private lives to maintain resilient networks of sociability, some of them—among merchants or planters—based on a common relationship to the forces of the market, and others, especially in the South, structured around institutions such as the courts.

In the important realm of high politics, the ideological legacy of radical English communitarianism, infused as it was in America with religious nostalgia, remained strong. Here was another anomalous if vestigial trait: in their economic reflexes and in other ways Britain's American colonies were closer to the abstract model of gesellschaft individualism than any other society had ever been, but this tendency was not carried over into the sphere of global political perceptions.

The history of the American colonies focuses on two contradictory themes: ideological communitarianism (of a kind); and, by French standards at least, a frenetically changing and dynamic economy. The common denominator of these two themes is the exceptionalist nonappearance of class, the absence in America of consciously stated and economically determined social ranking as the organizing and determining principle of American politics.

INDIVIDUALISM WAS MOST PLAINLY asserted in the thirteen colonies in their economic structures. Local supply was exceptionally responsive to urban and international demand. Between 1700 and 1780 America became a critically important producer of raw materials for an increasingly integrated, industrializing, and capitalist world economy dominated by England. The relative weight of Britain's imports from America shifted from tobacco (a luxury) to wheat, which workers ate, and cotton, the stuff workers increasingly spun and wore.

American industry was not unimportant, especially after 1760. The production of footwear, for example, was well developed in Massachusetts, at Lynn, where eighty thousand pairs of shoes were made yearly to be sold at home and abroad. From the first the colonists had been expert builders of ships. America in the mid-1770s also counted 250 iron works in both North and South. Pennsylvania alone had 73 such establishments, and the thirteen colonies together accounted for one-seventh of the world's supply of iron at that time. Nonetheless, in the eighteenth century the American economy, though incipiently industrialized, remained overwhelmingly agricultural. Initial economic development came through the production of staple crops which served to meet both local urban demand and the needs of Great Britain. Although England was a most efficient grain producer, its own production after 1760 could no longer meet the demand generated by its growing cities. British imports from America—and the Caribbean—sextupled between 1716 and the 1780s, a development that played no small part in Britain's determination to resist American claims to independence.

In the eighteenth century American farmers and planters—New Englanders and Virginians alike—grew specialized crops with an eye to selling. They were not peasants whose first goal was to support their families on self-sufficient, inherited family land. American landowners, like European peasants, did still grow and make a wide range of products in order to maximize their sales and minimize the volume of their purchases. A southern plantation might resemble a large village, with its own carpenters, smithies, weavers, bakers, and tanners. Gold coins were rare. Well over half of America's rural produce was used by the producers directly, as against a small fraction today. Whether farmers relied on trade and barter or tried to pay their taxes in kind, the end result was conceptually the same: even local trades were made with an eye to the larger moneyed whole.

American farmers specialized their production to meet market demand rather than—as was more common in France—to meet the needs of their private "domestic economy." A 1771 survey of farms in Massachusetts reveals that half of them had no cows or oxen, and that only one-third were self-sufficient in dairy products.[1] In the South as well, from the 1720s onward, planters learned to diversify their production. When tobacco prices fell after 1765, George Washington switched from that crop to wheat, which was fetching higher prices. The hinterland of Norfolk, Virginia, which was ill suited for tobacco, restructured its agriculture in order to supply the West Indies. Late colonial Virginia shipped almost half of its corn, wheat, and tobacco abroad. In the North, imports of sugar led to the creation of local distilleries; generally, the very shape of urbanization was dictated by the relationship of local conditions to the structures of North Atlantic commerce. By 1760 the smallest towns in New England were linked by road to Boston, Hartford, or Providence, many of them along old Indian trails. In Virginia, urban growth shifted from the Williamsburg-Yorktown area toward the James and Rappahannock rivers in response to a shift in international demand for agricultural products. The spectacular development of Baltimore in the 1750s as an entrepôt for the wheat trade is perhaps the most telling example of the interdependence between urban and commercial structures.

The volume of foreign trade in relation to the national production of commodities was larger in America than in France. More to the point, the structures of these exchanges were completely different. The French imported colonial produce and exported luxury goods. With some exceptions (such as a shift to wheat in southwestern France), their agriculture was not really affected by this trade. The reverse held true in colonial British America. The two sides of the British Atlantic were so closely tied that the underdevelopment of urban life in the American South, ordinarily supposed to express some economic lethargy, meant less than might at first appear: Virginian cities were small because Virginian tobacco was marketed, brokered, and insured abroad, after 1760 by Scotch "factors" whose urban base was Glasgow. American cities that failed to adjust to shifts in trade stagnated; Boston's population growth, for example, did not keep up with the rest of New England during the middle decades of the century. American imports rose from fifteen shillings per person in 1730 to twenty-six shillings in 1760, about three times the corresponding figure for France and a striking achievement in view of the colonies' unprecedented population explosion. American involvement in world trade was instinctive, and it grew practically without interruption in the eighteenth century. Ships were bigger, better used, and ever more numerous: four times as many vessels went from Philadelphia to the European continent in 1768 as had gone in 1733–34, and six times as many went in 1769–70.

America was the most resolutely capitalist society in the world. Everything there, including human beings, was bought and sold. "The only principle of Life propagated among the young People," wrote Cadwallader Colden in the 1740s, "is to get Money, and men are esteemed only according to . . . the Money they are possessed of."

And yet in this commercial welter where farmers, as John Adams put it, were "addicted to commerce,"[2] the celebrated "contradictions of capitalism" did not emerge as they did in every other European society when corporate agricultural traditionalism ceased to function as the matrix of social life. The nonappearance of social class as the determinant of political action is the central puzzle in the study of colonial social life. Therefore it is worthwhile to consider the economic and social trends that precluded the restructuring of American society along the lines that culture-bound European sociologists have for more than a century called normative.

THE FIRST OF THESE TRENDS was a shared prosperity. In America, capitalism really worked; the freewheeling American economy was a cornucopia. Even for those whose only property was their labor, America was, in contrast to Europe, a promised land. Perhaps as many as half of all immigrants to America arrived destitute or in some kind of bondage, however temporary. If they were white, many of them by their own standard soon did well. Meliorism as a principle was far more important to the French philosophes than it was to American publicists, who had little interest in the theme; but meliorism as a fact was far more relevant to life in America than it was to the everyday experience of the French.

In the cities, propertyless workers were relatively few in number: in 1771 only 7 percent of working Philadelphians were casual laborers; and 45 percent of the artisans who were propertyless in 1769 had acquired some property by 1774. Urban wages were so high that employers did what they could to keep them down through their control of local government. In another instance of American cultural innovation, workers were extremely sensitive to high levels of earning as opposed to the social context of labor. Many immigrants had come to the New World precisely because they had heard of its higher wages. White migrants from the Caribbean left those islands when the importation of black slaves depressed their own expectations. In the thirteen colonies labor costs massively affected both social status and economic structures. American entrepreneurs were forced to concentrate on those markets where they had a clear natural advantage and to avoid those where they did not: "Labor being much dearer than in Muscovy," wrote a seventeenth-century New Englander who was in the mast-exporting business, "as well as Freight, we can make no Earnings of it."

The high cost of free white labor was critical for both whites and blacks, originally as a powerful goad to the establishment and perpetuation of slavery and then, during the late eighteenth century, as a cause (along with slavery) of the gradual disappearance of indentured service for whites. In 1774 only 2 percent of Americans were so bound. When the longevity of blacks improved, a slave who might work a lifetime became a better investment than a more skilled but less coercible white indentured servant whose length of service was fixed by contract to seven years or less.

Urban wealth rose along the trade, and commerce was generally buoyant in the eighteenth century. The terms of trade changed in America's favor. In the 1740s, 100 bushels of grain were worth 150 yards of wool cloth; in 1765, 100 bushels of the same commodity were worth 250 yards of cloth. Simultaneously, the cost of shipping crops to Europe declined because the larger ships required fewer sailors per ton and because by 1720 the seas had been cleared of pirates.

Most Americans were country people, one step removed from the effects of the high cost of urban labor; but like their city neighbors, American farmers or planters (as even poor southern landowners were then called) also did well. America was "the best poor man's country." Seventy percent of all the cultivated land in America belonged to the people who worked it. Thomas Hutchinson estimated in 1764 that 2 percent of all white Americans were tenants. In England, by contrast, about a quarter of the arable land belonged to a few hundred families, and in Catherine the Great's Russia 90 percent of the peasants who worked the land belonged to the people who owned it or to the state. Per-capita wealth in England was close to what it was in America, but its distribution was skewed to the advantage of the very rich, who were much richer than the rich in America.

American rural prosperity had many causes. As the population increased, the price of settled land and of urban real estate rose. Originally penniless settlers who had managed to buy some land became well-to-do through no great effort of their own. In southeastern Pennsylvania, land prices trebled between 1730 and 1760. Real-estate speculation was a universal occupation. In later decades Washington and Franklin were heavily involved in operations of this kind. In Massachusetts, where the supply of public lands had dried up in the 1760s, towns had for nearly half a century been parceling out lands to influential speculators.

Much money was to be made by selling land and oftentimes by using it as well: American agricultural productivity rose steadily, thanks to better techniques, especially in the cultivation of such new staple crops as rice. Americans were unprecedentedly well off. The years around 1700 were a turning point in this respect. Items of silver, porcelain, or jewelry appeared in many American homes. Between 1745 and 1760 per-capita consumption may have increased by as much as 3 percent yearly. Americans drank steadily: two shillings, a day's wage, would buy a whole gallon of rum and often did so. Alcohol consumption came to about one quart of whiskey per person per week. Americans were the greatest meat eaters of their day. Because they were better fed than Europeans, they were also taller. Washington and Jefferson towered over Bonaparte and Robespierre in more ways than one.[3]

It is easy to give a materialist reading to Jonathan Edwards's belief that America at mid-century was something of a paradise—God's reward to his Chosen People, the gift of God for the people of God. The millennium, he knew, would begin in this new land. America, he explained, was that part of the world "pointed out in *Revelation* of God for . . . this glorious Scene." Many other Americans thought so too, if for reasons other than those that moved this great divine.

Prosperity, the first safety valve of colonial society, was thus an important obstacle to the conscious formulation of social class as the determining matrix of economic, social, and political life. Although the hatred of the poor for the rich often ran to fever pitch in the colonies as it had in the previous century during Bacon's rebellion in Virginia, it was usually disarmed not only by steadily rising standards of living but also by the availability of cheap land on the frontier and by westward migration. In this agricultural society, land was the essence of capital; and since Americans had no scruples about dispossessing Indians, land on the edge of European civilization was for them "dirt cheap"—an almost free commodity. From the beginning of settlement to 1800, the frontier moved westward at a rate of about three miles a year, an advance that, proportional to the size of the population, was even greater than that of the nineteenth century.

BECAUSE THE POPULATION of British North America increased very quickly, the opening of the West was a critical factor, and was, indeed, another trend that helped account for the nonappearance of a class society. The colonies' population grew at a spectacular and historically unprecedented rate of 2 to 3 percent a year, a rate of growth that is comparable to those of the most prolific underdeveloped countries of our own time. Between 1720 and 1780 the population of the colonies rose by more than a third every ten years. (From less than three million in 1776, for example, it rose to nearly four million by 1790.) The annual birthrate in America was twice as large as the death rate. In France, nearly a fourth of all infants died before they reached the age of one. (For foundlings placed by their presumably indigent mothers in the care of religious or state authorities, the death rate approached 80 percent within a year of birth.) In New England nearly four-fifths of all newborns reached the age of twenty-one. Life expectancy in late-seventeenth-century New England was comparable to that of old England in the late nineteenth century. The American people were more youthful and productive than any other people on earth, with the exception of French Canadians. Their age at marriage was also lower than that of any other nation settled by Europeans. Immigrants poured into the land at a dizzying rate: between 1760 and 1775 more than 220,000 migrants arrived in the New World, a figure which was nearly 10 percent of the colonies' total population at the time.

Westward migration made it possible to accommodate these growing numbers, whereas in eighteenth-century France such a population surplus became a potentially dangerous and politically mobilizable rural and urban underclass. In the Connecticut frontier town of Goshen, for example, nearly all of those who owned no land in 1771 had become owners of some property ten years later. In New Hampshire the fit was perfect between the size of farms and the size of population: when homesteads in any given town shrank to below sixty acres or so, the population ordinarily ceased to grow, a clear indication that landless men and women resolved their economic and social problem directly, by moving out. Differences in wealth, nonetheless, did exist in America, and in some respects they became more conspicuous during the course of the eighteenth century. In Boston, on the eve of Washington's presidency, 10 percent of the citizenry possessed one half of the wealth. But the colonial "poor" were oftentimes the children of propertied farmers, young people who were still tenants and had not yet had time to acquire "a small estate of their own by migration, savings, or inheritance."[4]

THE NONAPPEARANCE of modern class consciousness as the organizing principle of American social life hinged on other tangible factors as well. Of these the most critical was the ethnic variety of the American population. The transformation after 1789 of the Parisian sansculottes from an estate of sorts to a class of sorts, with the displacement of rankings based on birth and status by more economically determined stratifications, was furthered by a common experience, by shared ties of life in Paris (where more than half of the capital's sansculottes were born) and in many instances by recollections of recent communal country life. New arrivals to the French capital often congregated around precurrers from their home region or *pays*. The nature of American colonial immigration precluded a social or a political evolution of this kind. Even in seventeenth-century Massachusetts, which was ethnically and religiously the most homogenous of the thirteen provinces, some settlers came from the east of England where land had been enclosed or privatized, while others came from open-field country. With the exception of New England, whose dour reputation discouraged all immigrants except similarly minded French Calvinists, the colonies attracted migrants from all parts of the United Kingdom: more than a hundred thousand came from Ireland, north and south, and yet more from the Scottish islands, which were very poor, and the Highlands of Scotland, which had been savagely occupied by English troops after the abortive rising of 1745. After 1708 a hundred thousand Germans arrived from the Rhenish

Palatinate. By 1790, 20 percent of whites in America were not of British origin at all. In New York, whose original settlers had been Dutch, one inhabitant in two was not of English descent. One-fourth of the entire population—and in South Carolina two-thirds—was of African origin. In 1776 Tom Paine would make of this a political argument: "Not one third of the inhabitants of this province," he wrote of revolutionary Pennsylvania, "are of English descent. Wherefore I reprobate the phrase parent or mother country applied to England only, as being false, selfish, narrow, and ungenerous."

Social fission was in the nature of American life. Migrants to the New World were self-selected, adventurous men and women. Many were pulled across the sea by the prospect of self-improvement and a better material life. One migrant in twenty, and perhaps more, died on the way to the promised land, but that did not deter latecomers, so great was the hope of self-betterment. Many also yearned for America because of its religious freedom, even if such pressures were far less compelling in eighteenth-century Europe than they had been a century before. These two material and spiritual motivations might in any case entwine. It often happened that a personal and religious quest became something else in transit. The religious trajectory of French Protestants is revealing here. Ostensibly the Huguenots came here because Louis XIV in 1685 had withdrawn from them the protection of the crown. But within one or two decades most of these middle-class Calvinists—many of whom went into trade and especially into trade with Britain— realized the commercial advantage of establishing better English and official contacts; and with this mercantile epiphany came also conversion to the Church of England, even in Calvinist colonies like Massachusetts where Anglicans, though well placed, were quite rare.

Because of their world view, which was archaic in some respects, and because of their traditional or even tribal corporatist or anti-individualist social background (as in the case of African tribesmen or Scottish and German peasants) many of these immigrants might have reinforced traditional institutions, if these had existed. Ordinarily, however, the mix of settlers, as in the middle colonies of New York and Pennsylvania, had a disruptive rather than a stabilizing effect. Migrants were keen competitors, centered on their own personal advancement, which they naively chronicled in inviting letters to relatives mired at home. The poor, particularly in American cities, far from being a coherent class that defined themselves in opposition to men of property, were an unstable assembly of men and women who reasonably expected to improve their condition soon. Their collective sense of self was uncertain. Much is to be learned from "intraclass" urban riots, such as those in New York in 1740 that pitted poor urban whites against poor urban blacks, who accounted for one-tenth to one-fifth of the population not only of New York, but of Philadelphia, Newport, Baltimore, and Charleston.

RELIGION WAS STILL another aspect of colonial life which made for social fragmentation instead of class solidarity. The transcendental individualist and antinomian elements within Protestantism and Puritanism had always been pronounced. Boston was founded in 1630; Anne Hutchinson arrived in 1634, and by 1637 she had already become North America's first heretic. The hold of the churches, even in New England, had never been complete, and it declined steadily. Congregations and ministers haggled endlessly over stipends as well as doctrines. In the South, not much came from the efforts of the Society for the Propagation of the Gospel, which had been founded in London in 1701 to support Anglican proselytizing by the graduates of William and Mary, a college established in 1693 to improve the religious tone of the Old Dominion. In 1725 Bishop George Berkeley, more keen on the medicinal virtues of southern tar water than on southern mores, wrote that "there is at this day but little sense of religion and a most notorious corruption of manners in the English colonies settled on the continent of America . . . Small care hath been taken to convert the Negroes of our plantations who to the infamy of England and the scandal of the world continue Heathen under Christian Masters."

Individualistic or even inchoate tendencies, both institutional and ideological, were heightened by the Great Awakening, a wave of religious enthusiasm which began in 1739 with the arrival in America of the English evangelist George Whitefield, a man so eloquent that it was said he could make his audience weep by pronouncing the word Mesopotamia. Whitefield managed to sway even Benjamin Franklin, a most parsimonious Deist, to empty into the collector's dish (to Franklin's own amazement) the entire contents of his pockets: copper, silver, and gold.

The Great Awakening was a novel moment in the cultural history of the northern colonies. (Its effect in the South was geographically and chronologically more episodic.) The movement was intellectually ambiguous. Whitefield's own thought was trivial: though a graduate of Pembroke College, Oxford, where he had become a Methodist, Whitefield had never even read Calvin. By contrast, Jonathan Edwards, a graduate of Yale whose revivalist career reached back to the early 1730s, was a genuine and original thinker, a Lockean empiricist, and America's first great intellectual. Edwards's theology gave a new dimension to the religious autonomy of the self, and his passionate sensibility was almost preromantic. (Born nine years before Jean-Jacques Rousseau, the Reverend Edwards's dates, 1703–1758, were roughly coterminous with those of the preromantic Abbé Prévost, the author of *Manon Lescaut,* a novel of sensibility and passion also placed in an American setting.) Edwards wished to preserve the church for the truly faithful, whom he did not hesitate to threaten with eternal damnation, luridly described. In order to insure the sincerity of the redeemed faithful, Edwards was willing, like Roger Williams, to widen the separation between a holy church and the secular state, which he took to be irremediably corrupt. A millenarian and a pragmatist, Edwards was willing also to leave worldly affairs to "the logic of material necessity and self-recognition."[5] This he could easily do because in his Lockean and epistemological world view, practical concerns were not of much importance and only the psychological inner self was truly real.

Edwards's theological concerns, though learned and abstract, were not without effect: Yale, where Edwards had also taught, was forced to shut down in 1742 because many of its students, like the Russian narodniks of the 1870s, had gone to the people. The students, according to a shocked contemporary, "would neither mind their studies nor obey the rules of the college. Almost all of them pretended to an inward teacher which they ought to follow, and several of them made excursions into the country and exhorted people from town to town."

For many others, the philosophical questions that mattered so desperately at the academy in New Haven may well have been less than critical. Nonetheless, the intellectually modern aspects of the Great Awakening are obvious. It would be a mistake to see the converted New Lights, the followers of Whitefield or Edwards, as the premodern, backward-looking votaries of a traditionalist oral culture. They may have been that in some small degree, but for the most part this great revival was an adjustment of formal religion to a modern and individualistic spirit of personal autonomy. On the face of it, New Lights were more emotive and less reasonable than Old Lights. At a deeper level the New Lights' Arminian emphasis on good works, as against predestined and inscrutable divine grace, assured men and women that they could make sense of both life and the cosmos, an assumption which was a central value of eighteenth-century rationalism. The real contrast between Old Lights and New Lights was less that between learning and enthusiasm than that between lessons handed down and lessons that came from within.

Institutionally, the Great Awakening was also innovative. Its first effect was to weaken further the formal hold of the established churches. The already wobbly spiritual role of the American minister as intermediary between God and man was further eroded. Many religious communities in New England and elsewhere fell apart. Denominationalism was accentuated. "New Side" Presbyterians created a synod of their own in 1741, and the echoes of their doctrine seeped from Pennsylvania to the Virginian hinterland. South of that province, dissenting churches outnumbered Anglican parishes by 1750. In Massachusetts by 1760 most inhabitants lived in towns that encompassed an irreducible, organized, dissenting, non-Congregationalist congregation. In the South especially, religious enthusiasm also served to weaken established social forms because it sharpened the rivalry between rich and poor. Southern Baptists were, like the Quakers, originally hostile to slavery, and it was only in 1811 that Baptists created segregated congregations whites and blacks. In colonial British America, religion, political liberalism, and social change went hand in hand. That was hardly true in France.

The decline of religious authority during the Great Awakening affected the Americans' cultural world view in other ways as well. Often to the surprise of the most faithful revivalists, the public, that is, the economic and social, effects of their movement were the diametrical opposite of its private motivations: individualism in religion led to a still more intense drive for private economic gain. As Cotton Mather had mused some decades before, "Religion brought forth *prosperity,* and the *daughter* destroyed the *mother.*"[6] Because their solution to the lust for riches was to deepen the individualistic bias of American religious sentiment, the proselytizing New Lights inadvertently made personal self-seeking an even more acceptable social value than it already was.

The Great Awakening had unexpected libertarian political effects also, even if it is difficult to link the burst of evangelical piety in the 1740s to the revolutionism of the 1760s and 1770s. Many Old Lights, like that pillar of the Harvard establishment, Charles Chauncy, Jonathan Edwards's *ennemi intime,* resurfaced after twenty years as political liberals and partisans of Independence. But the connection between religion and politics holds more firmly at the level of cultural values.

The importance of this link can more easily be gauged when set against the patterns of other nations: in Catholic Europe, and in France more than any other European country, anticlericalism, preeminently provided the philosophes with an audience. In striking contrast, in America where a Protestant and dissenting society was transformed by the Great Awakening, religion and modernism went hand in hand. The French Revolution would develop as a struggle *against* religion; but the reverse was to be true in revolutionary America, where religious fervor had long since served to make individualism, especially in its transcendent form, an accepted principle of social action.

The individuation of religious feeling in mid-eighteenth-century America also explains the relative insignificance there of the Enlightenment as an explicitly defined discourse. Indeed, it might be suggested that America did not consciously experience that great cultural movement because it had no need for it. In France, the Enlightenment versions of possessive individualism as a social principle and of rationality as a justification for governmental action were socially and politically attractive—and revolutionary—because they ran against the grain of the Old Regime. This was much less the case in the thirteen colonies, whose ethos, in its Puritan variant at least, had started from premises that were close at times to the conclusions of the French philosophes.

Ramism, to be sure, was not Cartesianism. The Puritans' tangential interest in capitalist achievement was far removed from Joseph Schumpeter's justification of entrepreneurial zeal. And Winthrop *fils* was no Isaac Newton. Nonetheless, the spirit of individuating Enlightenment modernism did exist, latently at least, within even "traditional" Puritan American culture. In France, the geometric and ordered grids of avenues and *places royales* (the first of them in Paris dates from 1607) were cut, symbolically, into the fabric of the older cities. Large American cities, except for Boston, were from birth laid out in squares and circles. It is also worth noting that Rousseau's communitarian version of Enlightenment thought had little appeal for Americans, whose favorite European text was Beccaria's liberal defense of the individual's judicial rights made on grounds of common sense and fairness. Rousseau's *Social Contract* was not published in America until 1797. The more radical French texts had limited appeal for colonial Americans, whose favorite French book was Fénelon's *Télémaque,* a work whose first subject was the education of a sensible and patriotic king. In their daily lives, Americans were born pragmatists. America's greatest philosophe, Benjamin Franklin, was propelled to international fame by his practical applications of principles that Europeans found it necessary to invent but that were his from birth.

To be sure, within America's modern and meritocratic market culture could be found many social and institutional survivals of a communitarian, premodern type of life. Picturesque echoes of European feudalism survived here and there. In New York, politically grating feudal dues would continue well into the nineteenth century. In 1766 the Westchester "levellers," many of whom were from New England, refused to pay these small sums, which were levied on many people, especially after 1720, and which certainly mattered to the English magnates who collected them. In 1774 American feudal payments were worth more than twenty thousand pounds a

year to William Penn's descendants, and Lord Baltimore's did even
better. Overall, however, their intrinsic meaning for Americans was
negligible.

More significant as evidence of an extant American traditionalism
was the survival in the colonies of cultural traits typical of premodern Europe. Americans were hard-drinking, rough men. Though a
rudimentary knowledge of law was probably more widespread in
America than in any European nation, Americans also liked to take
the law into their own hands. Rioting was an accepted part of the
political landscape, and it was often directed to the maintenance of
traditional social goals, as happened in Boston when crowds attacked the local brothels.

Violence was endemic in America just as it was in France. Many
employers and slaveholders were sadistic persecutors. The persistent decimation of Indians was a form of genocide. Wife-beating
and child-birching were banal occurrences. In the 1770s aristocratic
French officers were appalled by the food that Americans delighted
in and also by their personal habits. Many of the southern colonists
could not be described as intense devotees of the Protestant work
ethic. Illiberalism and intolerance were still likely reactions, as Baptists discovered in the Episcopal South and in Congregationalist
Massachusetts. Blacks and Catholics were everywhere despised. Primogeniture, that cardinal principle of English aristocratic life,
which was in some American provinces a formal, legal institution,
was an informal institution in New England, where the eldest son
ordinarily inherited the family farm.

Many historians today, struck by the survival of such "premodern" values and institutions, have argued that colonial America
was still a precapitalist society. Much of the debate here has centered on the image of New England townships as "peaceable kingdoms," to use Michael Zuckerman's apt title.

Undeniably, a yearning for communal harmony did exist in many
New England towns. Lawyers, whose existence presupposes civil
discord, were few: in 1768 Massachusetts, with a population of
250,000, had only twenty-five of them. Some New England town
meetings passed decisions unanimously for years on end. The claims
of consensus were strong. The quasi-universal suffrage which prevailed in many places has been interpreted as a mechanism, not for

democratic dissent, but for social coercion—as a way of forcing all
residents to share in community actions. Thomas Hutchinson, the
loyalist governor of Massachusetts, lamented that in his province
"anything with the appearance of man" has the right to vote; but
since the upshot of that wide franchise was more conformist than
radical, he may have been unnecessarily distressed.

Such claims for the existence of a precapitalist American traditionalism are not convincing, however. Economically, the
"peaceable kingdoms" were market societies even if the mechanism
of this cash nexus had more to do with trade than cash. It was in
part for purely mechanistic reasons (that is, because fewer meetings
were being held) that fewer quarrels came to the fore at eighteenth-century town meetings. As time passed, overt disagreements
did become less common, but this was only because town, church,
and judicial authorities became less ambitious in maintaining public
morality. They knew that rigorous policies might cause the breakup
of established townships: the town of Stoughton went through
seventeen divisions in the eighteenth century. After 1704 Suffolk
County courts ceased to prosecute for premarital sex, an example of
moderation that was followed in the rest of Massachusetts after
1739 and in New Hampshire and Connecticut after 1750. The point
of prosecutions involving bastardy shifted from morality to child
support. The impression of harmony that appears in studies of
town meetings needs to be balanced by an investigation of the
private disputes that were resolved in typical American fashion,
through the courts or by arbitration—disputes between neighbors,
among relatives and heirs, stepchildren and stepparents, masters
and servants, towns and ministers, and between the towns
themselves.

The supposed harmony of colonial town life also has to be set
against the backdrop of the various collective economic safety
valves. Disgruntled younger sons, like the religiously dissatisfied or
the plainly landless, could transform their public situations privately
by moving to the city (if they were unusually adventurous) or to
newer towns on the frontier. In a European village setting, the
existence of a strong sense of community—and constraint—can be
inferred from the absence of social and political debate; but that
assumption does not hold for colonial America, where local ten-

sions existed but remained invisible because they were so often resolved by the contenders' departure. The Turner frontier thesis may not have applied to urbanized America in the late nineteenth century, when impoverished immigrants went no farther than the cities of the eastern seaboard, but it does have great relevance to America's earlier and agricultural past. Unhappy colonial Americans voted, not in the town meetings but with their feet. They left. It is not surprising that some historians have found eighteenth-century American villages even more harmonious than they had been a century before: if the earliest dissidents' first instinct was to complain, the later dissidents' impulse was to leave.

Two facts controvert the theory of a socially static American society: first, small American towns only appeared to be stable because they were able to export their social problems westward; second, only its rapid economic growth enabled the larger economy to absorb dissidents. The first principle of the colonial world that encompassed the seemingly peaceable kingdoms of village life was the competitive and "bourgeois" concept of autonomous entrepreneurial action. Boston crowds may have risen up to shut down brothels, but they acted likewise (in 1737) *against* municipal regulation of food prices—surely the only riot in favor of the laws of the market in any society anywhere in the world during the whole of the eighteenth century.[7]

Ironically, the only indisputably communitarian societies in British North America were those of native Americans. Reasons for the whites hatred of these "savages" range from racism and fear to religious hatred and a sense of social or technological superiority. Whites may also have felt guilty for having despoiled a people who still lived in organic communities that reminded them of their own supposedly "golden" past. Many whites who had been captured by Indians chose not to return to "civilization,"[8] presumably because in the world of native Americans they found advantages that their own society did not provide.

The hypothesis of colonial America as a conglomerate of peaceable kingdoms is flawed by its implicit reference to social models conceived by modern European thinkers with European conditions in mind. Though America did not become a class society in which the poor had a sharp sense of belonging to a group that they and others defined in terms of its relationship to the control of property, America had certainly ceased to be a society of caste and of corporatist community.

 AMERICA WAS UNIQUE. By the middle decades of the eighteenth century the colonists had come to understand that their society was different from all others. It is worth considering the various institutions in which their sense of individualism and their incipient nationalism found some measure of expression.

The colonists' newfound sense of themselves as members of a society where individuals had wider autonomy than in Europe was reflected first in the court system. Local tribunals extended their jurisdiction into the no-man's-land that separated English parliamentary legislation from local American and common law. Gradually an amended jurisprudence began to take into account the structure of the new society. The most famous but by no means the only instance of this evolution is the case of Peter Zenger, whose pragmatically minded lawyer dared to argue that any statement which was true could not be libelous, regardless of the existing English jurisprudence whose aim it was to protect the king and his agents.

The evolution of the colonial legislatures also bore witness to the growing particularist sense of the colonists and to their desire for self-rule. The population of the colonies was so highly politicized that by 1750 many Americans had become professional, full-time politicians. During the middle decades of the seventeenth century, many of the colonies ruled themselves with little regard for London's wishes. After that, in the 1680s, Britain reaffirmed her imperial power; but in short order the balance began to tilt once again toward greater autonomy for the colonies. The elected assemblies in New England were particularly strong. In Massachusetts after 1720 it was the General Court that paid the governor's salary and set the level of judges' pay as well. New York had reached a similar independence by 1750, and the southern provinces fell into line during the Seven Years War, which ended in 1763. The legislatures were not always successful in their bids for greater power. Decisions to allow the local printing of paper money, which was in great demand, were overruled by Westminster; but Americans did what they could to regulate the conditions of local politics and to control funding for specific projects.

The unique individualism of colonial life can be observed more directly, if informally, in the particular mix of private and public cultural values that characterized this epoch. Familial structures were hardly uniform. Conditions varied greatly from region to region and often from one religious community to another. Quakers were more innovative than other sects, but the overall trend in the eighteenth century was toward a growing respect felt by the parent for the child's autonomy. Locke's *Treatise on Education* was widely read. Though the death rate for children was extraordinarily low by the standards of the time, the fear of a child's death was experienced more vividly in America than in Europe. One-third of the portraits painted in early New England represented children, and it has been suggested that these paintings were commissioned by anxious parents who feared the premature death of beloved offspring.[9] Young Americans were not forced to marry against their will. Premarital sex was common, and age at marriage was lower than in any other country peopled by Europeans except, once again, French Canada. The parentally supervised but sexually ambiguous custom of bundling became quite common between 1750 and 1780: Jonathan Edwards did not like it much, but John Adams— at once dyspeptic and commonsensical—wrote of it in 1761: "I cannot wholly disapprove of Bundling."[10] In an account of his visit to Boston in 1782, the Marquis de Chastellux was struck by the fact that married children, though they lived near their parents, did live in separate apartments: "In a nation which is in a perpetual state of growth," he wrote, "everything favors this general tendency; everything divides and multiplies."[11] Divorce, though still infrequent, was a distinct possibility. The right of women to possess property and to make contracts developed more quickly in eighteenth-century America than it did in contemporary England. Attitudes toward life and death also changed rapidly in the colonies, especially in New England, where Calvinist rigor gave way to more Arminian or worldly concerns. In the last decades of the seventeenth century Puritan divines shifted their emphasis from death as a punishment for sin to the idea of moral self-betterment as the preface to a better death. On the gravestones of New England's burying grounds, cherubs and angels, typical of a more optimistic age, replaced the menacing skull and crossbones of the seventeenth century.

The evolution of American public values went in the same direction. Meritocratic and pragmatic individualism or careerist self-seeking were more highly praised than they had been before. Benjamin Franklin's notion of a good school was one where "the instructed youth will come out ... fitted for any business, calling, or profession."[12] The Puritans had warned against the sin of pride, but in 1777 Patrick Henry thought it proper to say that "it [has] ever been my wish to deserve the esteem of virtuous men, and to stand well in their opinion." Americans thought it proper to set clear limits on their obligation to others or to the state. British generals were surprised to find that colonial militiamen simply would not serve longer than the time for which they had contracted: Americans, it seemed to them, were indifferent to the call of military "honor," as privileged European officers defined it. By the middle decades of the eighteenth century, the cultural preconditions of a capitalist ethic (individual betterment as a goal, rationality as a fulcrum, and materialism as a frame of reference) had been thoroughly internalized by Americans and were a permanent part of American life, but in a manner particular to America. In its social structure, colonial America was distinctly *particular,* at once hierarchic, meritocratic, and in some ways egalitarian. With the exception of slavery, it knew neither caste nor class, as sociologists have ordinarily defined these groups. It was neither communitarian nor aristocratic in its public ethos.

A word about French society during the mid-nineteenth-century reign of Louis-Philippe, the bourgeois king, will clarify this point. It is customary to describe provincial France (or some parts of it at least) in that era as a transitional society wedged between caste and class, as not dominated exclusively by either landed aristocrats or rich bankers but by "notables"—some of them landlords, merchants, or financiers, and others intellectuals, lawyers, clerics, or army officers. French notables in the middle decades of the nineteenth century belonged to families that were rooted in a particular town or country place. They were people of some wealth whose social superiority, achieved sometimes through generations and at

great cost, was readily recognized in small provincial towns, especially when it was consecrated by the exercise of public office. The
domination of the notables was uncertain, however, because their
prestige was built on shifting social sands.

Something of the kind can be imagined for much of colonial
America, albeit more commercialized and, in consequence, more
unstable. Eighteenth-century America was not yet a democratic
society: from New England to Georgia, social and political life—
and especially local politics—was dominated by a handful of intertwined families. The aesthetic personae depicted in the portraits
which rich Bostonians and Virginians commissioned were essentially fraudulent. In the North, these portraits expressed the values
of a mercantile, quasi-Venetian aristocracy; in the South, they
showed the equally inapplicable image of a stable, Burkean, landowning gentry. But the same colonial portraits do convey the fact
that if some Americans were quite poor, others were quite rich—
and self-important. Many of America's prosperous colonial families
were related to one other. Nearly two-thirds of the delegates elected
to Virginia's House of Burgesses in the hundred years preceding
Independence belonged to about twenty intermarrying clans. The
social prominence of these American notables was, however, precarious. Few families were so prominent that the personal failings
of a single person might not precipitate the irremediable decline
and fall of an entire line. Newcomers could suddenly come to the
fore.

The uncertainty of membership in political assemblies is revealing. What first appears is the low rate of turnover in eighteenth-century legislatures, especially during the last two decades of colonial
rule. In Virginia, would-be members of the House of Burgesses
were informally vetted by their ensconced peers for their personality
as much as for their politics. Quite naturally, the mores and characters of their own aspiring relatives seemed most pleasing to seated
members, whether southern or northern. In the Old Dominion
between 1720 and 1776, four-fifths of the legislative leaders had been
born into families that had settled there before 1690. "Go into every
village in New England," wrote John Adams in the 1780s, "and you
will find that the office of justice of the peace, and even the place of
representative, which has ever depended only on the freest election

of the people, have generally descended from generation to generation, in three or four families at most."[13]

The political deference enjoyed by these prominent colonials in both North and South was nonetheless of an uncertain and fleeting kind. Elections were regularly held, and franchises were very broad. In Virginian contests, yeomen tended to send their more genteel neighbors to the House of Burgesses, perhaps in part because votes were by a show of hands that could be closely scrutinized by the local gentry. But the successful candidates, who were expected to be at home at election time, symbolically rose and thanked their more humble fellow citizens. In 1765 Virginia voters turned out of office one-third of the delegates to the House of Burgesses—those who had not responded to local feelings against the Stamp Act.

The backdrop of this political instability was a society both mobile and financially polarized. Americans moved up and down the social scale with surprising speed. Social rank was in large part a function of birth, as elsewhere, but also of luck as well as age and character. Americans' sense of caste was uncertain. Ruling factions could not expect that their members would close ranks. The borders were porous from group to group, and an Episcopalian gentleman in the South might suddenly resurface, horribile dictu, as a Baptist. Egalitarianism as a value was strongly felt, even among those who ought to have been most suspicious of it. Even prominent Virginians were hostile to the creation of an American bishop whose presence might have bolstered threatened the hierarchies of which they were a part. Notables, though few in proportion to the whole, were hardly of a single opinion about any issue: in Virginia they disagreed about such important matters as the use of western lands and public moneys. They were of a divided mind about their relationship to Britain and the Anglican Church. Rhys Isaac has very appropriately described late colonial Virginia as "an almost paradoxical compound of close neighborhood and the incessant mobility of restless striving."[14] This remark could also be made about the middle colonies, which were especially unstable, and about New England. From a domestic and even a parochial point of view, the differences between the social structures of the colonies were great. But when considered from a more general and comparative North

Atlantic and European perspective, the similarities far outweigh the differences.

AMERICA'S DYNAMIC ECONOMY was in a state of incessant structural change: capitalism in its pure form is a doctrine of constant revolution. Although most people improved their condition, the rich notables of yesterday were not necessarily the rich notables of tomorrow. Fortunes were easily made and unmade. The condition of the elite was unstable and so was that of the rank and file. After 1730 poorhouses sprang up in New York and Philadelphia. Between 1755 and 1775 the number of indigents in the City of Brotherly Love tripled. By the time of the American Revolution, the desperately poor constituted about 5 percent of the population in all of the major urban centers, a very low figure by comparison with European cities but expressive of a novel turn in American social life. Politically, it is true, these destitute whites, like the enslaved blacks, were ordinarily powerless, but their presence engendered a sense of unease which surfaced from time to time. Benjamin Rush of Philadelphia, a progressive-minded man who later became one of the first spokesmen for the abolition of black servitude, symbolized his era when he shuddered after visiting the houses of the poor in the 1770s and remembered that he "risqued not only taking their disease but being infected with their vermin." Every European society had its poor, but now, in America, their presence was differently felt: only with the advent of capitalism, which made the accumulation of wealth a central social function, did poverty become a genuine social vice. Many propertied Americans developed grave doubts about their society's ability to absorb not merely blacks but poor, and therefore undesirable, aliens as well.

The countryside was no more stable than urban society. Indeed, the greatest problem for America's already unstable elites was the shifting allegiances of middling rural whites, men of small or no property, who were more politically active than comparable groups in other countries. In the rural South, cleavages were obvious and growing, most notably between the eastern seaboard, dominated by great planters, and the newly settled backwoods areas, often peopled by Scotch-Irish Presbyterians who owned few slaves and were less involved in the market than the eastern "gentry." Religion in this instance was at once a crystallizing factor of social conflict and a rhetorical mode for the articulation of social differences. Not surprisingly, the Anglican planters' initial resistance to the revivalism of the backwoodsmen in the 1740s and 1750s was often brutally expressed. Beatings of itinerant preachers were not infrequent. Similar social divisions existed in the northern provinces. In rural New England the towns that had been created in the first four decades of settlement had run out of free land by 1720. This did not make for rural poverty, but it did make for a division between those who owned land and those who did not.

America's urban crowds were no more quiescent. The scarcity of labor, with the ensuing high level of wages, gave free American wage earners a strong hand in the social and political life of the larger cities. Strikes had been a feature of the American landscape since 1641, when some workers in Massachusetts decided to protest about the food they had been served. In 1760, at the other end of the chronological spectrum, white workers were strong enough to secure from the South Carolina legislature the abolition of the slave trade in their state, an act that was overruled in London. American printers, like their brethren in Europe, were particularly vocal. Workers and artisans formed friendly or philanthropic societies, the first of them in Philadelphia in 1767. Many sailors, the most proletarianized of America's urban workers, also joined marine or mutual aid societies.

This picture has another side, of course: identifiable, self-conscious local elites existed nearly everywhere in colonial America on the eve of the Revolution. (North Carolina, where most leaders of the legislature between 1754 and 1775 were first-generation immigrants, was an unusual case.) The situation of these leaders was structurally unstable, however, and it became increasingly so after the Seven Years War. The American poor were a political factor that could not be ignored. Even in rural New England, which succeeded in exporting many of its social problems, local magnates such as the so-called Connecticut River Gods had to defer to local forms of public opinion which they had not molded. Notables held a near monopoly of public office, but their freedom of maneuver was sharply limited. In the broader political sense, American notables followed and did not lead. Their right to rule was seldom brought into question, but in this fevered country the rich were often obliged to mind their fickle lower-class masters.

Many institutions of American social and political life can thus be understood as having been designed, unconsciously perhaps, to bind the poor to the rich. Because the hold of American elites on a mobile society was uncertain, many public or near-public functions, ranging from electoral campaigns to horse races and church services, institutionalized social ranking. Ceremonial occurrences can often be taken to prove the existence of accepted social norms, but the passion that went into southern assertions of display and rank can more plausibly be read as proof of an underlying feeling of unease.

The manipulation of judicial structures evinced a similar striving for social cohesion, an effort that made special sense since traditions of common law were broadly shared in America. Southern grand juries enabled great planters, after the 1720s, to involve yeomen in the process of government, but on their own terms. Another significant fact is the existence of slavery. The reduction of blacks to servitude and the perpetuation of slavery in America for two centuries is the most tragic facet of our history. Its origins and causes are innumerable, ranging from the age-old European suspicion of blacks to man's desire for easy domination. Another aspect of the problem is that by reducing one group of indigents or near indigents to slavery, rich planters succeeded in neutralizing the remaining poor politically and socially. The division of a potentially hostile social group was in itself a great gain for the labor-hungry landlords; and the enslavement of blacks gave poor whites an interest in maintaining an exploitative social system which they did not dominate. However destitute he might become, a poor white would never become black: this happy fact dulled any possible indignation. Laws on miscegenation can be read in the same light. The utter degradation of blacks was for poor whites a social promotion of a kind.

An awareness of the unstable, mobile structure of American society sheds light on many aspects of American life, including the hectic and, at first glance, trivial nature of American domestic politics in the eighteenth century. Local colonial politics was unprincipled and even corrupt because it reflected local conditions of patronage, flux, and change rather than differences of principle. In some colonies, such as Maryland, politicking had been stormy from the first. In Virginia during the 1670s the Greenspring faction (named after Governor Berkeley's plantation) had turned the lucrative control of administrative office into a fine art. Techniques of this kind gradually became more general, and after 1740 Americans often revealed themselves in their provincial capitals to be "a factious people." In a manner typical of clientele politics, local colonial magnates jockeyed for popular support and British patronage. They shamelessly betrayed old friends and principles. It was the province of New York with its varied ethnic composition and social instability that had the most twisted—and tiresome—local politics. In the absence of set parties, meandering mindless factions were brought together intermittently by strong personalities and evanescent interests. The constant skulduggery of these provincial politicians contrasted sharply with the vision, diffused at home and abroad, of Americans as earnest, public-minded, and sober citizen-farmers.

At first glance, colonial American politics does not seem to have amounted to much; in actuality, it mattered in important ways. In a positive and obvious sense, provincial America's agitated local politics is proof of the simultaneous existence of agitated civil structures. The configuration of local politics also shows that by the middle decades of the eighteenth century Americans had in their daily politics stumbled on the practice of popular sovereignty but not yet on its theory. They would take that fateful step later, during the War of Independence, when the explicit assertion of popular sovereignty became the first principle of a new, national American political culture.

IN THE MIDDLE DECADES of the eighteenth century colonial America was in most respects a "bourgeois" society, not only because of the peculiar, Calvinist origins of its culture but more particularly because of the individualist and pragmatic nature of its economic and social structures. The main exception to the rule of social and cultural individuation was the political theory which mediated Americans' perception of the world.

In their principles (but quite apart from the practice of their social life or local politics) Americans perceived themselves as a virtuous, bucolic people, endowed by God with a special mission. Conceptually, what seemed relevant to them was not their un-abashed desire for self-enhancement and material gain but their common morality, common purpose, and their sense of being a virtuous people. This cleavage between social reality and political ideology is the key to the unfolding of American history at the end of the eighteenth century.

Because America was a rough-and-tumble world, its political world view *ought* to have been Lockean, as its practical, local, or day-to-day politics had in fact become. Louis Hartz's argument for the critical influence of Locke's thought comes to mind here. The liberal and individualist if somewhat moralizing statements of Locke's *Treatise on Government* were very well known in America: Even Jefferson, who was some distance removed from Locke, re-produced a few key Lockean phrases nearly verbatim in the Decla-ration of Independence. Locke's views on education were as popular in America as his views on politics. Even Jonathan Edwards's Pu-ritan theology was epistemologically Lockean.

Americans perceived political reality not through Locke prima-rily, however, but through the prism of an anomalous Radical Whig ideology. This intellectual system did not acquire durable substance in America or even in New England until the early dec-ades of the eighteenth century. (John Milton's poetry, for example, was practically unknown even in New England before 1700.) Its origins nonetheless reached back to the seventeenth-century "Commonwealth men," however much the ideas of these English Puritans may have been transformed by their eighteenth-century English Whig descendants. The roots of this intellectual system lay in English history, but many of the Whigs' ideas were influenced by the writings of French Protestants such as Rapin and Hotman, whose *Franco-Gallia,* first published in 1573, was still being reprinted in London in 1775, and of such French Jansenists as the celebrated Rollin, a historian of Rome and sometime chancellor of the Sor-bonne. It is worth noting that the one French philosophical work which Benjamin Rush chose to have represented in Charles Wilson Peale's portrait of himself as a gentleman scholar in 1783 was Pascal's Jansenist masterpiece, the *Pensées.* Then too, the course of the history of France—the world's most powerful nation at the time—

with its drift toward absolutism and popery, was an important object lesson for both the English and the American Whigs.

The basic principles of this Radical Whig (or Commonwealth) doctrine were resolutely communitarian. The people were defined as a basically homogeneous entity. Differences of wealth were thought to be irrelevant. Although the Commonwealth men understood the advantages of their doctrine of a widely diffused system of property, they tended to underwrite existing arrangements of landownership. They thought of property not as exploitation but as a guarantee of political independence. One of their spiritual heirs, Madison, wrote some decades later to another of their ideological "step-descendants," Jefferson, that in America "a provision for the rights of persons was supposed to include of itself those of property." By virtue of their birthright and regardless of their wealth, thought the Commonwealth men, all freeborn Englishmen were by birth endowed with certain rights. All Protestants, in particular, deserved the protection of the state. Mercantilism did not appeal to these Whigs because they believed that all Englishmen, wherever they might reside, ought to enjoy equal economic rights and opportunities. Economic freedoms, like political ones, were for them inscribed in nature (though rather uncertainly) and sanctioned by history.

The British people, thought the Whigs, deserved freedom less because of their natural right to it than because they happened to have enjoyed that right in the past. As Blackstone put it in his juxtaposition of English freedom and French tyranny, the British were not free because they were more entitled to freedom's joys but because they had somehow decided to be free. This was a mechanism of thought which incidentally enabled Americans to exclude, with some ease, both blacks and women from their loftier concerns. Radical Whig theory was, indeed, doubly historicist because Whig thought was often expressed in ennobling comparisons with the classics or with historical descriptions of ancient Greece and Rome. Colonial Americans and Englishmen alike were pleased to present their ambitions as echoes of Graeco-Roman instances of self-sacrifice for the common good: "Give me liberty, or give me death" was a much cited line burgled by Patrick Henry from Addison's Roman drama *Cato,* written in 1713.

Englishmen, as the Radical Whigs saw it, were entitled by their English birth to personal security (habeas corpus), to personal liberty, to the defense of their property, and to the perpetuation of ancient and inherited, historically sanctioned, Saxon liberties. Politics in this view of life was a battle between the ruler (the king) and the ruled (a united people), whose shared sense of the public good would override whatever disunion might be implied by differences of wealth. A patriot king might from time to time respect the rights of his freeborn subjects as embodied in the prerogatives of Parliament; but the state as such was basically the people's enemy. Kings could ordinarily be supposed to conspire against their subjects because the spheres of freedom and state prerogative were antithetical. Corruption was the monarch's favored weapon. The British constitution was a rampart against monarchic ambition of this kind. Alert citizens should always be prepared to struggle militarily, if need be, to uphold their rights. A natural enmity separated the monarch from his subjects, and this view of politics allowed Whigs to feel sympathy for Lockean ideas of contract, which regulated the monarch's natural propensity to self-aggrandizement. Crown and people were antagonists bound together by contract.

These latter-day Commonwealth men were not egalitarian. The furthest the most radical of them would go socially was to defend mass education and a wider suffrage that would include, in addition to freeholders, some tenants. Nor were the Radical Whigs explicitly republicans. They accepted the British monarchy as a fact, just as they accepted the existing social order as a fact. It seemed reasonable to them that, as the people had their institutional expression in Parliament, so should landed magnates be represented in a House of Lords, and the crown too should enjoy some independence. Logically enough, the Commonwealth men believed in a separation of powers which, they thought, gave expression to this natural and social distinctiveness of commons, lords, and king. They assumed that judges should be independent, and that the first function of the judiciary was to support the people against the king. Their social view of government differed from the more mechanistic view of Montesquieu, who was interested in the separation of powers for its own sake, which the Greek historian Polybius had championed in the second century B.C. At the same time, the early Whigs did not much care about customary restraints on the autonomy of Parliament, because they assumed that Parliament would represent the people faithfully.

John Milton and Algernon Sidney were the votive figures of this movement in the seventeenth century, as were, in the first decades of the eighteenth century. John Trenchard and Thomas Gordon, whose letters to various journals, collected in 1724 as *Cato's Letters: Essays on Liberty Civil and Religious and Other Important Subjects,* were widely known. Though never dominant in Britain, the Radical Whig tradition did survive there after 1750 into a third generation led by Joseph Priestley the chemist; Richard Price, a publicist; John Cartwright, a rather eccentric soldier; and Catherine Macaulay, a historian. But in America, Radical Whig ideology did more than survive: it became politically supreme. Its intellectual dominance, along with the contrast between its communitarian ideology and the individualistic, unstable nature of American life, provides the key to an understanding of America's revolutionary politics.

Whatever its basic structural problems, Commonwealth theory was wonderfully appropriate to the immediate political circumstances of colonial American politics in the 1760s and 1770s. Conceptually, it made Britain's government a distant and negative force. While to the French in 1789 the revolutionary state appeared more real than society itself (whose extant forms seemed to the French elite to be uncertain material approximations of ideal truths), for Americans, society was real and the state distant. The Radical Whigs' negative view of power nicely corresponded to the Americans' instinct for minimalist power and to their practical experience with rapacious petty British customs and fiscal agents who owed their place to patronage and ordinarily thought of America as a kind of milch cow.

More practically, thanks to Radical Whiggery any English ministerial decisions the colonists did not like, and especially those that were manifestly counterproductive, such as the Stamp Act, were understood as proof of some secret political plan concocted on the Atlantic's other shore. John Adams, for example, surmised that the deeper purpose of the Stamp Act was to raise the costs of the printed page, to reduce American literacy, and to prepare Americans for political slavery. The efforts of the British government after

1760 to widen its powers over the courts by rescinding lifetime appointments and by deciding in 1768 to pay judicial salaries directly set off howls of pain in America, howls which the English elites did not take seriously because they did not understand the ideological background of American complaints. Jefferson stood for an entire tradition when he wrote in 1774 that a single act of tyranny might be coincidental, but that "a series of oppressions, begun at a distinguished period and pursued unalterably through every change of ministers, too plainly proves a deliberate and systematic plan of reducing us to slavery."

Taxation was the ostensible nub of American grievances, and here again Radical Whig theory was the framework within which they instinctively considered their problems. British taxes were very high in the late eighteenth century, higher even than in France; and England's land owners, on whose shoulders this burden mainly fell, quite naturally wished to shift some of it to the colonial beneficiaries of Britain's imperial protection. This was an ominous shift for Americans' de facto independence, especially as it coincided with a trend in British law that proclaimed the supremacy of Parliament and its right and ability to do anything but change man into woman. Americans interpreted all such fiscal and constitutional steps as diabolical political aggressions on their ancient and inherited liberties. This was the view they also took of Britain's efforts to rationalize its imperial trade. British errors of judgment—and unforeseen events, such as the Boston Massacre in 1770, whose first cause was the participants' loss of temper—were invariably taken by the colonists as conclusive evidence of conspiracy. Lord Bute, the king's friend and minister, and eventually George III himself, were suspected of conspiring against the colonies, and of doing so with the help of their malevolent American satraps. Governor Hutchinson's intercepted correspondence, which lent some credibility to the idea of a concerted antilibertarian action, became one of America's first publishing sensations.

After 1774 Americans, true to their Whig principles, widened the circle of their enemies from king to Parliament and then to the British generally: with surprising ease they extended the theme of American virtue versus monarchic, courtly corruption to include the English nation as a whole. Their commercial obsessions and local politics notwithstanding, Americans were convinced of being a yeoman people, perhaps the only one on earth. The English, they now realized, were by contrast either too rich or too poor, too aristocratic and too proud or too corrupted by need and want. This pleasing image of American virtue was of course absurd by the standards that prevailed in the colonies. Yet oddly enough, its power was felt not just at home but in continental Europe also, and especially in France. There the view of American innocence was reinforced by the association of white Americans with the Indians—all of them "noble savages" of a kind. Informed Frenchmen were convinced that all Americans resembled the Pennsylvania Quakers, a mixed imago that Benjamin Franklin at the court of Versailles squeezed for all it was worth. From a French point of view, Americans—like Corsicans, Poles, or the Transylvanians (much admired by Brissot)—were civilized but primitive as well, and uncorruptedly able to yearn for Spartan freedom.

Radical Whig theory not only explained events from day to day but was of some general applicability as well: like seventeenth-century Puritanism, which carried within itself the seeds of modern rationalism and individualism, Commonwealth ideology was in many ways suited to the needs of a modern, "bourgeois" society. It emphasized the political rights of individual Englishmen. It also defended property, albeit on its own grounds. And it stressed constitutionalism, legalism, and contract. Among the cultural values which it encouraged were independence, economy, thrift, hard work, frugality, and order.

At the same time, however, and in more fundamental ways, Commonwealth theory was strikingly irrelevant. The first of its values was virtue, especially the masculine virtue of courage in battle, a quality which the laws of the market were not designed to reward. Radical Whig doctrine made little allowance for social cleavages within society. For that reason, American Whigs would soon prove singularly unable to absorb the fact that an antimonarchic but oligarchic English Parliament might rule against some other part of the North Atlantic British nation. That dilemma they tried to resolve by proclaiming their loyalty to an ancient, lost, and better organized British constitution; but some puzzled and thoughtful Americans (such as James Otis, who eventually went mad) found this Commonwealth escapist line hard to swallow.

Commonwealth theory was also strikingly inappropriate for conveying the Americans' rejection of the British doctrine of virtual representation: if all the people were of one mind, as the Commonwealth men assumed, it did not matter too much who represented whom. But in America that issue soon came to matter a great deal. Local American politics was intensely pragmatic, and the issue of representation immediately took on critical, practical importance in the colonies. Fanciful schemes of American parliamentary representation were floated from time to time, as were plans for the creation of an American aristocracy, but these pipe dreams could not fill the theoretical gap that inevitably appeared when Americans ceased to think of themselves as an integral part of the British people.

Despite these limitations, Commonwealth theory held a dominant place in the political world view of otherwise freewheeling colonial Americans. Its influence, which had been incomplete in the late seventeenth century, widened steadily after the turn of the century, and by the 1730s it had made headway in the southern colonies as well. The existence of slavery there ought to have given planters pause; but they did not see, until after independence, the obvious contradiction between their own dependence on the oppression of black slaves and their resolute advocacy of political freedom for all. Indeed, the presence of blacks in their midst may have reinforced the whites' determination not to be humiliated in any way. German immigrants in Pennsylvania, through the German language press, also became familiar with the basic arguments of Radical Whig thought, which were passed on from one newspaper to another—from radical sheets in Britain to Boston and then to the rest of the continent, including Pennsylvania's German-language press. Whig principles attracted a broad audience partly because they overlapped with nationalist sentiment. At mid-century, the Hanoverian monarchy's victory over the French-supported, Scottish-based effort of the Catholic pretender to capture the British throne was greeted not just as a victory for King George but as the triumph of the principles of 1688 and the spirit of Magna Carta over tyrannical and popish superstition.

The durability of the Commonwealth arguments in the face of

their social and, to a degree, political irrelevance is a central theme of American history. One explanation of their continuing presence is self-referential. By 1776 Radical Whig theory was more than a century old. It was well articulated and admirably developed. Even its opponents gave credence to some of its principles. Many English statesmen, for instance, were convinced that American complaints were the handiwork of a small group of corrupting conspirators who might easily be ferreted out and destroyed. Commonwealth principles were accessible in America even to those who were not literate; they had spawned a wide iconography, which blossomed during the travails in Britain of John Wilkes. The persecution of this disreputable man by the British crown during the 1760s made him immensely popular in both Britain and the thirteen colonies, where his difficulties were taken as another instance of growing monarchic corruption. The Radical Whigs had not only their mythic heroes but also their favorite villains, such as the Catholic James II and George Jeffreys, the seventeenth-century "hanging judge."

A second and more interesting reason for the popularity of Commonwealth doctrine was the hegemony of Britain's culture in her thirteen colonies: Americans subscribed to the Radical Whig ideology because their range of ideological options was limited to the cultural panoply that existed in Britain. Within that range they might choose what best suited them, but it was culturally impossible for them before the 1770s to conceive of other possibilities. The prestige of Britain in the colonies was immense. The victories of the Seven Years War carried England's naval might to unprecedented heights. Its institutions, social and political, seemed almost too perfect to have been designed by mortal man: "Could the choice of independency be offered the colonies or subjection to Great Britain upon any term above absolute slavery," wrote Otis in 1764, "I am convinced they would accept the latter."[15] Aesthetically, Americans relied on indigenous English styles exclusively (even the English did not do that), so that Boston and New York were more naively English than Bath or London. From a twentieth-century perspective, one could describe Radical Whiggism as an early expression of an immigrant cultural nostalgia for the golden past of "the old country."

In the third place, the Radical Whig ideology derived great

strength from its overlap with indigenous Protestant, especially
Puritan, culture. Some of their shared traits were old and others
new. Radical Whiggism and American Puritanism both emphasized
the idea of a single chosen people, destined for a special mission.
Both of them dwelt on the need for virtue, on contractualism and
covenants as a barrier to decay, and on the natural depravity of
mankind. The Radical Whigs were often dissenters who knew how
the authorities could capitalize on man's propensity to sin. Ironically, Radical Whig ideology and American Puritan thought were
both out of step with American social reality. Both systems shared
a vision of a golden past and believed in the need for restorative
atonement. In 1776 American republicans were politically bold beyond any other people, but their natural assumption was that their
first goal was to recapture a lost Arcadian simplicity. Americans
moved easily from religion to politics and back again: Jonathan
Mayhew of Boston, a Congregational minister whose predecessor
had become an Anglican, raged and fumed about "the stamping . . .
and episcopizing [of] our colonies [which] were . . . only different
branches of the same plan of power."

Radical Whig thought and America's religious heritage gelled,
and they were further solidified by the complex relationship of both
doctrines to incipient American nationalism. This relationship is
not easy to follow, however, because the ideological force of nationalism in America was exerted in opposite directions before and
after Independence. *After* 1776, the institutionalization of nationhood enabled Americans to overcome their sense of political inferiority. In the late 1780s a successful American nationalism displayed
in its ideology a number of social and institutional innovations that
earlier had found pragmatic expression only in American local politics, but had been forced to remain inchoate at a higher level as
long as the thirteen provinces were under British rule. Only after
Americans had become a nation were they able to formulate a
wholly novel and pluralist system of politics. *Before* Independence,
in the third quarter of the eighteenth century, Americans' growing
sense of national separateness had had an opposite ideological effect: this new national consciousness had strengthened the ancient
ideological and communitarian resolves which were commonly
identified as the key to Britain's imperial triumph.

Before it threw off English dominance, America was, as it were, on a two-way street: incipient American nationalism strengthened the appeal of established ideological patterns that were British in origin but could seem distinctively American because they were not espoused by Britain's aristocratic elite: thus traditional antimonarchic politics helped the still dependent American nation to become itself. In the 1760s and early 1770s Radical Whig thought, however inappropriate it was to America's social and economic structures, fed the feeling of American national identity. Conversely, that growing sense of nation strengthened the appeal of Whig thought. Americans' heightened and patriotic consciousness of themselves as a distinct people bolstered their resolve to claim their rights as freeborn Englishmen.

These complications suggest that eighteenth-century American nationalism should be considered in greater detail than has ordinarily been done. In the 1760s and early 1770s, nationalistic thought was an essential part of the American political equation, even if its apparent function seemed at the time to be overshadowed by its effect, that is, by the hardening of the more visible and traditionalist Radical Whig rhetoric.

The roots of America's sense of nationhood were manifold. Americans, particularly in the southern provinces, were united in resenting the low esteem in which they were held in England. A gap existed between the planters' optimistic view of themselves as genteel men of culture and leisure and the British view of them as expressed in the English press, a gap that was widened by the contempt with which they were treated by resident English officials and army or navy officers.

Americans gradually acquired a sense of place, and from the 1750s onward a market developed for provincial and continental maps that provided them with a visual representation of their homeland. In New England most families had local ties that were by then more than a century old. Governor Hutchinson was fond of evoking the memory of his antinomian ancestor: "The frenzy," he wrote of his own travails, "was not higher when they banished my pious great-grandmother."[16] In an inverse trajectory which, paradoxically, also encouraged the growth of American patriotism, many colonials acquired a sense of America's oneness by achieving prominence after moving away from their original colony, as did Benjamin Franklin, John Dickinson, Jonathan Edwards, and the Bayards of Philadelphia, whose cousins lived in New York and Boston.

Religion was another unifying bond that straddled provincial borders: though Jonathan Edwards's Calvinism was no longer popular at Harvard, it was still well regarded at Princeton, where he assumed the presidency shortly before his death. In a different but related vein, the Great Awakening was America's first indigenous, "nationwide" cultural movement. Americans were a Protestant, unepiscopized people. John Adams's description of the Catholic service that he witnessed in Philadelphia conveys a tone of intrigued, anthropological amazement.

By 1765 America was economically far more mature than it had been only forty years before. The lessening dependence of the upper South on Britain's importation of tobacco and its growing reliance on exports of grain to southern Europe made British mercantilism increasingly constraining. By the 1770s America's production of iron already totaled one half of Britain's. Moreover, intercolonial commercial links were tightening: between 1768 and 1772 half of the ships that left Boston harbor were bound for some American destination. Gradually Americans realized that in some ways they were all alike, and that their interests differed from those of Englishmen, Frenchmen, Spaniards, or native Americans.

Americans were proud of the role they had played in pushing the French off the North American continent. Coming as it did on the heels of a great Anglo-American military fiasco—the failed siege of Cartagena in 1741—the capture of Louisbourg in 1745 after another costly siege was hailed by many as a divine sign. Much of that glory was theirs, thought the colonists, and many of the ignominies were attributable to Britain. As Franklin later pointed out, it was Braddock's blundering redcoats, and not Britain's more sagacious provincial allies (Washington among them), who had been decimated by the French in 1755 on their way back from Fort Duquesne. It is not farfetched to regard the great enthusiasm that was felt in New England, especially after the fall of Louisbourg, as the first important secular manifestation of America's religious sensibility. Here was a new and powerful application of the myth of God's chosen people. Popery had been for New Englanders synonymous with tyranny. Now their own religion seemed to them to be an obvious guarantee of unimpeded liberty. Henceforth, Americans were able to ponder their religious past in a new light: in 1736 Thomas Prince, in his *Chronological History of New England in the Form of Annals,* had opined that the founders of the colony deserved to be imitated still, "not only for their vital and pure Christianity, but also for their *Liberty* both *civil* and *Ecclesiastical.*"[17] This theme acquired ever increasing power between 1745 and the 1760s, when it found full expression in John Adams's text of 1762, *A Dissertation on the Canon and the Feudal Law.*

Though Americans argued their case in terms of legalistic rights and wrongs, their true concern was for America's "natural" and historic rights. The raging debate on internal and external taxation, a wily distinction dear to Benjamin Franklin, can be understood as an unconscious reference to this same nascent nationalism. America's first claims to internal sovereignty were set within the protective context of British imperial might.[18] Even as he railed against the Stamp Act, James Otis wrote: "If I have one ambitious wish, 'tis to see Great-Britain at the head of the world, and to see my King, under God, the father of mankind."[19] So also the Stamp Act Congress of 1765, which had drawn delegates from nine colonies, sent London a double message: Americans would not pay the tax, but they did nonetheless acknowledge "all due subordination to King and Parliament."

But as Americans developed a greater sense of nationhood, their political theorizing on this issue was miraculously transformed. By the late 1760s most Americans had come to reject the distinction between internal and external sovereignty. It had become clear that they should consent to import duties only if the purpose of the duties was to regulate imperial trade. Henceforth any British attempt to raise taxes in America for whatever reason, internal or external, would not be acceptable.

Increasingly aware of themselves as a people and energized by a political philosophy which provided a convincing map of international politics, Americans in the early 1770s were ready to assert themselves as a nation. They were on the verge also of forging a new and indigenous political theory that would blend popular sovereignty with localist pluralism. The achievement of national independence, and with it cultural and political autonomy, would bring this pattern to fruition.

That America should have achieved independence at the end of the eighteenth century is not in itself surprising, but the way in which this was done deserves attention. It mattered a great deal that America's yearning for nationhood should have been expressed through a communitarian ideology that could not in itself be sustained but whose legacy could not be dismissed, a legacy that even today can be found in some parts of the American ethos—no longer, perhaps, in our political system, but in the particular configuration of our civil society and its capacity for human empowerment.

4

Possessive Individualism and Universalist Illusion in Prerevolutionary France

OMINOUS, SUSTAINED, and growing contradictions character-ized French social and cultural forms in the last decades of the Old Regime. France was divided against itself. Its cultural forms were uncertainly shaped. Its social structures had become blurred. The gap had widened between the principles of tradition, which re-mained critical politically, and the new rationalistic, optimistic, individuating message of the Enlightenment. The breakdown of the French Revolution, with its sequel of class war, terror, and statist centralism, was in large part the political consequence of these prerevolutionary social and cultural ambiguities. Although it is less important to understand the economic and material contradictions of prerevolutionary French life than its cultural cleavages, these economic contradictions have loomed large in historical writing.

The economic problem is best approached indirectly, through the experience of England. It may well be that each European country—even each region—has had to find its own path of eco-nomic change and industrialization; certainly the specificity of every nation's economic history has to be borne in mind. Nonetheless, in the second half of the eighteenth century England provided France with the most obvious model for growth. In fact, what happened in Britain is a forcible reminder of what *might* have happened in France but did not.

Georgian England was a ship in full sail, as the French realized with envy. Informed Frenchmen did find day-to-day British politics turbulent and its urban population unruly: "Riots in London," wrote Louis Sébastien Mercier in an unpublished manuscript of 1781, "are more frequent than in Paris; or, rather, they are as frequent there as they are rare here." Many other aspects of English life, however, seemed admirable. Britain's constitution, for example, was seen as a general model for mankind in prerevolutionary France just as it was in prerevolutionary America: "All the long and brilliant career of the Roman Empire," wrote Chastellux in 1772, "is not worth the latest period of English History, that is, the time which has elapsed from the revolution [of 1688] to the present day."[1] Montesquieu, who lived in England from 1729 to 1732, celebrated, on his return to France, the balance of British crown, commons, and Parliament.

What really impressed the French, however, was England's dramatic rise as a political and economic world power after 1700, with the consequent loss for France of prestige, wars, and such colonies as Canada, the Ohio Valley, Louisiana, India. And behind the English fleet, they knew, was England's credit, her spectacular and wholly unprecedented ability to borrow. Behind that, in turn, they perceived the weight of British trade, the development of its agriculture, and the rise of its industries. French intellectuals were well aware also of the English and the Scottish Enlightenment, with its social and economic message of benevolent progress toward modulated, individuated forms. Voltaire, Montesquieu, Diderot, and Rousseau all lived for some months or years in Britain or in Holland, and Benjamin Constant studied in Edinburgh in the early 1780s. Indeed, the French sometimes adapted Anglo-Scottish thinking for their own ends. Sieyès, for example, used Adam Smith's views on the technological division of labor to justify the political delegation of the nation's broad and popular sovereignty to its selected deputies.

It is important for French history, therefore, that economic individuation was the shorthand notation for the economic history of Britain in this period. Back in the 1640s the collapse of Stuart absolutism and the dismantlement of its burgeoning bureaucracy had facilitated the capitalist transformation of England's commerce and agriculture. Land was gradually enclosed—that is, privatized and fenced—a process that had begun under Henry VIII in the sixteenth century and was to continue until the first decades of the nineteenth century. The customs of communal village life were gradually given up. The sustained efforts which both the Tudors and the early Stuarts had made to force the sale of grain at a low price during hard times were abandoned. Village commons were put up for sale. Nationwide, a growing domestic rural market for cheap industrial goods such as textiles, coal, and pottery provided a sound basis for overseas commercial development. Though restraints on the export of machinery were retained until the next century, export taxes were abolished. Trade and growth were closely intertwined. Colonial staple products (sugar, coffee, rice, indigo, cotton) were not just locally consumed as pepper had been a century before. They were refined or transformed into industrial goods that were resold the world over, and at the lowest prices.

During this period of economic growth landowning gentry did not lose its hold on British politics. It combined its vestigial prestige as an Anglican aristocracy with its new, moneyed power as a possessing class. As justices of the peace and members of Parliament, the gentry landlords and their merchant allies, many of whom also became landlords, ran the counties in the assizes. From the Parliament at Westminster they also ran the country to great personal advantage: though the operations of the state—which they controlled and from which they profited—were less visible than in France, the state was an efficient orchestrator of war, a most efficient collector of taxes, and the active dispenser of vast networks of patronage.

English landlords were rural capitalists of a kind, converting vast acreage from grain to wool. Sheep ate men. In the 1760s Britain, though it had (with Flanders) the world's most efficient agriculture, also began to import grain to feed the growing population not just of commercial London, Europe's largest city, but of the growing industrial cities in Yorkshire and Lancashire. British ships were everywhere. In western Europe, half of Lisbon's better properties belonged to English merchants, whose financial losses after the great earthquake of 1755 were greater than those of their hosts. In eastern Europe, most of the vessels which put in at Saint Petersburg flew the flag of Saint George. The French could not rival these capitalist and mercantile achievements.

Britain's greatest success was its growing colonial empire, including, of course, the thirteen North American colonies. Before the seventeenth-century crisis, that is, before the first decades of the seventeenth century, world trade had functioned within military empires, whose worth was computed largely in terms of the precious metals they might yield. Spain was the first world power in this field. In Mexico and Peru, Spaniards forced the natives to work in mines; they killed those that would not work. By the beginning of the eighteenth century, however, a new imperial system was in operation, and here England took the lead. Trade grew among the "advanced" nations and even between one colonial empire and another: Americans, for example, had extensive if illegal dealings with the French Caribbean islands. Henceforth the core countries valued their colonies not for treasure but for their slave-grown staple crops—agricultural supplies for the burgeoning industries of the mother nations. Because contemporaries were determined to maintain established preferences, cross-national colonial trade was ordinarily hampered or even forbidden by laws, of which Cromwell's Navigation Acts were the Anglo-American variant.

France's place in the eighteenth-century world of commerce was defined by its ambiguous relationship to this rapidly shifting world system, which Britain ruled. The French remained the second industrial and commercial power in the world. Their society did not go into a tailspin, as those of Spain and Portugal had done in the late seventeenth century. In absolute volume, French trade roughly equaled that of Britain. The population of France was more than twice that of its northern neighbor, and in terms of the absolute power which either state could mobilize, the lower per-capita production of France was more than balanced by its greater numbers. As Portugal had become de facto an informal British colony, so had Spain become a French dependency of sorts, ruled by monarchs of French origin (cousins of the king of France) who accepted the French domination of Spain's overseas trade.

The gap between France and Britain was nonetheless considerable, and, unfortunately for the French, more a matter of quality than of quantity. They differed more in regard to their type of involvement in world trade than in the volume of goods they sold abroad. England's whole economy was involved in the capitalistic world system. Propertied individualism was more generally accepted there than in any other European country. *Robinson Crusoe*, with its solipsistic and widely read reconstitution of social and economic forms, was a highly symbolic text. Even women became for Englishmen a kind of marketable property, and Addison, on whose prose the young Benjamin Franklin modeled his own style, spoke for his age and class when he explained that man valued female chastity so highly because it gave him "a Property in the Person he loves, and consequently endears her to him in all ways."[2] Neither the economy nor the culture of France was transformed in this way. France largely remained as it had been, especially when contrasted with colonial America, whose economic individualism and material prosperity were the limiting case of British growth. French involvement in this new capitalist, commercial, industrial, and financial world system was real, but decidedly more peripheral.

The French internal picture was not uniformly dark: with some exceptions, mostly in eastern France—that is to say, close to the German border—French peasants were free men who could come and go, buy and sell, and marry as they pleased. In most of France serfdom had not existed for centuries. In central Europe, by contrast, it was not abolished until 1848, and serfdom continued in Russia until 1861. French land tenure was relatively modern also. In the eighteenth century, leaseholds whose provisions incited long-term tenants to improve their lands gained at the expense of the most destructive, annually reviewed share-cropping. After 1720 the currency became more stable. Discrepancies in prices from region to region waned as communications improved. And as prices stabilized, so did the death rate, which fell in France from more than forty-one per thousand per year in 1740 to about thirty-five in the mid-1770s.[3] The population of France grew sizably in the eighteenth century from less than twenty million to twenty-six or twenty-seven million. This rate of demographic increase, though well below that of Britain and much lower than that in the thirteen colonies, was in its way quite high: in this preindustrial society where so many lived on the margin, a significant rise in population necessarily pointed to improvements in the organization of distribution and to some improved ability to produce foodstuffs. Until the mid-eighteenth century the curves of death rates, like those of agricultural prices, zigzagged wildly across the graph: in 1709, for example, widespread starvation was rampant except in Brittany. But this was the last instance of generalized famine in France, despite great scares in 1741–42, in the late 1760s, and on the eve of the Revolution as well. In Britain, the last famine dated from the sixteenth century; in America, none had ever occurred; in Russia, tens of thousands of peasants starved to death in 1894. These dates are a useful barometer in the comparison of rural technologies and networks of distribution.

Everywhere in Europe the return on planted seed was extraordinarily low by modern standards. Agricultural yields were never more than ten to one and were often as low as four to one. French agriculture was poorly organized and rigid in its structures. In America, the nature of crops and the very location of settlements were functions of rising prices and new opportunities. Rural France was, by contrast, a collection of "immobile villages." The shape of settlement and the very layout of fields and fences reached back to the Middle Ages or beyond. In America new cities, such as Baltimore, which thrived on wheat exports from their agricultural hinterland, could achieve maturity within a decade. In France during the seventeenth and eighteenth centuries only three new cities were created, one of them Versailles, a largely parasitical mini-metropolis that was the administrative capital of France and the site of a bloated and increasingly despised royal court. Since the thirteenth century there had been no French frontier to setttle. By 1700 very little suitable land remained untilled in France; and the state's efforts to encourage new clearings through tax exemptions were largely unsuccessful. Some swamps were drained, some forests cleared, and some areas reforested; but rural life went on much as it had since the sixteenth century when France had emerged from its late-medieval doldrums.

Eighteenth-century France, unlike England, did not experience a sustained enclosure movement. Economic individualism did not transform French agriculture during the reign of Louis XV (1715–1774) any more than it had in the reign of Louis XIV (1643–1715.) Most French peasants did not produce primarily for the market. Theirs was ordinarily a familial economy. They did not, as individuals, rationally adjust a varied choice of crops in order to meet urban demand. Their first goal remained what it had been for centuries: to hold out until the next harvest and to maintain the unity of their households. France was a vast "wheat factory." Peasants were there by the millions, but French farmers were few and far between. Landless Frenchmen moved within their regions, from one master to another, in order to maintain some independence; but relatively few of them migrated from one end of the country to the other, or to cities in order to find an altogether new kind of life and employment. Even fewer of them went abroad as permanent migrants. During the whole of French colonial rule, fewer than thirty thousand Frenchmen migrated to Canada, where, incidentally, their prolific descendants number today more than seven million.

French peasants, though independent-minded, were suspicious of social individualism and frightened by the implications of the market. They might be litigious, acquisitive, eager to round off their holdings, and often envious of their neighbors: in a word, they had a petit-bourgeois world view. But they detested entrepreneurial risk-taking. Their condition shows that capitalism and bourgeois life, though perhaps coterminous in time, are not by any means one and the same thing. Rural communitarianism was much more unusual in France than it was in eastern Europe. The Russian mir with its annual redistribution of land was unthinkable in France. Extended families like that of the Yugoslav Zadruga were few and were becoming less common, even if their communitarian organization struck the imagination of Parisian intellectuals, suddenly enamored of primitive social forms. The agricultural hinterland of even the busiest harbors might remain a world unto itself. "Mon Dieu!" wrote the English agronomist Arthur Young when he arrived in 1788 at the seaport of Nantes, whose backcountry was tangentially involved in the modern textile trade, "do all the wastes, the deserts, the heath, ling, furze, broom and bog that I have passed for three hundred miles lead to this spectacle? What a miracle, that all this splendour and wealth of the cities of France should be so unconnected with the country!"[4]

It was of fundamental importance that France's significant involvement in world trade did not extend inward as it did in Britain. The configuration of French life and culture would have been very different if commercial capitalism had engendered a rural capitalism in turn. But with some exceptions—such as the area northwest of Paris where the future revolutionary communist Babeuf grew up— that change did not occur. French peasants in the late eighteenth century were in an intermediate situation. They were anticapitalist, negative-minded individualists. They could unite (but only to resist rather than to act) against outsiders, the state, the city, and after 1789 the "revolutionary bourgeoisie." Only gradually after 1789 did peasants become citizens of the Grande Nation, thanks to universal military conscription, state-sponsored education, the wider use of the French language, and the development of railways in a monetized market economy.

Agricultural stagnation had broad social effects in France. In particular, an essentially unreformed agriculture narrowly constrained the possibilities of urban growth. Many French cities were, to be sure, active centers of trade and manufacture. Bordeaux, Rouen, and Marseilles were far more dynamic than the dormant cities of the Rhineland or of Italy, which had been stagnating for two centuries and whose total population fell during the eighteenth century. Industrial and artisanal production counted for more than a third of the French national production of commodities. Lyons silk was sold all over Europe. Nonetheless, an eloquent contrast may be drawn between Paris, an administrative center whose growth was tied to a swelling royal bureaucracy, and London, the world's largest seaport in the eighteenth century and the staging area for Britain's exportation of manufactured products. England produced mass consumption goods, such as Wedgwood's earthenware. The French were better known for their tapestries, stately mirrors, and elegant porcelain. Fashions were set in the French capital, and elegant dolls attired in the latest Parisian fashions circulated throughout late-eighteenth-century Europe, but the cloth that was used to make these dresses usually came from Britain. That Marie-Antoinette's English percale gown (in the portrait of her painted by Mme Vigée-Lebrun) should be resented by the public as yet another personal and perverse proof of her antinational, monarchic insouciance was quite unfair.

Thoughtful Frenchmen understood that their society was becoming more commercial, technologized, and industrial. They realized also that Britain was moving more quickly than France toward these new goals; and it was in part because French industrial development seemed incomplete that the able civil servants of the ancien régime often rushed in to fill the gaps in ways that private entrepreneurs had been afraid to try. France's international and colonial trade was closely nurtured by the state. Bankers were actually more dependent on the favors of *le roi très chrétien* than nobles were. In the eighteenth century many industries were kept afloat by tariff protection. Government expenditure in state-run armaments industries and navy yards grew by leaps and bounds. French professional schools—the ancestors of today's Grandes Ecoles, were created by the monarchy to meet its own technological needs. (The School of Roads and Bridges dates back to 1755 and the School of Mines to 1783.) State-guided capitalism was well developed and may in fact have retarded growth, because the celebrated royal manufactories—many of them created by Colbert in the seventeenth century—funneled scarce skilled labor and capital into wasteful luxury industries.

French urban growth was, in sum, structured awkwardly. The basic pattern was one of failure, but only by the standards that had been set by Britain and her thirteen North American colonies. French urban and economic growth from 1720 to 1789 was in many ways respectable, especially during the middle decades of the century. Between 1715 and 1789 France's European trade quadrupled and her Caribbean commerce rose tenfold. The production of coal, chemicals, and metals expanded rapidly. France acted as a second clearing center for world trade by importing and exporting colonial produce to eastern and southern Europe. French bankers were heavily involved in these transactions. The faces of many coastal cities, such as Nantes and Bordeaux, were reshaped. Paris itself experienced a prerevolutionary building boom.

Here as elsewhere ambiguity was the touchstone of French life, and what was true of the economy applied also to the nation's economic ethos. The aristocratic contempt for money, like the Catholic suspicion of wealth, ran deep: when Louis XVI solicitously asked the bankrupt Prince de Guéménée how much was owed to his creditors, the frivolous and insolent courtier replied that he would be sure to inquire so as to satisfy his sovereign's curiosity. The very serious Physiocrat Marquis de Mirabeau, whose dates are nearly coterminous with those of Benjamin Franklin, expressed the same sensibility in a different register when he defined "a society where wealth and cupidity have undisputed preeminence" as "an assembly of overt or covert thieves, of civilized brigands."[5] And yet, of course, the prestige of trade did grow in eighteenth-century France, and with it the prestige of economic individualism. Bourgeois and provincial nobles alike learned to keep accounts.

A significant symbol of this cultural shift toward a new and official valuation of the pursuit of greater wealth was the renewed curtailment by the French state of the traditional rules of *dérogeance*, or "denobilization." In the past these disabilities had been invoked by the crown (as well as by nonnoble merchants eager to defend their corporate privilege) to hurl into a social void those enterprising nobles who had ventured into trade. Now these restraints were partially repealed, and the French state actually ennobled some successful merchants. In the patent of nobility that was granted in 1775 to a merchant at Rouen, the monarch, or more precisely his bureaucratic civil servants, explained that although in the past in France wealth had merely been the means by which a successful family passed into the nobility and gave up trade, the thirst for riches needed to become a freestanding principle of social action. It was important, ran the document, "to make it known to the nation that trade is at once honorable and useful."[6] Between 1750 and 1789 hundreds of merchants and bankers, as well as artists and intellectuals, were ennobled for their achievements. Ironically, some of these former bourgeois were to be executed as nobles in 1794.

The progress of the French economy toward capitalism was undeniable but badly flawed. In a way, France received the worst of both worlds. Such growth as took place engendered grave illusions. In a society where many economic relationships were still encumbered by feudal dues or, less formally, by customs and traditions of deference and community, the monetization of social dealings seemed to promise a great deal. In the late capitalist societies of the twentieth century the problems implicit in monetized relations have long since become obvious: money is power, and relationships of power are as a rule asymmetrical, involving the rich and the poor, men and women, the young and the aged, the productive and the parasitical, workers and employers. In the perspective of eighteenth-century French life, where incipient individualist values had sapped the culture's tolerance for feudal deference in general and for rural feudal dues in particular, money seemed instead coterminous with freedom. The monetization of feudal relationships appeared very promising. Voltaire in his writings on England waxed lyrical about the transformative power of the London stock exchange. In the past, he explained, Christians and Jews, Catholics and Protestants, Anglicans and Dissenters had been at one another's throats. Now, he observed complacently, all of them competed peacefully— if avidly—as greedy stockjobbers on the London exchange. Avarice, it seemed, could transcend cruelty. The idea was an unusually pleasing alternative to grating corporate arrangements. Yet from the moment of its actualization this theoretically acceptable vision of individualized and capitalistic relations engendered unsuspected problems, as when the sansculottes suddenly discovered in 1792–93 that they would starve if the laws of the market were left to operate without restraint—if the state, that is, withdrew from civil society as the revolutionary elite had decreed it should. A more complete involvement in the capitalistic system might well have lessened the anticorporatist zeal of reformers in the eighteenth century and during the Revolution as well.

France was the most backward of the modern nations and the most modern of the backward ones, halfway between America, Britain, and Holland on the one hand and continental Europe on the other. In consequence, France in the 1780s was in a double crisis. Its modern sectors suffered from a broad cyclical downturn in the world economy. Rates of growth were well below what they had been between 1740 and 1765. Within that broad and negative context, metallurgy and potteries were somewhat affected, but the textile industry suffered especially, due to the increase in British exports resulting from the free-trade treaty signed with England in 1786 for essentially diplomatic reasons. Industrial price and wages fell. Peasants involved in "proto-industrial" activity through the putting-out system suffered a great deal: in the Vendée, not far from Nantes, the ensuing animosity between town and country, between unemployed peasants and cost-cutting urban entrepreneurs, was to be an important factor in the counterrevolutionary insurrection of 1793.

For a different set of reasons the untouched rural sector also waned as the Revolution neared. As the size of the rural population grew and per-capita agricultural production stagnated, the number of landless peasants swelled. Food prices rose by 60 percent between 1726 and 1789. During the 1780s a large proportion of the population, perhaps as many as 20 percent, lived in "an economy of makeshift," by occasional employment, beggary, ingenuity, and theft. In especially hard times, large bands of desperate people roamed the countryside. Because propertied peasants were determined to defend themselves if no one else would do so, their fear of these vagrants had much to do with rural uprisings in the summer of 1789.

MANY HISTORIANS HAVE made economic travails the first cause of the decline of the Old Regime. This argument, though bolstered by much impressive research, cannot be sustained. The economically ambiguous nature of French society on the eve of the Great Revolution is important because it introduced and in some measure explains the ideological and cultural ambiguities that were basic to France's decline. France had not one economy but two; and French culture was no more monolithic than its economy. Different systems of thought, some individualist and the others not—and none of them uniformly shaped—existed side by side in that nation's culture.

One system of thought was lived from day to day and was basically oriented toward communitarian, or at least corporate, group action. Another, more ideological in its origin, was conceptually geared to the pursuit of tangible and private gain. Defensive individualism did bridge the gap between these various doctrines: all Frenchmen, for example, whether disciples of the philosophes or members of a guild, increasingly despised and feared an arbitrary state. Nonetheless, the distance between the two broad world views—individualist and communitarian—was very wide. The conflict between these two systems and the ambiguities within each were the necessary if not the sufficient cause not just of revolution but of the radicalization of politics after 1789. A bright thread runs from the uncertain and contested prerevolutionary world view of the propertied elite to the successful assertion of republican virtue over private rights between 1792 and 1794.

Contemporaries concerned with the high culture of their times did not primarily understand it as a struggle over the limits of individualism, even if that value was important to them. Voltaire's slogan "Ecrasez l'infâme," like Kant's "Sapere aude" in Germany, said more about man's struggle against the institutionalized forces of darkness in the world than about man's alienated and divided self.

This difference of perspective between ourselves as observers and those living in the eighteenth century whom we observe—between their obsessions (clerical obscurantism, for example) and our own interests (the rise of individualism and capitalism)—should be a cause for concern but not for despair. As Hegel explained, it is at the dusk of History that the owl of Minerva takes flight, which is to say, in terms of Marxist rhetoric, that men do make their own history but seldom understand what it is they are achieving. The writing of history is a dynamic interplay between the past as it was lived from day to day and as it is now conceptually perceived. The Renaissance as a historical construct was not invented until the middle decades of the nineteenth century. In the same vein, it would be hard today to describe eighteenth-century Europe without making reference to the idea enlightened despotism, but that term was practically unknown at the time. Particular events or trends ceaselessly acquire new meanings. To insist on making individualism a pivotal element of broad eighteenth-century cultural change merely reflects our knowledge that the rise of liberalism and capitalism would soon become the central theme of European history in the nineteenth century.

This is not to argue either that history is what historians say it is or that the present always condescends to the past. It is to suggest instead that the trends in our lives, which often seem inexorable in retrospect, invariably surprise us as we live them. The determining instances of our personal existence and of our collective histories are not always, or even often, the ones that seem important day by day.

To restate this view in the context of eighteenth-century French life, the cultivated Frenchmen of the Enlightenment may well have been less concerned about asserting individual rights than they were about knocking down the Old Regime. They were certainly less interested in the economic consequences of anticorporatism than in the destruction of a governmental system which they took to be an intolerant and intolerable web of privilege and abuse, of absolutism, and of clerical, obscurantist repression. The nature of their thinking, however, does not make it wrong for us to sense that the Old Regime was far more avuncular than they thought; that its fate was sealed in any case; and that what really mattered in 1789 were the implications, limits, and contradictions of the individualist ideology which they only tangentially invoked to justify their great task. From our late-capitalist perspective, it is clear that what was most important in eighteenth-century France was not the foreordained fall of the Old Regime but the kind of democratic and industrializing system that would replace it. After traditional corporatism, what next? A system that emphasized narrowed but open-ended liberal values in politics and economics? Or a more determining and communitarian system of virtue that emphasized not just the public good but the assertion of "socialized" property as well? It is largely because of the continued relevance of these choices that we still care about the definitions of individualism that were given in France before 1789.

TWO BROAD CULTURAL currents are discernible in prerevolutionary France, neither of them homogeneous: the popular culture of the masses and the high culture of the educated elite.

Most Frenchmen in the eighteenth century continued to live in the inherited affective world of the seventeenth century that has been described in the second chapter of this book. At the general level of cultural instinct, their sensitivity was to the world of sounds and smells, to the spoken word rather than to print. Loyalty to inherited ways and means was the touchstone.

This popular culture coexisted, however, with a very different set of values whose relevance had been growing steadily since the seventeenth century. Its centerpiece was the assertion of secularized individualism as a purpose, and of reason as a method. A broad cultural shift was articulated around these two values, which are not only the central themes of the high Enlightenment in France but also the basic principles of capitalism (a nexus of economic and social relations which emphasizes the rational maximization of private interest). In this novel context, the future mattered more than the present or the past; the management of life took precedence over the management of death.

At the highest level, in the Parisian salons and academies, the educated elite was enthralled by the development of ordered and ordering meliorating science. Newton was more often apotheosized on the banks of the Seine than he was in London. The most curious of the visionary plans drawn up by the late-eighteenth-century utopian architect Etienne Boullée was a gigantic, planetlike cenotaph to Newton's memory, a sphere that would visibly represent the philosopher's successful encompassing of the cosmos. Voltaire's companion, Mme du Chatelet, who was soon to die in childbirth, wrote an elegant abbreviation of Newtonianism for the ladies. The findings of expeditions sent by the French Academy of Sciences to South America and to the polar circles in order to measure the circularity of the globe were eagerly awaited in Paris. The Enlightenment public thrilled to every scientific discovery: to Cook's discoveries in the unexplored South Seas, and to those of the Comte de la Pérouse, whom the young Bonaparte decided at the last moment not to join, and whose two vessels disappeared with all hands in 1788. Physics and astronomy enjoyed particularly high prestige. Benjamin Franklin, who became Europe's first American hero, thanks to his lightning rod, was much admired by Parisian intellectuals, who no doubt were agreeably surprised to find that their interest in physics could have immediate and practical effect. The ramifications of the new rationalist and individualist world view were legion. No aspect of social life or culture was left untouched. Transparent, rational simplicity was everywhere praised, and imposed, even where one would least expect it: "With regard to counterfugues," wrote Rousseau of the type of music which Bach's genius had just brought to perfection, "double fugues, inverted fugues, ground basses, and other difficult sillinesses that the ear cannot abide and which reason cannot justify, these are obviously remnants of barbarism and bad taste that only persist, like the portals of our Gothic cathedrals, to the shame of those who had the endurance to build them."[7] With mesmerism, even credulity assumed a pseudoscientific guise.

The French Enlightenment was an age of learned taxonomy
rather than of analysis. Buffon, who had categorized the whole of
nature, concluded that "we must resign ourselves to describing as
cause what is a general effect, and abandon attempts to advance our
knowledge further. These general effects are for us the true laws of
nature." The spirit of the age was often naive: for Condorcet the
accumulation of evidence, and the statistical study of this mass of
information, held out the promise of near-perpetual progress. Undeniably, from our modernist perspective, such limitations of Enlightenment thought are grating. Nonetheless, Diderot's great and
subversive *Encyclopedia*, published with the complicity of the Bourbon state, was a vast catalogue of human achievement and a paean
to man's ability to decipher the laws of the universe. Enthusiasms
and scientific fads were often comic, but on the positive side they
had a determining effect on the development of scientific knowledge, notably in mathematics, astronomy, and the physical sciences
generally.

Religion and magic became simultaneously less seductive. The
physical world was less threatening and death less problematic but
more troubling than before: the subjects of Louis XVI might worry
less about dying in a state of religious grace than had those of Louis
XIV, but they were more disturbed by the waning prospect of life
after death. Everywhere in France, but especially in Paris, reformers
campaigned successfully to remove cemeteries from the inner cities.
Medical arguments do not suffice to explain their unease. What was
the purpose of life if mankind had not been created in God's image?
What was the true nature of pleasure? Fear of ennui coincided with
a thirst for novel experiences. Sexuality appeared more interesting
than before and became a persistent theme in the high culture of
the epoch: in the widely read and still popular novel the *Liaisons
dangereuses* an artillery officer named Choderlos de Laclos, who
would later become a prorevolutionary pamphleteer and one of
Napoleon's generals, sketched out the lives of characters whose
existence revolved around their sexual selves and who schemed
rationally to exploit their sexual advantages in order to dominate
and humiliate. The unreasonable and unnatural Catholic interdict
on clerical celibacy was held up to persistent ridicule: Diderot, in
his seventies, mused on his youthful escapades when he enjoyed a

visit to the brothel in the company of Montesquieu, Buffon, and the Président des Brosses. Though not well known at the time, the works of the Marquis de Sade, who was briefly imprisoned in the Bastille, appear to us today to have intersected many of the most important cultural currents of the age. Bodies were more fascinating as souls became less so. The prestige of physicians who tended bodies rose—rather surprisingly so since the advice of doctors was usually destructive. The high standards of British domestic comfort were much admired. Extremes of heat and cold seemed less tolerable than before. The smells and filth of Paris, of which no one had taken much notice in the past, became the object of national debate.

Traditionalist and modern cultural traits were not necessarily mutually exclusive. Many Frenchmen carried within themselves echoes of both strands, just as their lives were often meshed into different economic systems. Louis XVI's reactionary brother, the Comte d'Artois, invested heavily in chemicals; and Voltaire did not think it wrong to hope for profit from the slave trade. History is not neat, and the distinction made between high and low culture is too schematic. In many respects—medicine, for example—eighteenth-century French folk culture was an adaptation of seventeenth-century high culture. Rationality was hardly allotted by class. French peasants were very calculating, just as French bourgeois Jacobins were emotive rhetoricians who searched for conspirators under every bed. Age and education may well have been a more telling divide than social status.

Disclaimers, however, do not tip the scale: it is still possible to draw a line between the social audiences of the two world views. The propertied and intellectual elites, which largely overlapped, were more touched by the new rationalist and individualist ethic than were peasants or the urban masses: "Within a nation," wrote Voltaire, there is always a people that has no contact with polite society, which does not belong to the age, which is inaccessible to the progress of reason, and over whom fanaticism maintains its atrocious hold."[8] At the level of the collective zeitgeist and, more prosaically, in the everyday business of life, cultural and social discontinuity was the rule. The Enlightenment cultural climate that prevailed at the top was by no means generally representative. Changes in the sexual habits of the elite (about which we are reasonably well informed) do not by any means imply, for example, some corresponding evolution in the lower reaches of society. In all likelihood, the rising rate of illegitimacy for young working women was *not* a reflection of the romantic disposition that affected elitist literary circles: a more plausible explanation for rising rates of popular illegitimacy may be the greater incidence of sexual exploitation as defenseless young peasant women tried to find urban work to raise a dowry, and as sexually active and mobile young men became increasingly reluctant to marry against their will. This situation contrasted strongly with that in colonial America, where individualist concerns, at once pragmatic and transcendental, secular and religious, were diffused from top to bottom on the social scale.

Although the new cultural systems directly affected only a small minority of the nation, their impact on the upper reaches of society was broadly felt. The French Enlightenment was both radical in theory and widely taken up by the nation's social elite. Whether one considers the philosophes to have been the expression of a wider sensibility or the creators of either a novel or a renewed "public opinion," the fact remains that Enlightenment writers did speak for one side of their age.

The new possessing class even took its particularist ideological and cultural desires to be the expression of "natural," broadly societal, self-evidently correct, and therefore "public," opinion. Whether the philosophes were cause or effect, there is no mistaking the extent of the event of which they were a part: a somewhat eccentric archbishop who became prime minister in the late 1780s was rumored to be an atheist. The good word of the philosophes was spread across the land in hundreds, possibly even thousands, of cafés, salons, local academies, and Masonic lodges, some of them opened to women. (It is thought that one in eight of the four thousand published writers who lived in France at this time was a Freemason.) In the 1780s the French book trade was a vigorous and unscrupulous business. A provincial press appeared after 1770. Rates of literacy, though class-specific, rose overall throughout the century. For the commercial professions especially, private and public reading in cafés and in the newly created public libraries became a common exercise. Bourgeois and nobles were voracious readers of newspapers, many of them printed abroad but allowed to circulate in France. Book collecting became a sign of discernment: during the seventeenth century Colbert, a bourgeois bureaucrat, accumulated the largest private library of his time. Small cities could boast a salon, a local reading society, an academy, or perhaps a chamber of commerce, all of them instruments of a renewed sociability and, as such, the elitist analogues of the more popular and traditional *confréries* and *chambrées*. Censorship was erratic if not desultory. Nearly a quarter of the prisoners put into the Bastille from 1660 to 1789 were connected with the book trade; but few of them stayed there for any length of time, and a number of them made their fortune on the basis of that very imprisonment. Booksellers did not hesitate to smuggle into the kingdom contraband books which would sell well, and over the century the changing titles of the books they sold indicate changing values. After 1750 the more successful illicit books tended to have a pronounced political and anticlerical character.

THE HIGH CULTURE of the mainstream philosophes was strikingly different from the popular culture of the urban and rural rank and file. It stood apart also from the anti-individualist strand of elite culture, a tradition that is harder to sort out and has been much less studied. Taken as a group, or sect, as they were called by their enemies, most of the philosophes diffused new values which both justified and furthered the new individuated and capitalist modes of social and economic life. Many other writers, however, went against the grain and supported, tangentially at least, the view that communitarian values ought to frame most social choices.

Theirs was an ancient wine put into new bottles. The united voice of nature and reason, they suggested, did not lead to individualism, taken as autonomous self-assertion, but to the individual's pronounced responsibility for the social good. Reason and nature dictated that men, and more particularly women, should place public or familial good before their own private economic and cultural well-being. "Philanthropic" writers renewed traditional themes of Christian charity. Simon Linguet, a bourgeois journalist who was to be decapitated in 1794, argued before the Revolution in favor of a populist and monarchic despotism. In short, vocal intellectuals were by no means united in praise either of individualism or of strict, dessicating rationality. Although Rousseau's *Social Contract* was republished only twice between 1761 and 1789 and was not nearly so well known as Montesquieu's *Spirit of Laws*, which was republished twenty-two times between 1748 and 1750, the preromantic Rousseau best reflected the deep sensibility of the French reading public—better than either Montesquieu the aristocratic liberal or Voltaire the rational classicist. Rousseau's novel *La Nouvelle Héloïse,* which expressed in appealing form his praise of social complementarity (and female self-effacement), was the best-seller of its day and was reprinted seventy times between 1761 and 1789. Fascinated readers wrote effusively to express their gratitude to Rousseau for having helped them to discover their true selves. Mme Roland, wife of the Girondin minister of the interior in 1792, an intelligent, well-educated, and forceful woman, found Rousseau's *Social Contract* indigestible but wept over the fate of his Julie and Saint-Preux.

A growing sense of nationhood, fueled by humiliating defeats (in 1763) and gratifying victories (in 1783) was another overriding and ideologized communitarian value which Rousseau and many other authors did a great deal to enhance. Social and material factors were of relevance here: better roads, the increased circulation of goods and men, and greater use of the French language (half of all Frenchmen ordinarily used some other language in their daily lives.) The social background and social situation of writers and publicists were also relevant. Many of the major and minor philosophes or writers were rich or even titled; but not being anchored in any corps, these deracinated men and women were often seduced by the "sublimity of nation," a new and seductive abstraction, quite different from the old, more tranquil concept of *patrie* that historical figures such as Joan of Arc had represented for centuries. The myth of "the nation," which had heretofore found expression in the quasi-religious cult of the monarch, was now increasingly centered on the idea of a French people and a geographically determined homeland, shaped by nature and history. The French language—its orgins, grammar, and structure—became a subject of lively intellectual concern.

Among the modernizing but communitarian impulses sustained by anti-individualist philosophes (if such a self-contradictory term can be momentarily allowed) one could also find yet another strain, the rough counterpart in France of the Anglo-American Radical Whig cult of ancient virtues. Montesquieu, for example, was a friend of Bolingbroke and an assiduous reader of Machiavelli, whose work was the starting point of much radical English theorizing. For Montesquieu, "virtue" was the mainspring of republicanism, and in *The Spirit of Laws* he described Britain as a republic of a kind. Though Montesquieu, himself a noble, also concluded—perhaps to his relief—that his age was not wholly virtuous, many of his enlightened readers thought differently: Montesquieu was the favored thinker of Saint-Just, Robespierre's most faithful friend.

Charles Rollin's history of ancient Rome was as widely known in France as it was in America. *Cato's Letters*, by John Trenchard and Thomas Gordon, was repeatedly translated into French, as well it might have been because the argument of the seventeenth letter explained the ruin of modern countries in terms that were obviously written with France in mind: wars, corruption, luxurious distractions, and the impoverishment of the people. Catherine Macaulay counted Mme Roland among her French readers; and, surprisingly, Marat's first political tract, *The Chains of Slavery*, which he wrote in 1774 while in England and had reprinted at the beginning of the Revolution, was fully within the Radical Whig tradition, with its defense of individualism, its eulogy of the people, and its bitter suspicion of all authority.

Nonetheless, neither the philosophes nor the classicists were the principal cultural prop of anti-individualism in eighteenth-century France. That role fell to the church and to the Catholic religion, which remained a vital force until the Revolution. The occasional conjunction of the communitarian-philosophical and the clerical-traditional had ironic consequences. Catholic intellectuals detested Rousseau as much as they did Voltaire, but Rousseau and the Catholics were in an objective sense antiliberal fellow travelers. Many eighteenth-century Frenchmen who invoked natural law to define man and society did no more than secularize the ancient principles of canon law. These believers and unbelievers shared a common suspicion of cities, commerce, industry, technological specialization, and individuated social forms, that is, of modern bourgeois life.

The situation was complex because in some ways the French Church was itself a modern institution. Just as some dissident, *passéistes* philosophes were seduced by the ancient communitarian models of Greece and Rome, so were some modernist clerics keen to accept their own epoch.

The French Catholic Church was far from fossilized. Many strands within it were very close to the spirit of the times. Hundreds of parish priests, some of whom would soon side with the revolutionary party, were Richerists who believed that the powers of the bishops should be curtailed and those of the lower clergy be strengthened, as had been true in the early church. At the other end of this modernizing Catholic spectrum were the worldly and compromising Jesuits, a few of whom were covert admirers of Voltaire, and the Calvinistic Jansenists, whose anticapitalist individualism was well suited to the ambiguous temper of bourgeois life in France. Many clerics worked to reconcile the teachings of the church with modern philosophy. In the last decades of the seventeenth century Malebranche strove to fuse Cartesianism to religion, and this reformist frame of mind lived on. It inspired some Jesuits and dominated the life of the Oratorians, a teaching order whose influence grew suddenly when Jesuits were banished from the kingdom in 1764. (Many Oratorians, such as Fouché, who later became Napoleon's chief of police, were to play important roles in politics after 1789.) These varied modernizing and Catholic strands were to receive formal consecration during the Revolution in the Civil Constitution of the Clergy, a document that stands as a link between Jansenism, Gallicanism, and the enlightened Catholicism of the eighteenth century, on the one hand, and, on the other hand, the beginnings of Christian democracy in recent times.

In most ways, however, the Catholic establishment was intellectually unimproved. Its spirit was certainly more "bourgeois" in that it was, with some few exceptions, exemplary in its morality. (Though recourse to prostitution was not an offense in France, the police in Paris, at the prompting perhaps of its archbishop, went out of their way after 1751 to apprehend the few clerical patrons of the capital's twenty thousand prostitutes.) In its philosophical opinions, however, the French clergy remained very hostile to modern ideological forms and to individualism in its various incarnations, a circumstance that was to prove fatal for the unfolding of the French Revolution and for the subsequent course of French history for nearly two centuries. In the eighteenth century the Roman Church was in France a bulwark of cultural traditionalism, and it was a far more vigorous bulwark than many of its opponents liked to think. The church opposed religious tolerance, and it successfully blocked the extension of civil rights to Protestants until 1787. Divorce did not exist in France. Suicide remained a punishable offense until 1789. The church insisted on the doctrine of original sin. Although the Jesuits had agreed to take material progress as a proof of virtue, mainstream Catholic doctrine, in contrast to Protestant theology, generally had little room for the philosophes' vision of a heavenly city on earth. The ties between the church and the increasingly discredited monarchy remained very close.

PROPPED UP AS IT WAS by most churchmen and by the dissenting, minority wing of the philosophic movement, anti-individualism remained a strong element of the French elite's cultural life and of the intellectual discourses of the time, both on theory and on politics. Many debates hovered uneasily between the two principles of autonomous individualism (defended by most philosophes) and determining anti-individualism (supported by many other thinkers, both religious and secular).

At the highest level of abstract thought, many philosophes, including those most convinced of the new principles of social life, hesitated to make the rights of the one the first and absolute principle of modern ethics.

Nearly all French thinkers of the eighteenth century did in one way or another start epistemologically with the individual's consciousness. It made little difference whether they supposed, as did such empiricists as Locke and his French disciple Condillac, that men and women (who were often held to be alike in this respect) understood the cosmos by accumulating sense data, or whether they thought, as did the Cartesians, that consciousness flowed from man's innate ideas. Individual consciousness was still the common denominator in every theory.

But it was also widely thought that the individual self, whether it had realized itself through ratiocination or accumulated sensation, could not ethically stand alone. Isolated intellectuals might reason, as La Mettrie did in his 1748 work *On Happiness*, that a sense of well-being was a psychological condition rather than a social reward for virtue; but the members of the French elite did not so perceive the issue. An individual, thought most philosophes, could not morally justify his action self-referentially. Rousseau's political theory was an unending effort to sort out the limits of the *moi commun*, that is, man's responsibility to others, and of his *moi humain*, or his responsibility to himself. The General Will could not be denied; every citizen must yield to it. But that state was best, he thought, which legislated least and left each man to his own devices. (Women, by contrast, he held to have an individuality that sought its wholeness in a dependent complementarity to man.) In the end, and quite typically, Rousseau sidestepped rather than resolved the issue: he advised those who wanted to reconcile man's private and public impulses to separate laudable self-love from culpable selfish love and to moralize the state. (Robespierre's Republic of Virtue was embedded in Rousseau's political sensibility.) Rousseau also urged them to evade the issue by keeping their public ambitions to a minimum. Rousseau recognized (in an anti-Lacanian mood, as it were) that language, which was the fruit of social intercourse, enabled mankind better to conceptualize its thought and, in so doing, to realize its true potential. A truly wise man might, nevertheless, have to resign himself to solitude. All sexual relations, however empowering and natural they might seem, were fraught with danger because sexual gratification almost always involved a thirst for domination—an idea, incidentally, which was soon to please the Marquis de Sade as much as it horrified Rousseau.

In the same vein, a raging debate on luxury placed those philosophes who saw the gratuitous consumption of costly, useless items as a desirable solvent of private ennui in opposition to thinkers who perceived luxury as the selfish origin of corruption and public decadence. Unable to decide between these contending views, many people successively argued on both sides of the same case.

A similar inability to connect empowered individualism with a concern for the public good was visible in the more mundane but (for our purpose) more important realm of political theory. Here also the articulate public was typically of different minds. In terms of the friends and critics of individualism, three broad groups can be discerned: the utopians on the left, Physiocrats on the right, and between them the mass of the French elite (who will be discussed later).

On the left the Utopian Socialists, as Marx contemptuously described them, were resolutely anti-individualist. Gabriel Bonnot de Mably published in 1763 his most famous work, the *Entretiens de Phocion sur le rapport de la morale et de la politique*, where he argued for a politics of public morality and denigrated progress in the arts of civilization. A state religion, together with an interdict on new religious forms, seemed to him the necessary cement of social life.[9] (It is, incidentally, suggestive of the universal use of Graeco-Roman images in the North Atlantic world that Alexander Hamilton, who stood for everything that Mably despised, should in the 1780s have used the name Phocion as a pseudonym in signing two of his essays.) Some of Mably's writings enjoyed wide circulation: even Robespierre owned one of them. Morelly, who also wrote in this vein, had fewer readers.

While Britain was the obvious historical model for those on the right, for many of the philosophes on the left the individualism of northern Europe was less attractive than that of two other cultural models standing halfway between ancient Greece and modern Britain: first, the supposedly communitarian revolts of such southern or eastern European "primitive" peoples as the Corsicans, Poles, or Rumanians; and second, the American Revolution, which, Parisian progressives naively believed, proved the modern relevance of a more simple and communitarian "ancient" liberty. It was quite characteristic of the Abbé Robin, who had accompanied Rochambeau's troops to America, to urge Americans to defend their united, republican simplicity by adopting a common religious belief, as befitted an uncorrupted nation.

On the other shore of political thinking lay the rightist strand of French thought, which aggressively extolled social and economic individualism of a narrow and materialistic kind.

The modern theory of capitalism begins with the French Physiocrats and Dr. Quesnay, who died in 1774, the physician to Louis XV and founding father of the Physiocratic school, to whom Adam Smith first intended to dedicate his *Wealth of Nations* (1776). Between 1756 and 1778 the Physiocratic body of thought, which Mably despised, was developed also by the eccentric Marquis de Mirabeau, the father of the great demagogue of 1789; by Gournay, a government supervisor of trade and industry; by his friend Turgot, Baron de l'Aulne, the last great minister of the monarchy; and by Pierre Samuel Dupont de Nemours, whose son Irénée was to found in 1799 in the United States what is today one of the world's largest industrial conglomerates.

The individualism of the Physiocrats was rigidly unbending in many areas that were to have critical cultural and political effects. The idea of the self is a dynamic concept whose makeup reflects not only existing social or material forms but cultural legacies as well. It can easily be modulated by either sustained ideological argument or determined institutional pressure. It mattered to French culture and politics that individualism in seventeenth-century France was often aristocratically or negatively defined, that is, defined not in terms of cooperation or innovation but of aristocratic resistance and Jansenist aloofness. It mattered also that the Physiocrats and their philosophic allies, many of whom were in government service, cranked that atomistic ratchet wheel even further.

In Physiocratic thinking, individuals were defined socially in terms of their relationship to property. Individual profit became the mainspring of national well-being. Turgot, who conceptualized the celebrated "iron law of wages," embedded his principles in both nature and reason: the supply of land was limited while mankind's capacity to reproduce was unlimited. Necessarily he concluded, the supply of labor would always outstrip demand. Wages could not rise above the minimum required for survival. But fortunately, added the Physiocrats, the capitalist's ability to turn an effortless profit by charging more than he had paid out benefited everyone. The size of his gain determined his ability to invest in such things as better plows, scientific breeding, and drainage, which promised further growth. The poor would never become rich, but they could multiply. In Turgot's scheme, all that was needed to secure the march of progress was to give the market free rein. Physiocrats were bitter foes not just of urban and rural corporatism but of governmental interference, because both were obstacles to growth through competition.

Though it was profit-bound and savagely individualistic, Physiocracy was also curiously closed-ended. Most peculiarly, the Physiocrats, with the exception of Vincent de Gournay (1712–1759), were unrepentant ruralists who held industry in great contempt because they reasoned, rather childishly, that the net added value of artisanal work was nil, since the value of the goods that an artisan produced was invariably matched by the cost of the food needed to sustain him. The contrast between France as the Physiocrats thought it should be and Britain as it already was in the 1780s is suggestive. Britain had long since become a capitalist society, transformed at first by enclosures or commerce and increasingly by industry. In Quesnay's time, British jurisprudence had been adapted by Blackstone and his successor, Lord Mansfield, to suit the contractual needs of merchants and manufacturers in ways which the Physiocrats could hardly conceive. The specifically political thought of the Physiocrats was also decidedly backward-looking, even in French perspective, since the goal was to create a state that was at once all-powerful and powerless. In their mind's eye, the monarch should rule as despot, unencumbered by advisory representative assemblies. (Turgot and Dupont did not agree with this view.) Generally speaking, the Physiocrats thought that the function of the state was merely to clear the decks for the laws of nature, which, as it happened, overlapped those of supply and demand. Once it had done that, the omnipotent state would become the idle spectator of an ongoing and natural social and economic system.

Two facts emerge: first, that French thinkers were very divided; and second, that their modern and individualist wing was at once extreme and backward-looking. A wide chasm separated the ideas of Quesnay from the transcendental, individualist statement of late-eighteenth-century America, a statement which in the thirteen colonies was not only informed by religion but was more spacious in its political possibilities than Physiocracy ever could be. In the theoretical and practical vision of Madison and his friends, political individualism found embodiment in the idea of direct rather than virtual representation, but for most Physiocrats self-rule was an encumbrance, an obstacle to efficient reform.

THE AMBIGUITIES of French economic life and of its cultural, ideological, and political currents before 1789 make deeply puzzling the breakthrough after 1789 of possessive individualism in all its forms—political, economic, and social—and the equally dramatic breakdown of political individualism in 1793–94. If anti-individualist, corporate traditionalism was strong in French society before 1789, why did the French Revolution unfurl so stridently the banner of rampant individual rights? And after that initial victory, if adamant individualism had managed to sweep all before it between 1789 and 1791, why did its political forms collapse so completely during the Terror of 1793–94?

The solution to this complicated puzzle is central to an understanding of the period as a whole. Essentially, the answer presented here is that the limited ideological impact of possessive individualism in prerevolutionary France had less to do with the inherent appeal of that principle than with the decay of existing corporate institutions. In other words, individualist ideology thrived less in its own right than in consequence of the discrediting of corporate institutions. The French in 1789 *thought* themselves to be partisans of an autonomous and classical bourgeois individualism, but they thought so in large part because the guardians of the inherited corporate order (king, church, nobility, parlements) appeared to them to have betrayed their trust. Although between 1789 and 1791 the French daringly restructured their society in an anticorporatist way, they were in many respects little more than disappointed partisans of social solidarity.

Prerevolutionary feelings of disappointment over existing communitarian and corporatist institutions were of various kinds. They were in many ways skin-deep—as events would soon prove—but in sum they seemed to cover the field: "Imagine a country where there are many corporate bodies," wrote one of France's leading Protestants, "the result is that . . . one hears only of rights, concessions, immunities, special agreements, privileges, prerogatives."[10] Different parts of the population were differently dismayed, but everyone was affected.

For the urban masses what mattered most was the decay of urban economic corporations. These had been intended to exclude outsiders and to regulate the labor market, but they were being used to exclude insiders as well, or were thought to do so. Corporations were expected to be broadly fraternal. They were not. They were riddled with internal strife which frequently spilled over into the law courts. Young masters, the *modernes,* not only oppressed and cheated their apprentices and journeymen but were cheated in turn by their superiors, the *anciens.* Feelings ran very deep, especially in Paris. Workers objected to their masters' betrayal of the corporate spirit, but the masters' indifference had little to do with an espousal of individualist values. Workers might simultaneously wish to set up their own shops and think it necessary to control the labor market. They wished to do well, but they still believed in an age-old ethic of corporate solidarity, generosity, and conspicuous consumption.

Guilds had few admirers in late-eighteenth-century France. In advanced centers such as Paris and Lyons, disputes and strikes became increasingly common after the 1730s as employers and employees began to realize that their interests did not overlap. (The French word for strike, *grève,* taken from the site of Paris's informal labor market, was coined in 1785.) Ordinarily, both apprentices and masters (ancients and moderns) still thought that their trade should and could be a naturally harmonious whole, but they also reasoned that perverted ill will had destroyed a golden past. Guilds were blamed by the poor for difficulties of all sorts: workers attributed to them, and to personal conflicts within them, problems that had to do instead with shifts in the competitive situation of industries in a technologically changing environment. Between the Physiocrats and philosophes, who hated guilds on principle, and the working people, who disliked them in practice only, the connection was quite thin; and the difference between the two points of view was bound to emerge later, as it did in 1793–94. In the short run a common enmity sufficed to discredit these fundamental institutions of corporate life. Sébastien Mercier spoke for his age in 1781 when he said of the corps or guilds that they had become "opinionated, stubborn, and hoped to isolate themselves from the machine of politics: every corps today only responds to the injustice which its own members are made to feel. It considers as indifferent to its own interests the oppression of any citizen which doesn't belong to its own self."

Another kind of disappointment mattered a great deal to the lawyers, who were the heart of the French bourgeoisie. This resulted from the decline of the nation's ancient corporate administrative and legal institutions, the parlements, or courts. These courts too were increasingly perceived as bastions of selfish privilege, as obstacles to administrative reform and fiscal justice. The technical incompetence of many parlementaires who had inherited their offices and purchased their university degrees was much resented.

The parlementaires often defended their selfish prerogatives by invoking Enlightenment principles, including the right of the nation to self-government. The nation did exist, they thought, and they conveniently reasoned that it was ordinarily represented by themselves. This nationalistic anti-absolutism was much praised. Then, too, in some depoliticized and unostentatious ways, the parlementaires did really represent the interests of the propertied elite as a whole. They did useful administrative work. They also became more rigorous in their punishment of crimes against property—in the second half of the eighteenth century, 80 percent of the cases on which they ruled in Paris involved theft—and they became more and more lax in their condemnation of religious or moral misdemeanors: Sabbath breaking and heresy; infanticide, abortion, and suicide; bigamy, adultery, and gambling.[11] These attitudes won them at times the semblance of public approval. On balance, however, the popularity of the parlements, like their own commitment to change, was quite insubstantial. Many of the philosophes, including Voltaire, were bitter foes of these aristocratic courts. Mably—much read in both France and America—was another critic. His most important work, entitled *On the Rights and Duties of the Citizen*, has relevance to the fate of the parlements. Mably began his book as a defense of this institution, which was then embroiled in a dispute with the king; but the focus of his text drifted from antimonarchism to a defense of the courts, and finally became a radical defense not of the parlements at all but of the Estates General and of social egalitarianism everywhere.

Vaguer, more general, and more difficult to pin down was disappointment over the church. The mass of Frenchmen, including the larger part of the elite, was not really irreligious, but dislike of the church as an institution and as the willful defender of an obscurantist ideology was widely felt. The close and enduring ties that bound the Catholic establishment to a discredited absolutist state and feudal social system were resented. These were sensible objections: the church had largely turned its back on the modern spirit fostered by the elite. It did not allow much room for individualism, as Pietism did in Germany and Methodism in England, and as the Great Awakening did in America.

The church antagonized much of the elite, and it was unable to retain the loyalties of the masses. Its handling of poor relief was increasingly inadequate. In the eighteenth century it made no allowance for popular millenarianism, or chiliasm, which was an important religious extension of an affective culture. In Paris, chiliasm surfaced as a popular and vulgarized offshoot of Jansenism. Convulsionaries performed miracles on the tomb of the deacon Francois de Pâris (who had died in 1727) in the Church of Saint-Médard at the bottom of the popular rue Mouffetard. The church collaborated with the state to suppress these popular rites: "De par le roi," wrote a wag, "il est interdit à Dieu de faire miracle en ce lieu."[12] In an age of absolutist Enlightenment and dessicated clericalism, popular messianic eschatology could not assert itself peaceably in France. After the Revolution of 1789 it emerged again, albeit in secular and irreligious form. But before that time chiliasm found a voice in France only briefly in the early 1700s in that isolated strand of rural French Protestantism which exploded during the Camisard revolt of Calvinist peasant guerrillas in the Cévennes Mountains of southern France.

The situation of religion and the church in France illustrated the place of corporatism and corporations generally. Anticlericalism was strong, but it was shallow because it focused less on religion than on the failings of the church as an institution. Fundamental irreligion, though growing, was still rare. The books that the working people of Paris read before the Revolution were religious and devotional works: first the Bible, and along with it missals, hymnals, and vesperals. Peddlers carried religious pamphlets and broadsides to the countryside. The French of all social classes took communion at Easter time. The flowering of a preromantic sensibility, present in the works of Rousseau and of many of his widely read contemporaries, including Bernardin de Saint-Pierre, the author of the sentimental and exotic novel *Paul et Virginie*, held promise for a dramatic resurgence of Roman Catholicism during the Revolution. The "Moral Economy of the Crowd" in whose name the poor resisted the application of modern principles of supply and demand, was close to the moral teachings of the church.

The failure of the Catholic Church in eighteenth-century France was perhaps the single greatest misfortune of modern French history. If the church had answered the secular call for a more efficient distribution of charity, or if it had managed to revitalize its educational institutions more consistently, as the Oratorians had begun to do, the possessive individualism of the elite, tempered by the application of Christian principles, would perhaps have been more acceptable to the poor, who by and large were still devout. A philo-Christian ruling class might also have been less aggressive after 1789 in its application of economic individualism, and the ensuing "liberal" settlement might have been less criticized in 1793. As it was, the refusal of the mainstream French Church to move with the times held the promise of major political conflict, because the church, though weak, was also strong, stronger than it itself suspected. When in 1789 the political institutions to which it had unnecessarily bound its fate were destroyed, the church would soon reacquire its ability to resist.

The last massive disappointment that explains the countervailing but ephemeral prestige of negativist individualism in eighteenth-century France centered on the role of the monarchic state in the last three decades of the Old Regime.

Certainly in the 1770s, and possibly even in the 1780s, a resolute king might have renewed the monarchy and avoided revolution. A reformist state might perhaps have rescued the monarchic principle by furthering the social consolidation of a new elite. The integration of nobles and bourgeois into a single class along the lines of what had happened in England by the first decades of the eighteenth century might have been used to revivify the crown with the help of a renewed, reformist bureaucracy. Such a pattern was developing in Prussia at the time. In France a solution of this kind might, under the umbrella of a respected monarchy, have reconciled the new principles of Anglo-American bourgeois liberalism with a sense of social concern derived from France's religious and corporatist past. The French administrative machine could then have played a paternalist role similar to the one vainly envisaged by the Prussian bureaucracy in the first half of the nineteenth century.

Mutatis mutandis, an ecumenical solution of this kind—a blend of innovative liberalism and traditional monarchic and communitarian longing—would have been structurally comparable to the republican amalgam of tradition and innovation elaborated by the Founding Fathers in 1787 when they adapted America's radical and transcendental ideologies to the pragmatic, possessive, and individualistic realities of American life.

The urbane, informed, and well-meaning servants of the Old Regime certainly tried to rally public opinion by carrying out reforms that might have defused the French political tinderbox. The French state under Louis XV extended some of the modernizing functions it had acquired in the seventeenth century. It even subsidized pamphleteers and journalists at home and abroad to inform the public. Royal officials thought of themselves as dedicated public servants. In Burgundy some of them tried to invigorate rural communities in order to thwart the partisans of revived feudalism. Part of Turgot's plan was to create a system of representative institutions which would allow owners of property to formulate their needs.

The French state also provided a reasonably effective shield under which French Atlantic and colonial trade could thrive. In the end the results were mixed: the Seven Years War was a catastrophe; India, which had been under French more than under British suzerainty, was lost; Canada was abandoned; and Louisiana was ceded as compensation to Spain, France's most loyal ally, to make up for that country's even more grievous losses. But many bright spots remained. Santo Domingo (Haiti today), which belonged to the French, was the world's richest slave colony. Guadeloupe and Martinique (where Empress Josephine was born) were sources of great wealth. During the War of American Independence France briefly gained control of the high seas. Indeed, since General Cornwallis was forced to surrender to George Washington because he could not evacuate his troops by sea, the battle of Yorktown was, in a sense, the most important victory in the entire annals of the French Royal Navy. For some months in 1778 the possibility of a French descent on the Isle of Wight and on Britain's southern coast was a real possibility.

The monarchic state protected capitalist development by protecting French trade abroad; and in some measure, it allowed free industrial development at home. The ennoblement of successful merchants became more frequent. Interdictions on the putting-out system (never too stringently enforced) were lifted in 1762. Merchants were allowed to bypass urban guilds and were authorized to involve peasants in manufacturing. The merchant cloth maker, instead of paying high wages to urban artisans, was allowed to sell his thread to peasants and to repurchase from them, at a low price, a semifinished product. The state also quickened national commerce by improving internal communications. In Britain, private enterprise financed construction of new and better roads through the turnpike trusts. In France the engineers of the newly created state board of works, the Ponts et Chaussées, designed the time-shrinking, stone-paved, stately, tree-lined highways that linked the provinces to Paris, if not to each other. Related to the theme of ambiguity and the interweaving of the old and the new is the preference, from the 1730s onward, of these technicians of communication for forced, corvée labor. Because they feared that the money which the state might collect from a commutation of these labor dues would be siphoned off by other governmental agencies, these determined modernizers chose to rely on the most primitive method of capital accumulation.

The monarchy's most daring act, however, was not economic but plainly political. Suddenly the parlements, which had become the aggressive vehicle of insolent aristocratic and corporatist privilege, were dissolved. In 1771 the aged Louis XV staged an informal coup d'état against the courts. He dismissed or exiled to the provinces the ennobled judges who owned their offices and were as a rule hostile to fiscal reform and sometimes to administrative change. New courts were created. With the help of a young man named Charles Lebrun (who after 18 Brumaire 1799 would become, with Bonaparte, one of the three ruling consuls), René de Maupeou, the King's new Chancellor of Justice, laid the foundation for a complete overhaul and codification of the French legal system. His fellow minister, Joseph de Terray, even more hated by the parlementaires than he, repudiated part of the royal debt and attempted to arrest the chronic imbalance of income and expenses. Goaded by the fiscal stresses that had been occasioned by the Seven Years War, the French state and bureaucracy that had tried to reform itself episodically since the late 1740s finally confronted aristocratic privilege head on.

Unfortunately, with Louis XV's death in May 1774 this first major attempt at administrative and fiscal reform came to an abrupt end. The French state, which could perhaps have transformed itself, and could in so doing have met many of the grievances that exploded in 1789, failed the hopes of the elites. Louis XV, a shy, furtive, and dissolute old man who had lived too long, now proved to have died too soon. The monarchy, which was still a credible institution, accelerated its own decline. In August 1774 the obstructionist, aristocratic parlements were recalled by the new king, Louis XVI, the grandson of the deceased monarch, a very uncertain and poorly advised young man of average intelligence who was much too eager to please the traditionalists and the rationalist publicists who had united against Maupeou's authoritarian reformism. The revived presence of the aristocratic parlementaires dealt the crown a grievous blow. It meant that for the next fifteen years the absolutist bureaucracy and the traditionalist parlements would wear each other down and, in so doing, clear the decks for two other rival principles of government: parliamentary liberalism and a more democratic, salvationist, Rousseauist politics.

The collapse of the Old Regime was some time in the making. In July 1774 Louis XVI, just as he was about to recall the parlements, authorized the last great attempts at change from above. The aim of Anne Robert Jacques de Turgot, Louis XVI's new first minister, was to reproduce in France some aspects of the English social model. An aristocrat whose family had a long record of administrative service, Turgot was also a brilliant intellectual and a convinced if authoritarian and hurried Physiocratic individualist. As an administrator in the Limousin, where he served as an intendant during Maupeou's reforming ministry, Turgot had concluded from his superior's failure that a head-on attack on traditionalist fiscal exemptions would not work. The parlements, to whose recall he had acceded, were somehow too strong. Turgot was not overly depressed about their return, however, because he also thought that the answer to the monarchy's fiscal problem was to increase its tax base by developing the wealth of the kingdom as a whole. Turgot's recipe was simple to a degree. Between 1774 and 1776 he abolished as many of the economic guilds as he could. He also authorized the internal free trade of grain which had been briefly tolerated in 1763, as the export of grain had been allowed in July 1764. Turgot's aim was to use the power of the state to permit the "natural" and improving forces of property and economic individualism to assert themselves.

What the long-run effect of such anticorporatist measures would have been in town and country is hard to say. If Turgot had remained in power, a more expansive capitalism might have transformed France, and the kingdom would perhaps have drawn closer to the English social and economic model. In a society so transformed and individuated, Robespierre's universalist call for republican communitarian virtue would probably have elicited a far weaker response. But opposition to Turgot's hastily assembled plan was too strong. In the outskirts of Paris, thousands of peasants rioted in the streets, to the delight, surely, of many traditionalist parlementaires, whom Turgot suspected of having encouraged the rebellion. The king was unable to withstand these pressures. In 1776 he dismissed Turgot, and a Prussian solution of reform from above ceased to be a realistic possibility until it was revived by Napoleon after the collapse of both the neofeudal Old Regime and the democratic Revolution.

After Turgot's dismissal, the ancien régime lived for another decade on borrowed time and money. A disappointed public grew visibly more impatient. The execution in 1762 of the Protestant merchant Calas, falsely accused of murdering his suicidal son, and in 1766 of both the young Chevalier de la Barre, who was said to have mutilated a crucifix, and the aged Baron Lally de Tollendal for treason, came to be regarded during the 1770s and 1780s as proof of the state's wide-ranging inability to control either the obscurantist Catholic Church or the unreformed parlements. The Enlightenment elite gradually veered toward thinking that it, rather than the absolutist state, should become the arbiter of social and political contentions. Matters were brought to a head by the monarchy's decision in the late 1770s to intervene against Britain on behalf of the rebellious American colonies—a decision which was taken against the advice of Turgot, who rightly foresaw that this international conflict, fought as it was on many continents, would be ruinously expensive for the French. The War of American Independence was not only successful but very popular in France: it fed the doctrinal and nationalistic passions of the day. Financed through loans, it was also the first war of the Old Regime which did not lead to an immediate rise in taxation. These were short-run gains for the crown; but the long-run effect of the massive debt that had been incurred to pay for it was to bring the monarchy to its knees.

The last important statesman of the Old Regime, the dour and fatuous Swiss Protestant Jacques Necker, who had grown rich in banking and grain speculation, did not aim so high as Turgot. As the king's first minister in 1777–1781, his limited goal was to effect minor administrative repairs. Though he understood what was to be done and consistently hoped that Louis XVI might become an enlightened despot of a kind, Necker never thought it worthwhile really to challenge vested, traditional interest.

By the late 1780s, because the state had failed not only to give society a lead, as Turgot had wanted, but also reform its own judicial or fiscal structures, as Maupeou and Necker had hoped, it could not even pay its way. Its expenses were one-fourth larger than its receipts, and more than half of these went to service the debt. Only minor reforms were within its grasp: in 1784 some Jews were exempted from a discriminatory personal tax; the cases of prisoners under arbitrary arrest were reviewed, and most of them were released; in 1787 Protestants were granted the de jure freedom of worship which they had enjoyed de facto for about three decades. Torture was abolished, as was the peasants' forced labor for road building, the celebrated corvée. The state of the French military establishment and particularly the state of its artillery were improved—a fortuitous precondition of Bonaparte's subsequent victories and irresistible rise to fame. In 1788 another first minister, Archbishop Loménie de Brienne, rather desultorily first attacked and then recalled the parlements.

These were not steps that could win over a disaffected public. The failure of the state seemed inevitable, and at this very moment the bureaucracy revealed its political helplessness when it failed to push through a plan to abolish internal customs and make France a single trade zone. In 1789 the absolutist monarchy still had no proper budget. Indicative of its disarray were the local assemblies whose creation it had ordered here and there, institutions which did not play a great role but which did remind the public that alternatives to monarchic absolutism could be found. Unable to direct the flow of politics, the crown seemed to be digging its own grave.

Only the prestige of the king might have bolstered the regime. As a person, however, Louis was unimpressive and his character could not make up for the decline of the crown as an institution. His wife's interfering ways and her supposed love affairs (she was falsely rumored also to be a lesbian) may have done the monarchy great harm. Louis XVI was neither a conquering monarch, as Louis le Grand had been in the seventeenth century, nor a model of domesticity, as was his mother-in-law, Empress Maria Theresa of Austria—a successful monarch, a loyal wife, and the dutiful mother of innumerable royal children. Many Frenchmen were convinced that Louis's predecessor, Louis XV, a womanizing and secretive man who had run a private diplomatic service behind the backs of his foreign ministers, had also speculated in the grain trade and profited from his subjects' misery. It would take Louis XVI's humiliation and death in 1793 to revive, even in part, the prestige of the crown.

The mystique of the French monarchy was much diminished. Kingship was "desacralized"; it lost its magical aura. In the past the king had represented the nation. Now the monarch was identified merely with the distant state, and the nation was vested increasingly in the people. Whereas the third Estate had been nothing, it would soon be everything. The history of France had in the past been the chronicles of its kings. Henceforth, from Mably to Boulainvilliers (the apologist of the aristocracy's right to rule), from Montesquieu to the parlementaire Maultrot and the Jansenist Rollin, Frenchmen became increasingly concerned with the history of their nation as a justification of antimonarchic sentiment.[13]

DISAPPOINTED IN THE CORPORATE structure of the economy, the courts, the church, and the state, French society in the 1780s was neither persuaded by the individualistic ideas of the Physiocrats nor by the communitarian ideas of the utopians. It was adrift. Ostensibly, the rejection of the social status quo was complete: "The organisation of Indian society in castes rising one above the other," wrote the Abbé Raynal in the Aesopian language of his immensely popular *Histoire philosophique et politique des établissements et du commerce des Européens dans les deux Indes*, "is typical of the deepest corruption, and the most ancient slavery. It reveals the unjust and revolting preeminence of priests on the rest of society; and exposes the stupid indifference of the first legislator for the well-being of the nation."[14]

In their innermost selves, however, the French continued to yearn for a society of interlocking institutions that would buffer individuals against the vagaries of life, economic upheaval, and social change. The feudal and corporatist values of prowess and clannishness, bravura and loyalty, survived; but they were no longer anchored to any stable set of institutions. Everything was in flux, including French social structure—an indeterminacy that was to have a major effect on the unfolding of the Revolution.

By the end of the eighteenth century French social structures were uncertainly shaped. Like the economy, the institutions, ethic, and political culture of eighteenth-century France, social forms oscillated between highly antithetical principles of organization.

France remained in many ways a traditional, neo-medieval society of corporate orders. Significant differences divided nobles and nonnobles. In the 1780s access to the officer corps was restricted to young men who, though they might be poor, were of impeccably noble birth; this foolish law, whatever its motivation, confirmed the bourgeoisie in its belief that the state was a milch cow for an incompetent nobility. Nor were they completely wrong: the French army lost many wars, and the top ranks of the military, as well as of government service and the church, were indeed aristocratic preserves. Even the bureaucracy, which a century before had been staffed by the new legal bourgeoisie, had become more aristocratic and self-perpetuating. Sales of ennobling offices dried up, and some parlements ruled against the admission of nonnoble lawyers, however rich they might be. Even the rich bourgeois in the 1770s and 1780s took a dim view of aristocratic privilege. Though nobles were not uniformly rich and often paid their share of taxes—as in southern France—it was commonly assumed that they did not pay their way. Rich commoners did not stop to think that the Parisian rentiers who owned government bonds paid no tax whatever on that income; they preferred to think that aristocrats did not work and that nobles were idle, corrupt, feminized, and sexually debauched. Ennobled former members of the Third Estate, who ought to have been the object of bourgeois admiration, were often despised for bringing together the supposed vices of the two social orders: envy and corruption.

In theory and to some degree in fact, nonnobles still saw themselves in the 1780s as part of a distinct social order. At times, however, that vision yielded to a more modern, or at least to a more Anglo-American, understanding of social forms. In many respects the French Third Estate lacked cohesion: the gap was wide between Parisian bankers and illiterate, semistarved peasants in central France. The estates of the French body politic no longer were coherent wholes. Uncertainly composed, they were organized around uncertain economic facts and principles.

Most bourgeois in 1789 were not industrialists or rentiers with class interests different from those of the aristocracy. Like the nobles, they were working landlords whose lands (like those of the nobles, the peasants, and the church) were not involved in a dynamic market economy. Industrialism was little more than a promise in 1789; and international trade had had few repercussions on the rural hinterland. The material interests of the French bourgeoisie, though very different from those of the landless peasants, were not significantly different from those of the Second Estate, the noble landlords or seigneurs. The range of wealth within both the Second and the Third Estate was impossibly broad: tens of thousands of bourgeois were far richer than tens of thousands of nobles, some of whom were practically destitute.

For the nobles also, France was no longer a society of interlocking, corporate orders. Over the centuries the centralizing action of the state had reduced the institutions of feudalism to cyphers. Nobles obeyed the injunctions of the intendants just as the bourgeoisie did. Among country nobles feelings ran high on the greed of the court nobility: "All things considered," wrote one of the most thoughtful noble delegates to the Estates General in 1789, "I would just as soon that John Doe think himself my equal as that some great Court noble think me his inferior."[15] Nobles from the provincial parlements still felt that Versailles was the corrupting preserve of condescending court nobles whose equals or superiors they were. Divided among themselves for traditional reasons, the nobles were also rent by their varying reactions to capitalist entrepreneurship. In a noble population of about forty thousand families, thousands of individuals were fully integrated into the most modern aspects of contemporary life: the industrialists, scientists, academicians, and free-lance intellectuals. Others played a role in shipping, banking, or the Caribbean trade, such as the Ségurs and the Lameth brothers, who were all to be key political figures between 1789 and 1792. Most of the approximately six hundred forge masters in business in the 1770s and 1780s were either noble or ennobled. Indeed, nobles may well have been more sympathetic to the ethos of possessive individualism and economic or technological progress than any other social group. Many of them were indifferent to feudal dues, either because they did not collect any or because they owned many other things. Many were in the forefront of those demanding political reform.

The audience of the Enlightenment included tens of thousands of nobles, many of them members of local academies. It could be considered a "ruse of history," to use Hegel's phrase, that the first affirmation of "bourgeois" individualism (that is, the French Enlightenment) was often the work of aristocrats, as was the first general critique of that same bourgeois view (that is, European romanticism). The eighteenth-century philosophes were often nobles, like Buffon (a somewhat inauthentic aristocrat, it is true), Montesquieu, d'Alembert (a noble foundling), Holbach, Mably, and Condillac; and so, in the next, romantic generation, were Lamartine, Vigny, Musset, Shelley, Byron, Alfieri, Hardenberg, and Kleist. Like the bourgeoisie, and often before them, French nobles subscribed to the new Enlightenment world view, with its changed attitude to death, happiness, and the family. They favored a more equal definition of roles in marriage and were more conscious of the formative importance of childhood experiences. For bourgeois polemicists the assertion of these values could be a means to power. Nobles were often less self-serving. As the Comte de Ségur later wrote in his memoirs of the prerevolutionary French aristocracy, "Voltaire enthralled our spirits, Rousseau had touched our hearts. We felt a secret pleasure in attacking the old edifice [of the ancien régime], which seemed gothic and ridiculous. In the theater, we applauded republican dramas."

Separated by institutional fiat, bourgeois and nobility were often united by a joint opposition to the state, by age-old *arrivisme*, and, most important, by modern cultural change. In 1788 the dream of many French bourgeois was, as it had been for centuries, to become noble, to "live nobly," and to ensconce their children by marriage and by influence in the aristocracy, as the hero of Molière's *Bourgeois Gentilhomme* had tried unsuccessfully to do a century before. The prestige of government service was very high. "People did not want nobles to be superior in any way," wrote an acute novelist, Mme de Charrière, in 1795, "but they also wanted to become noble themselves."[16] Before 1789 a curiously large number of prominent revolutionaries-to-be had tried to pass themselves off as of noble birth, among them Roland de la Platière, Creuzé de la Touche, Brissot de Warville, and de la Revellière de Lépaux (who were all Girondins); and, among the Montagnards, Barère de Vieuzac, Billaud de Varenne, d'Anton, de Robespierre, de Saint-Just, and "Monsieur de Marat"; and on the far left, among the spokesmen of feminists and the sansculottes Leclerc d'Oze, Taboureau de Montigny, Olympe de Gouges (her father was a butcher named Gonze), Théroigne de Méricourt, and the Dutchwoman Etta Palm d'Aelders. The playwright Sedaine specialized in the production of plays whose heroes were up-and-coming bourgeois who had successfully internalized aristocratic codes of behavior. These literary fictions often acquired practical embodiment, as in the case of the father of the painter David, an ironmonger who died nobly, in a duel.

The bourgeoisie's longing to enter the magic circle at the top and its ability to do so were reinforced also by the effect of new and enlightened values. The socially mixed memberships of salons, academies, and Masonic lodges had the explicit purpose of providing a common ground for people separated by honorific distinctions which could not otherwise be suspended. The pull of new cultural forms united them, and this pull was all the more strongly felt because of the weakening of the ancient estates.

In short, a consciousness of caste survived, but fitfully and by no means universally. As Tocqueville pointed out a century and a half ago, Frenchmen of the Old Regime were, socially speaking, simultaneously similar and different. The two groups—bourgeois and noble—were drawn apart and pulled together by both modernity and tradition. Though still strong in some respects (and still hated), the ranked corporate society of orders was also very weak. The noticeably worsening political running war between the traditionalist parlements and the absolutist state, which had been taking place for nearly half a century, discredited the social principles of privilege, birth, hierarchy, and tradition. These principles had been weakened also by the spread of Enlightenment values: in society as in politics, economic and cultural change worked to destroy the society of orders and to bring into existence new social forms.

For reasons old and new, by 1789 bourgeois and nobles had tentatively come together in many ways within a new, single, and propertied elite, united by a common world view and also commonly hostile to the stifling web of traditionalist absolutism represented by an inefficacious state bureaucracy and the self-seeking parlements. It was this united front of nobles and bourgeois, allied to the philosophes whose work they read, and to down-at-the-heel journalists whom they subsidized but who exerted little autonomous cultural or political force, which brought down the monarchy between 1787 and 1789, essentially by abandoning it to its own fate.

ALL SOCIETIES ARE forever in transition, but this banal truism has seldom been more dangerously true that it was for France in 1789. On the eve of revolution, everything in France seemed possible; few Frenchmen had any sense of the problems that were inherent in modern social life. They underestimated the extent of urban and rural disorder in their country: "A popular riot that would degenerate into open sedition," wrote Mercier in the 1780s, "has become morally impossible." Elites basked in a warm glow of universalist self-indulgence. Historical experience shows, or so Marx resolutely thought, that every class which rises to the fore likes to present its particularist goals in universal terms. Franco Venturi has likewise written about the mix of reformism and utopia that characterized all of continental Europe in the 1770s and 1780s. But seldom has this been more evident than it was in France during the last decade of the ancien régime. The first particularity of the prerevolutionary propertied French elite, partly noble, partly bour-geois, was its resolve to institutionalize possessive individualism—and with it, of necessity, capitalism—in the name of fraternity and community. The American Founding Fathers were less ambitious in 1787, and their task was in any case far less difficult: in the newly emancipated thirteen colonies a theoretically transcendental indi-vidualism and a more flexible definition of the public good were far easier to reconcile than were the negativist individualism of the French elite and the strongly communitarian, neo-corporate yearn-ings of the French nation. The working people of France did not at all perceive market forces to be immanently natural or humane.

The gap between the actual circumstances of the times and the French elite's ideological perception of them was evident in many respects—for example, in their conflicting attitudes to the problem of poverty. The poor were widely feared and increasingly conspic-uous. French standards of living were roughly comparable to those of the advanced Third World today, and the poor seemed a race apart. "The workers" of Lyons, wrote an observer in 1783, "live a life very different from that of well-off people. They are usually thin and shrivelled, short of stature; the contamination of the air they breathe, the poor quality of the food they eat, the lack of exercise, the filth in which they live, the cramped position in which they have to operate their machinery completely changed their nature and made them entirely different from the other inhabitants [of the city]."[17] The number of these poor was swelling just as organic ties of place were weakening. In the day-to-day business of life, it was widely assumed by the rich that the indigent were individually responsible for their condition. Some thoughtful propertied writers even reasoned that true charity precluded monetary help, because alms only confirmed degraded individuals in their errant ways.

And yet the poor, though feared and despised in practice, were as an abstract entity the object of constant elitist solicitude. Count Rumford, an ennobled, germanized New Englander who lived in Paris, invented Rumford soup, an unusually nutritious mixture, he argued, and fortunately quite cheap to make since it was mainly composed of water. Necker and his wife, two paragons of bour-geois virtue, endowed a hospital for small children. In the late 1780s, the Parisian Société Philantropique had hundreds of members who subscribed millions of francs for charity. The word *bienfaisance* (beneficence) was coined in the eighteenth century.

Here, as elsewhere, the elite's perception of reality was fanciful and self-indulgent. The basic problem of social engineering, they reasoned, was to blend self and selflessness, and they were much comforted by the discovery that such reconciliations had in fact already taken place, and could, they thought, be easily reproduced in France. They paid little attention to the gap that separated their own country from the social contexts of the societies they admired, with their varying traditions and strikingly different historical destinies.

The first of their models was the ancient Graeco-Roman polis with which the French elites had become familiar in schools and universities. In the 1750s Lafont de Saint-Yenne, perhaps the first modern art critic, a man sensitive to the nature of his times, praised representations drawn from Roman life in a period when the love of every citizen for the "gloire de la Patrie" knew no bounds. It was true, he mused, that in those days, for "every private person having his part in governance, the good constitution of the State became his private and personal interest."[18] Innumerable Parisian commentators were sure that the first characteristic of the Greek and Roman city-states had been that very harmonization of the private and public which they craved for themselves and France. As the materialist philosophe Helvetius explained, "If Greek and Roman history are so replete with heroes, and if the annals of despotism have nothing to compare with them, it is because in tyrannies, particular interests are never linked to the public good."[19] Some time later, Diderot was even more effusive: "The same patriotism that bubbled in the depths of the soul of a Greek or a Roman, bubbles in the same way today in the depth of every patriotic soul."[20] French artists, thought Diderot, echoing Saint-Yenne, should paint as the Spartans had spoken. Shortly after Diderot's death, the painter David did just that and became immensely popular. His vast, public-minded canvasses of pretentious, masculine self-sacrifice seem in retrospect to have been an obvious prolegomenon to the moralizing of Terror. Amazingly, however, it was not to disenfranchised, bourgeois subscribers that David sold his work, but to the decaying Bourbon state. This militant classicist, who was also a shrewd businessman, was the portrait painter par excellence of the propertied and enlightened elite.

The elite's second historical model of social harmony was, of course, the newly independent thirteen colonies, where nature and progress seemed to the philosophes to be happily and harmoniously entwined. It was on the banks of the "Oyo ou du Mississippi," mused Mably, that Plato today would create his Republic. Rousseau had thought it necessary to choose between virtue and the arts, between the *moi commun* and the antithetical *moi humain*. In the 1780s, however, French commentators habitually supposed that America had proved him wrong forever and for every place. In his *History of the Indies*, a critical description of European colonialism which was one of the most influential books of the epoch, the Abbé Raynal argued that in America free pioneers had miraculously reconciled patriotism and wealth: "This countryside has brought together the era of biblical patriarchs and the blessings of our own times. One finds in American cities . . . all the arts of Europe. All branches of science have their practitioners. A simple and generous simplicity has mellowed and embellished all the virtues."[21]

Pierre de Lacretelle concurred and thought that the thirteen "peuples législateurs" held in their hands the destinies of the world: "It is by your example," he concluded, "that modern peoples will know within the next fifty years if republican constitutions can still be upheld, and if healthy mores are compatible with the great progress of civilization." Lafayette, who in 1776 was charmed by the unspoiled simplicity of American social life, wrote in a letter to his wife that "the richest and poorest are on the same level here; and although some people are immensely rich, I defy anyone to find any difference in the way the rich and the poor behave toward each other."

French commentators, significantly, were unable to understand the fundamental evolution of contemporary American politics. The modern French penchant for describing France in their descriptions of American life has secular roots: when Voltaire wrote that vice was unknown in Philadelphia, a Pennsylvanian journalist commented dryly: "Wish [that] it were so!"[22] This pattern of incomprehension deepened during the 1780s. Frenchmen could not grasp that American society had developed a new ideological stance which had harmonized the idea of a virtuous people with the institutionalization of social and geographical pluralism. Turgot found American federalism incomprehensible: "All public authority should be one," he wrote, "namely that of the [single] nation," an opinion that John Adams later considered to be "as mysterious as the Athanasian creed."[23] When André Morellet translated Jefferson's *Notes on Virginia*, he conveniently forgot to translate those passages that described Virginia's constitution with its indirect elections, its lower and upper houses. Parisian commentators who, like Diderot, suspected that America like other nations might eventually go into decline invariably supposed that excessive individualism would be to blame. Mably in his *Observations sur l'Amérique* warned Americans about the twin evils of women, "who have introduced corruption in all republics," and commerce, which implied the creation of artificial needs and luxurious consumption.

Incapable of measuring the extent of its contradictory desires, unaware of the difficulty of reconciling individualism (as it understood that value) and community (as the poor expected it to be), the nascent propertied elite in France on the eve of revolution were unusually self-confident. They had much contempt and little use for the ancient model of French corporate life. The term "privilege," which in the past had meant the exercise of a right of liberty within a corps circumscribed by the rights of other corps, had become synonymous with abuse and particularist self-seeking. The French elite nurtured two alternate modes of thought. They were enthusiastic about the emancipatory possibilities of individualism and they were deeply moved by the Rousseauist, salvationist emphasis on the common good.

It is difficult for us today to accept the idea that the prospects of such a reconciliation should have been so widely diffused. Intransigent, possessive individualism and an acute sense of the social and economic rights of the community are for us two opposite ends of a very long and divisive social and political spectrum, whose tormented and salient points are the revolutions of 1848, the Paris Commune of 1871, the Russian revolutions of 1905 and 1917, and the fascist counterrevolutions of 1922 and 1933. Today we clearly see the divergences which existed in the eighteenth century between these two views, which became during the second half of the nineteenth century the bedrock of conservative, bourgeois "liberalism," on the one hand, and of revolutionary socialism, on the other hand.

In 1789, however, when the categories of modern social life were still in gestation, the possessive individualist-universalist myth of the new, socially composite elite seemed eminently feasible. Rich and poor might be very close: at Versailles the king whiled his time away as an amateur artisan (he was a first-rate locksmith), and Marie-Antoinette played out her hours as a shepherdess.

The elite's new, schizophrenic social vision was deeply felt and (since, unfortunately, largely devoid of substance), very wide in scope. It reconciled in much too facile a way not just possessive individualism and a strictly defined public good but, by extension, the one and the many, nobles and nonnobles, rich and poor, nature and the arts, reason and imagination, men and women, the aged and the young, the learned and the untutored, the present, the past, and the future. The French enlightened elite assumed that individual happiness and public virtue would effortlessly overlap. In describing the French utopia of 2040, Mercier fancied that the "insolent luxury" of his day would soon be replaced by an undefined "luxe d'industrie . . . utile et nécessaire." By being himself, the emancipated (male) citizen could work for the good of all. With many thoughtful reservations, Adam Smith in 1776 had likewise reconciled the greed of the one with the interest of the many. But his "invisible hand" was a mechanistic device that was held to work within the world as it then existed. To achieve a similar goal of conciliation between opposites, the French elite banked on the unfolding—especially in the minds of the poor, and thanks to the achievement of an unprecedented social and political liberty—of a heretofore unknown side of human nature. On the eve of the Revolution, the propertied elite's cumulation of liabilities and illusions formed the true ingredients of political catastrophe.

THE EVOLUTION OF the French Revolution needs to be explained in reference to prerevolutionary ambiguities in culture and ideology and to the fragility of the compromise that the elitist revolutionaries aimed to establish between divergent forces that could not really be reconciled.

Had French society been less advanced, the lure of a possessive, capitalistic individualism might have seemed less strong and aristocratic survivals less shocking. France like Germany might not have had a revolution at all. Had France, on the contrary, been more advanced, and opted in the seventeenth century for unfettered economic individualism instead of state-guided, Colbertian mercantilism, then the dangers of "bourgeois universalism," of associating determining community with the claims of intransigent individual property rights, would surely have become more obvious. French society of its own accord would have been better able in the 1790s to arrest a process of political change, or *dérapage*, that was set in motion by the monarchy's inability to reform itself.

The incomplete nature of French social and cultural forms in the 1780s meant simultaneously that no political solution seemed self-evident and that every solution seemed possible of achievement. French culture and society was, if not in fragments, in a state of rapid, disintegrating change; and in this cultural and sociological rubble many fantasies could take root. In the New World, when Independence was achieved, when Americans proceeded to elaborate their own national ideology, definitive solutions quickly fell into place. Revolutionary France, by contrast, gyrated wildly from one political system to another, from the traditional corporatism of the Old Regime to individualist and constitutional monarchy, to tyranny and republican virtue, to a proposed communist regime, and finally to Bonaparte's military authoritarianism of 1799. Every artifice of modern politics emerged in those years, from corruption and indirect elections to purges, coups, runaway inflation, and wars of nationalist aggression. "In a wisely constituted Republic," wrote Academician Daunou in 1793, "personal interest is indissolubly linked to the public good." It took the Terror for the French propertied elite to find out that this was a very difficult, a well-nigh impossible, goal to achieve in France.

In 1789 the French were incapable of conceptualizing their new (and indeterminate) social and cultural situation. They had rejected corporate organicism as a model, but had no true understanding of the imperatives and limits of a modern liberal society and also no sense of the structures of class that it might engender. It was this opacity that permitted a false optimism in 1788–89 and after 1791 made it difficult for the propertied elite to control a radicalized Revolution that created new and unmanageable social groups (such as the sansculottes) as, torrentlike, it swept everything away.

The price of prerevolutionary social and political irresolution and confusion would then be paid, and that price was to be very high. From its very nature French society, unstructured as it had become, could find after 1789 no inner social or cultural balance which might arrest a revolutionary process of universalist radicalization that was in its origins simultaneously fated and demagogically fortuitous. In the 1780s a resolute monarchic policy of institutional modernization might have saved the day; but that did not happen, and the effects of this political failure quickly appeared after the Revolution because of the inchoate shape of French society and the divided nature of French thought. A unique concatenation brought together in the late 1780s the ingredients of the unique political catastrophe of the middle and late 1790s, marked by the emergence of Terror and the Bonapartist, authoritarian suspension of parliamentary politics.

The postrevolutionary shock of awakening was very harsh for both the elite and the poor. It took some time and many disappointments for the universalist and propertied elite of 1789 to understand the constraining nature of modern politics and of its own narrow place in history. Its drift from 1792 to 1794 toward a compensatory and terroristic rhetoric of communitarian ideology as an alternative to a popular call for genuine equality was to be the first measure of its confusion. Everyone would suffer from these mistakes: the poor who were deceived and the bourgeoisie itself, which had called up demons that it could not control.

5

Public Good and Transcendental Self in the American Revolution

THE CAUSES OF the American Revolution were of two types, material and imagined: very real differences set the colonists at odds with the government of Great Britain, but no less important were American perceptions of what had caused these problems.

After the Seven Years War, the British political class—great landed magnates, country gentlemen, prosperous merchants, members of the professions—reconsidered the shape of their empire and, within that context, the nature of America's economic relationship with England. The development of Britain's North American colonies, which had been one of the first objects of its diplomacy for more than a century, became a cause of hostile concern. The spectacular growth of America's population was being echoed in reverse by the near depopulation of some home areas, particularly in Scotland. At times it was suggested in London that further emigration from Britain to the colonies should be made illegal. Coincidentally, in order to avoid a repetition of bloody and costly Indian insurrections, British statesmen forbade white settlements to the west of the Appalachian Mountains. The provisions of an act of 1763 to that effect were reinforced in 1774.

Most annoying to the colonists was the English government's determination to make Americans shoulder a larger share of the cost of empire. Americans were imperial free riders. The liabilities to them of British mercantilism were more than outweighed by the value of the protection given by the British navy to American commerce. It seemed abnormal to English country gentlemen that per-capita taxation in England should be ten times higher than in America, especially as the ostensible cause of the English debt had been the financing of imperial wars and the defense of the thirteen colonies against French attacks.

In the aftermath of the Seven Years War, imperial and fiscal concerns came together in the British elite's decision to raise the import duties for Americans, and in their continued resolve to prohibit the issuance of paper money, already forbidden to New England by the British Currency Act of 1751. Tolerated abuses and customs evasions, such as those that occurred in the colonials' West Indian trade, were no longer to be allowed. In March 1765 Parliament decreed that a stamp tax should be levied on all American legal documents and newspapers. Americans complained bitterly. In an unprecedented show of continental unity, thirty-seven delegates from nine colonies met in October 1765 to petition the crown to repeal the tax. The Stamp Act was soon withdrawn; but it was followed in 1767 by the Townshend Acts, which legislated a new set of import duties. In the face of sustained opposition and economic boycotts, these were repealed in 1770. Under pressure the British government reversed itself in practice, but it did not give up its claim to the right to tax Americans. From Westminster's point of view, colonial American assemblies were like ad hoc committees, empowered only to propose "temporary bylaws" in the absence of definitive rulings from London. In 1773 the issue surfaced a third (and final) time with the Tea Act. Designed to bail out the East India Company by draining off its surplus, the new legislation might well have lowered the cost of tea to Americans: what the consumer paid in higher tariffs might have been compensated by lower retailing costs. Americans would have none of it. On December 16, 1773, Sam Adams, with about 150 Bostonians disguised as Indians, dumped England's tea into Boston Harbor. A direct confrontation of this kind necessarily elicited a strong response: the British elites regarded Americans with cultural and political contempt. They feared that concessions to America would lead to unrest in Ireland and perhaps to the breakup of the British Empire everywhere: even Jamaican planters were petitioning Westminster for greater home rule. Britain's rulers decided to force the thirteen colonies into submission. The Coercive Acts (known in America as the Intolerable Acts) ordered the virtual annulment of the Massachusetts charter of 1691, as well as the military occupation of Boston under the command of General Gage, who replaced Hutchinson as governor.

The various legislative decisions the British Parliament had taken would certainly, in time, have had some practical effect on the lives of many Americans; potential migrants to western lands, readers of the public press, ironmasters and hatmakers, consumers of molasses, rum, or tea would all have been involved. The Currency Act of 1764, which forbade the issuance of paper money in the colonies, was resented, especially in Virginia. Nonetheless, there was an obvious gap between the narrow and rather sensible material scope of British legislation and its devastating political impact on America. The American response was stronger than the situation called for, an indication that the American Revolution was no more about taxes than the French Revolution was about the financial failure of the monarchy. In this respect it is particularly ironic that the per-capita tax burden shouldered by Americans after independence was ten times higher than before, just as the French paid more tax under Napoleon than they had under Louis XVI.

The politicized *perception* of economic fact rather than the tax burden itself was the real problem. At every step American resentment was filtered and expanded by the Radical Whig perception of politics. In 1776 that doctrine provided not just the vocabulary but "the grammar of thought" for the men and women who wanted independence. Americans believed after September 1774 that the king and his ministers were conspiring against the liberties which Americans considered their birthright as "freeborn Englishmen." American patriots assumed that American loyalists had been corrupted by patronage and the prospect of private gain. The proposed installation of an American Anglican bishop was surely designed to institutionalize this spirit of corruption, just as the newly established customs commissioners would soon reduce Americans to slavery. The shooting fray between British soldiers and a threatening crowd in Boston in 1770 was a "massacre" that proved British malevolence.

In 1776 Americans thought of themselves as persecuted, embattled farmers. So, too, did their opponents in a way—a mistake that led English statesmen to suppose that the British army would soon make mincemeat of these posturing civilians. And so did, in their own way, the French; it was commonly thought in Paris, for example, that the fire which broke out in New York after its occupation by the British was set by Plutarchan and self-sacrificing American *femmes patriotes*. Only after 1815 would America be perceived in France as embodying a materialistic and vulgar culture. In the early nineteenth century the very thought of New York City filled the novelist Stendhal with overwhelming ennui, but before 1800 Parisians considered Americans to be virtuous, abstemious, latter-day Spartans, albeit of an Athenian kind.

Ideology galvanized American indignation, and ideological mobilization in turn expanded the audience of Radical Whig thought. An economic boycott—or, as the last one was called in Massachusetts in 1774, "a solemn League and Covenant, respecting the disuse of British Manufactures"—is notoriously difficult to enforce. Yet the value of British exports to America fell in 1770 by £700,000. The success of formal political mobilization was even more striking. The Stamp Act brought into being a network of self-styled Sons of Liberty, many of them merchants and prosperous artisans, who efficaciously intimidated their loyalist opponents: the destruction in August 1764 of Andrew Oliver's house in Boston, with his renunciation the next day of the office of stamp collector for Massachusetts, was a suggestive omen. North of Georgia, not a single stamp was ever sold.

Ideological mobilization, already pronounced before 1775, was compounded after 1776 by the logic of ideas and by the material effects of war. Revolutionary thought and action drove Americans toward new political forms, and Americans had ample material cause to reflect on the particularity of their political situation. The practicalities of their war-torn lives forced upon them new reflections, just as war and shortages would be, in revolutionary France, the catalyst of new ideological crystallizations. Wartime disruption in America was much greater than is often supposed, greater in many respects than in revolutionary France. Of the new nation's three million inhabitants, 231,950 are said to have served in some military capacity. One-fourth of the adult white males were involved, and in some areas, such as Rhode Island, a large number of blacks as well. Service in the state militia was compulsory. A history of the Revolution, as John Adams later wrote to a French correspondent, would have three main headings: the courts, the institutions of local representation, and the militia (which was at once a military force and a revolutionary, paramilitary political organization).

The prerevolutionary political consciousness, which was first crystallized by Britain's stated intents, was further expanded by the widespread destruction of American property by the British during the Revolution. Americans often assumed this havoc to have been perversely intentional, and in a way it was. After their defeat at Saratoga in upper New York state in 1777, English generals shifted their attention southward. Instead of trying to destroy Washington's elusive army they decided to secure, through overriding strength, the loyalty, or at least the obedience, of an intimidated people. They turned from the rebels' army to the rebels themselves. New England, whose population seemed resolutely hostile, was for the moment given up, and New York City was retained only because it was easily defensible. The thrust of Britain's war effort moved to the south. Southern patriots would be cowed and southern loyalists comforted. British naval forces might also shuttle more easily between engagements in the American South and raids on the French Caribbean islands. Between 1776 and 1778 destruction had already been widespread in a broad area of northern New Jersey and western New York, where twelve thousand farms had been abandoned and hundreds of buildings burned. Between 1778 and 1782 the southern states were torn by full-fledged civil war. Armed bands crisscrossed the area. At the Battle of King's Mountain, a small army of American patriot irregulars destroyed a small army of American Tory irregulars, some of whom came from as far north as New York. The Tory Guy Tarleton became infamous; and Francis Marion, the Swamp Fox, became an American legend in his own time. British assaults on American towns made a strong impression: all Americans knew about the burning of Falmouth in Maine, of Charlestown outside Boston, and of Newport News in Virginia. Particularly ominous were British plans for the creation of an "Ethiopian" battalion and for an offer of freedom to black slaves; Jefferson may have had these plans in mind when, in the Declaration of Independence, he accused Britain of confiscating American property.

Economic disruption amplified the social travails caused by the war. As a trading nation, America was dependent on foreign commerce and domestic coastal trade, and its economy had become habituated to infusions of British coinage paid for American goods. The suspension of British war purchases after the Peace of Paris in 1763 had led to a serious economic downturn in the colonies. Four hundred million dollars' worth of paper money was printed by the Continental Congress with predictable effect: by 1777 these bills were worth in gold one-third of their nominal value, and by 1779 two cents on the dollar. (Cheap and shoddy goods were "not worth a continental.") Bartering and black marketeering were commonplace. Debtors found sudden relief. Fortunes were made and unmade in military contracts and shady dealings. Workers struck for higher pay. Urban social life was particularly affected by the war, if only because the British, at one point or another, occupied all of America's major cities. The war momentarily reversed the trend of population movement to urban centers: in 1790 less than 6 percent of the total population lived in cities as against 7 percent in 1776. New York's population fell by half. Tens of thousands of people loyal to the crown left the country. Property was confiscated. Patriots fled when the British army moved in; loyalists were harassed when it moved out.

At the local and provincial level, in New England and the southern colonies especially, many voices were heard demanding the imposition of price controls, a dramatic step in a society accustomed to prices set by supply and demand. Building on precedents provided by sumptuary law and by those provisions of the common law that forbade "regrating" and other such "unfair" practices, Massachusetts passed in 1777 an act "to prevent monopoly and oppression."[1] In 1779 when the British left Philadelphia, rioting broke out and a town meeting voted to set a ceiling on the prices of thirty-two products, another ominous step: in revolutionary France the catalyst of sansculotte politics was precisely the crowd's desire to lower the cost of food. Many people were impoverished, while a few did quite well. In the rebellious American colonies a republican concern for virtue could be nicely fitted to an assertive sense of political righteousness and a typically American desire for profit: so it was that Mercy Otis Warren took no small satisfaction in dating her patriotic letters from Governor Hutchinson's confiscated Roxbury mansion, now become her own. More property—in proportion to total wealth—changed hands in God's new nation than in France during its great Revolution. All of the new states with the exception of South Carolina passed acts confiscating loyalist properties.[2]

It was impossible to live in America without feeling the effect of war. Material hardships hardened political resolve. Political ideas were expressed in new and more convincing ways. At the level of the spoken and the written word, revolutionary orators like Patrick Henry developed a new, more emotional, more accessible political rhetoric, the secular analogue of the religious preaching made familiar by the itinerant revivalists of the 1740s. Writers like Tom Paine did the same for the printed word. With the Stamp Act of 1765, pamphleteering had become a regular fixture of the American public scene, and the most successful of these efforts—Tom Paine's *Common Sense*—sold 120,000 copies within three months of January 1776. Plainly written and studded with familiar biblical references, this ungrammatical tract was novel in both style and content. Gouverneur Morris, an elegant patrician who would in time fine-tune the wording of the federal Constitution, despised Paine—"an adventurer . . . ignorant even of grammar"—and this, precisely, was his strength. In Paine's work, the language of dissenting, Whig Protestantism was reshaped to carry a new and more popular message of political revolution.

Americans restyled their inherited grammars of thought so as to dignify their struggle. They had rebelled against taxation and on behalf of the historicist restoration of Britain's ancient constitution. They now found themselves involved in a struggle whose scope was far greater than any of them had supposed possible. Americans did more than merely "realize . . . the theories of the wisest writers," as John Adams wrote. They transformed them; and thinkers, like John Adams, who persisted in seeing America's national fate and struggle in the strict and narrow context of learned and classical republicanism gradually became irrelevant.

Rejuvenated republicanism was often expressed in a borrowed and occasionally exotic rhetoric of enlightened natural right. Even before the Revolution, Americans had admired foreigners like John Wilkes in Britain and Pascal Paoli in Corsica. Through observation they had learned to consider their domestic travails in a wider context of world history. Revealingly, it was an outsider, a very recent immigrant, Tom Paine, who had only lived in America for a few months, who best managed to express what it was that Americans thought they were doing. While Burke wrote of the "real rights of men," Paine referred America's struggle to the more abstract and immanent rights of man.[3] In the same way, a significant difference of tone distinguished Jefferson's provincial *Notes on Virginia* from the philosophic correspondence of the Parisian Jefferson in the late 1780s. Americans who before 1765 had been the dutiful colonial subjects of a European if patriotic British king now suddenly discovered that they were not just the heirs of premonarchical Hebrew tribes but citizens of a new world: "Why send an American youth to Europe for education?" asked Jefferson in 1785. "It appears to me . . . that an American coming to Europe for his education, loses in his knowledge, in his morals, in his health, in his habits, and in Happiness."

This ideologization and ennoblement of America's "sacred cause" was visible at many different levels. In 1751 Franklin, in his *Observations on the Increases of Mankind,* had written in grandiose terms of America's economic and demographic future, albeit within a triumphant British Empire. Over the years his declining Anglophilia and rising Francophilia were two good barometers of America's growing cultural self-confidence. When he arrived in France, in 1776, this calculating and amorous man, who had explained in 1735 that "self-denial is not the Essence of Virtue," and who had for years after his retirement—at the age of forty-two—cultivated the image of a British gentleman-scholar with a gift for scientific research, began to develop yet another persona—that of an elaborately fashioned, sartorially appropriate, politically correct, and deceptively Quakerish "American." His was the vulgarized and most successful analogue of Jefferson's elevated ideological nationalism, a living pictorialization of the themes that assured the fame of Saint-Jean de Crèvecoeur's *Letters of an American Farmer,* a superficial French eulogy of American simplicity published in 1782.

America gradually emerged from its provincial dependence to become a national political-cultural entity in its own right. The new American ethos was a powerful combination of enlightened and historicist versions of natural law (some of them indigenous, others not) and of a secularized religiosity. Many learned Enlightenment thoughts and phrases had popular echoes—like Jefferson's Lockean "pursuit of happiness"—because they had also figured in Puritan or other Protestant discourse. Americans were a religious people, and though less religious than they would become with the Second Great Revival, they were already more religious than they had been. In the northern provinces in the 1700s most Americans, most women especially, were regular churchgoers. Though the Great Awakening had weakened the formal institutions of religion, its long-range effect had been to strengthen religious feeling by making it more direct and personal. Americans in 1776 felt that theirs was a divinely sanctioned cause: "God," explained Joseph Warren in 1772, "had always owned the cause of liberty in North America." Defeats were so many mortifications imposed by God on a chosen people that had momentarily failed Him. Chastened loyalists, who were likened by the victorious patriots to repentant sinners, were in Connecticut required to declare themselves "penitent of their former conduct" and to present their new opinions as "a matter of conviction."[4] "Religion," Edmund Burke shrewdly observed in 1775, "always a principle of energy, in this new people is in no way worn out or impaired; and their mode of professing it is also one main cause of this free spirit."[5] This was a truth, incidentally, which Burke's initially more successful rival, Tom Paine, did not understand. His violently anticlerical *Age of Reason,* written in a French jail in 1794, was soon to be a source of considerable embarrassment for Paine's American supporters.

Perfervid nationalism was another by-product of military conflict. In September 1774 a majority of the delegates to the Continental Congress looked forward to some kind of conciliation with Britain, but in the early summer of 1776, after the battles of Lexington and Concord, John Adams wrote that "every post and every day rolls in upon us independence like a torrent." The war heightened America's sense of nationhood, which had been steadily growing for decades.

In the newly independent thirteen colonies, loyalism, which had begun as a political option, became a kind of national betrayal. New patriotic rites were invented to express unprecedented feelings. At York, Pennsylvania, which was for some months the temporary capital of the new United States, floats were paraded on the anniversary of Independence Day and to celebrate events like the French alliance and the burning of Charlestown. The artist David, in Paris in 1794, would not have disavowed these efforts. Military parades exalted local pride. The death of heroes was mourned. American propaganda, which had centered before 1775 on the rights of Americans as freeborn Englishmen, was refocused to exalt the newly discovered and natural rights of free Americans. So strong was nationalistic passion that it soon spilled over into xenophobia and race hatred: Americans grew to hate both the British and their Indian allies. The saga of Jane McCrea, scalped in 1777 by Britain's redskin hirelings, was widely known. For some months in 1779 Americans appeared to be more concerned about fighting Indians than about struggling against the British. Large parts of western New York were ravaged by American militias: the Iroquois people, which numbered ten thousand in 1776, was only half that size ten years later. In Georgia, entire Cherokee villages were wiped out. American nationalism was not a passive doctrine.

England and English culture remained in some respects models for Americans after independence as they had been before. But where Americans before 1750 had imitated British habits because they themselves were more British than the British, they now did so because England happened to be the world's richest and most modern nation. English ways of thinking, of making money, or of organizing social and judicial life might still be copied but in a different and consciously nationalistic American spirit which gelled at the moment of independence. Britain's moral corruption was universally decried: "Luxury, effeminacy, and irreligion," wrote Timothy Dwight in 1778, "were causes of her fall."[6] Britain's loss was America's cultural gain.

So great, then, were the physical and moral transformations of American life that what most needs to be explained is a "nonevent," namely, that "the struggle for home rule" never became a genuine "class struggle" about who would rule at home, or (if that seems an overstatement) why the political struggle over independence never became a clear-cut social conflict about the shape of home rule.

Some considerable political and social changes, obviously, did occur in the embattled colonies. As with the French Revolution, which can be imagined as a dérapage, or "sliding out from under," so was American society affected by seven years of conflict. The French possessing class, which aimed to create an aggressively pro-individualist regime, found itself confronted in 1793 by popular, communitarian demands which it had itself encouraged. Faint analogues of this drift—called by Bernard Bailyn a "contagion of liberty," can be found in America as well.

The most conspicuous examples of the American "sliding out" were institutional. As has often been said, "authority was fragile" in the colonies, and the specific shape of American institutions (if not their overall purpose) was uncertain. More than other concern, institutional forms attracted the attention of eighteenth-century Anglo-American radicals: for them what mattered was the political setting of social change, rather than social change per se. Opponents of local aristocracies focused on the destruction of legislative upper houses that would give constituency to groups they did not like, rather than on the destruction of aristocracies as such. Whig thought vigorously asserted that the people ought to advance from the principle of the defense of their rights against monarchic encroachment, but the way in which they should do this was often left undefined. Before the Revolution, that very vagueness had allowed the theory to be adapted to local circumstance. Now, that same institutional plasticity worked to a different end.

The call of the Continental Congress for revisions of state constitutions in May 1775 set off a flurry of popular interest in potentially destabilizing lawmaking. State constitutions appeared and disappeared with alarming speed. South Carolinians drafted three such documents. In Massachusetts independent-minded voters actually rejected a proposed constitutional draft. To ensure the permanence of a revolutionary spirit, eight state constitutions contained a self-nullifying provision. Vermont and Pennsylvania had boards of censors to alert the public to the need of constitutional amendment. The thrust of these documents was not to insure the representation of interests but to encourage the political participation of the people taken as an indivisible whole. In a surprising move, which ran against the genius of American life and was not durable—but which would have inspired French revolutionaries, had they known of it—the censors of the Keystone State ruled in 1784 to annul the charter of the University of Pennsylvania on the grounds that no "corporation" could stand between the people and the state. Typically also, the Pennsylvania constitution—much admired by Parisian philosophes and translated into French by Brissot, the future leader of the Girondin party in the French Convention—encouraged the enactment of legislation that guaranteed virtue and prevented vice.

Not surprisingly, most of the documents that emerged were far more populist than the ones they replaced. In New York the governor was to be elected directly, and Pennsylvania had no governor at all. The ability of the state executive to appoint officials, which had been narrow in colonial America, was nearly everywhere reduced. Popular recall for judges was permitted in many states. Electoral franchises were broadened. In America, as in revolutionary France, the very poor were indeed excluded, but on the grounds that they might easily be coerced or bribed.

The hold of the established churches was diminished further. At the local level the connection of church and state was not everywhere abolished: Congregationalism remained the established religion of Massachusetts until 1833, and the constitution of New Hampshire authorized religious assessments until after the Civil War. In some places, at war's end, non-Protestants still experienced various political disabilities. Nonetheless, the religious role of the states was everywhere curtailed. In some places it simply lapsed. Virginia in 1772 had imposed certain restrictions on Baptists, but these were repealed in 1776. Baptists were not given so free a hand in New England as in Virginia, but they were exempted from paying religious taxes to the established churches.

New institutions sprang up and new men came into politics both at the grass-roots level of the towns and in the state legislatures. The proportion of merchants, lawyers, and rich planters in high political office fell everywhere, even in the South, where elites had seemed more firmly entrenched and where the gap between rich and poor was wider. In the northern states, where 17 percent of delegates had owned property worth less than £2000 before the war, 62 percent of those returned after the war were in that bracket. Property requirements were not abolished, but they were often lowered. Farmers in New York were more likely to voice their economic complaints against the "lords of the manor," as Massachusetts farmers did against their more prosperous neighbors. The poor were more likely to sue in the 1780s than before. Indentured white servitude essentially disappeared. In the South, the War of Independence saw the extension and politicization of the running conflict between the eastern planters and the backcountry Regulators.

The effect on blacks of a war which whites were fighting against whites was illustrative. In the late 1770s, petitions pointing out the anomaly of maintaining slavery in a free and newborn nation were widely circulated, one of them by blacks in New Hampshire. In Pennsylvania in the 1760s isolated voices had already been raised, including that of John Woolman, who refused to eat sugar because it was produced by black slave labor. The number of such complaints swelled during the Revolution. In 1780 slavery was banned in Pennsylvania. In Massachusetts the war brought to a climax an unease about slavery that dated back to 1712, when the importation of Indian slaves to the province was outlawed. In 1767 a punitive tax was proposed on the importation of all slaves; and the General Court in 1771 actually voted a cessation of the provincial slave trade. In 1783 a state court interpreted a law of 1780 as a ban on slavery. In the northern and middle Atlantic states, involuntary servitude also gradually disappeared, and Congress in 1787 forbade the importation of slaves into the Northwest Territory. Many of the northern colonies (and Maryland also) resolved that blacks who had served in the revolutionary army would be freed. Even southern magnates whose way of life rested on slavery became uneasy in the 1770s and 1780s about involuntary servitude, which had been legal everywhere before the War of Independence but was fast becoming a "peculiar institution." In the early eighteenth century, Virginians had seen themselves through British eyes—it was in the 1720s that the imported myth of southern laziness was taken up from Britain by the southerners themselves—but in the last decades of the century, Virginians began to perceive their most distinctive social institution through the prism of another and more troubling ethic, that of the

American Republic. Individual manumissions became more common: ten thousand blacks were freed by their masters during the 1780s. William Binford of Henrico County, Virginia, freed twelve bondsmen in 1782 because he was convinced that "freedom is the natural right of all mankind."[7] Washington's will provided for the freeing of his two hundred bondsmen.

Republicanism affected the situation of women as well: after 1776 the social space of married women was defined even more than before, by reference to the legal rubric of "coverture," an ancient concept of common law which restricted the rights of married women by placing their husbands' prerogatives between them and the public legal system. But in spite of this continuity, the idea gradually emerged that coverture was antirepublican. Although the short-and long-run effects of the revolutionary settlement diverged on this issue, the eventual and liberating effects were the more important. The radical role of women in the French Revolution was more visible than in America, but the achievements of the American feminist movement in the nineteenth century, grounded in the bedrock of American religion and republicanism, proved more substantial, precocious, and durable than those of the more flamboyant French feminist tradition. It is perhaps more than a curiosity that the 1776 state constitution of New Jersey tacitly enfranchised both blacks and women and allowed them the vote until 1807.

All of these institutional and social dérapages created a mood of openness. At times it seemed that widespread social change might occur in America after all. Indignation mobilized collective energies. In the larger cities the merchants, mechanics, and sailors all formed political organizations or committees. Here and there, from Boston to Philadelphia and as far south as Charleston, worrisome crowds milled about, often led by individuals of equivocal prominence, who seemed eager to turn the political War of Independence into a real war of national regeneration. In 1773 the New York Sons of Liberty put up their liberty pole next to the poorhouse. In the celebrated "Fort Wilson" episode of October 1779 the rioting poor of Philadelphia besieged the house of James Wilson—an enemy of price controls and of the Pennsylvania constitution—whose guests that day included Robert Morris the financier and Thomas Mifflin, a general in the Continental army. Philadelphia, with its pool of

German immigrants, "renegade Quaker" egalitarians, populist militia, Jack Tars, and well-organized ships carpenters (the celebrated "Hearts of Oak"), seemed a likely breeding ground for avowed radical revolutionaries, the likes of whom would soon accelerate the course of the French Revolution. In 1776 some Philadelphia radicals even proposed to insert in the new state constitution an explicit denunciation of large properties. Dr. Thomas Young, a recent migrant from New York, where he had learned to hate the "dirty pultroons" and their neofeudal dues, seemed a likely candidate to become an American Marat.[8]

Interesting also as a potentially radical figure was one of Tom Paine's new friends, Charles Lee, a British officer who had fought in Spain in 1763 and had also visited Poland and Hungary, where he had seen that the consuming hatred of peasants for their foreign overlords could be mobilized to fight popular wars of national liberation. Lee, who distinguished himself at the siege of Boston, and had in October 1775 proclaimed the need for American independence, was impatient of "Hyde Park tactics" and critical of Washington's determination to fight the British more or less on their own terms. Washington did his best to avoid pitched battles —and wisely so, since he lost such engagements with some regularity—but he wished to lead an army that was properly enrolled, well uniformed (in a manner of speaking), and on government pay, in theory at least. What Lee's radicalism might have led to is purely speculative because he was captured a few months later and soon afterward was disgraced in a military trial for having disobeyed Washington's orders at the Battle of Brandywine; but his initially successful career is suggestive of the radical potential of the War of Independence.

And so was, of course, his eventual failure, for in the end the American *dérapage* could not be sustained. By the determining standards of the French Revolution, which remains the central event of modern politics, social consciousness changed very little in revolutionary America. Social conflict, though sharpened, did not lead to the emergence of an unprecedented class consciousness in the newly independent nation. The American urban poor did not reconceptualize their social or political situation. There was no American Gracchus Babeuf.

Contemporary neo-Marxist historians, oppressed by their sense of America as an impoverished culture, have tried to present mob actions as expressions of some particular political will based on a separate social sense of self. A comparison of the natures of the American revolutionary crowd and the sansculottes will reveal the difficulties of this social interpretation of the American Revolution.

At the heart of the difference between the two popular political cultures was the American crowd's perception of itself as an agent of society taken as a whole, rather than as a representation of only one of its constituent parts. Colonial rioters ordinarily presented themselves as defenders of a generally accepted, historicist system of rights. For example, leaders of the "Meeting of the People of Boston, and the neighbouring Towns," whose informal and sometimes riotous membership numbered in the thousands, went through legal motions and did what they could to have Britain's tea sent home peaceably before they decided, in concert with other local figures, to heave it into Boston Harbor. Crowds composed largely of transient sailors, bottled up at times in icebound ports, were admittedly less deferential, but they were less representative as well. The myth of American rioters was legalistic and starkly different from that of the sansculottes, who believed in direct, violent, and blatantly illegal action, including murder and even dismemberment, while the Americans believed that resistance to oppression was a quasi-legal right and even at times a religious obligation.

What moved the Parisian working people, or "petit peuple," was not a respect for law at all, but its very reverse, moral indignation. Characteristically, Parisian rioters were unable to draw a line between the public and the private. As one of them explained in a pamphlet curiously entitled (in translation) "Conversations between a Citizen of Philadelphia recently arrived in France and a Republican Frenchman who had served under Washington": "To be respectable [*pour être honnête homme*] you must be a good son, a good husband and father, and unite—in a word—all the private and public virtues . . . Only then will you have the true definition of the word 'patriotism.' "[9] Here was a view of politics that galvanized private indignation but made it difficult to find long-term allies in politics.

One could argue the relative strengths of the two popular movements ad infinitum. The sansculottes sense of apartness was both a source of power and of weakness. On account of their cultural particularity, the sansculottes were quicker to defend their rights. They might easily decide, for example, to invade legally elected assemblies, a step that would have been unthinkable for an American crowd. But once the sansculottes had done this, they stopped: however badly treated, they could never bring themselves to supplant the bourgeois, propertied Convention, because, unlike the American crowd, they did not have the sense of being a microcosm of the entire nation. Their ideologically stunted particularism enabled them to rise, but not to rule.

What matters historiographically, however, is not whether American crowds were more or less efficacious, but whether their undoubted and important presence can be taken as proof of the existence of a distinct popular consciousness, such as existed in Paris. Clearly this was not the case.

Some points of ideological and social comparison can of course be found. In both countries the crowd was socially mixed: many Parisian popular revolutionaries were petit bourgeois, as was also true in Philadelphia, while some of them were shopkeepers or rentiers. But the difference was great when measured in terms of cultural and social distance. In Paris, everyone understood the gap in status, influence, and method that separated the middle-class Jacobins from their more popular counterparts, the sansculotte Sociétés Populaires. In America, by contrast, instances of continuity between the crowd and the elite were the rule. Many leaders of the early revolutionary popular movement, such as John Lamb of New York (whose father, an indentured servant, had been saved in extremis from the gallows), resurfaced later as respectable, mainstream army officers. Lamb himself became a general. Decades later, many former members of the American urban crowd completed their cursus honorum as more or less respectable Republican party stalwarts. Numerous plebeian Sons of Liberty of 1765, who were quite close in method, ideology, and social composition to the French bourgeois Jacobin clubs, which they were often accused of aping, figured prominently in the more respectable Democratic-Republican societies of the 1790s.

The difference between the self-images of the French and American revolutionary crowds is of methodological consequence, and the negative conclusions it implies regarding the existence of American class consciousness appear in other domains as well. In France, the crowd passionately hated the counterrevolutionary aristocrats who soon came to hate and fear the crowd. It would be difficult, however, to prove that the urban poor in revolutionary America ever went much to the left of classic Radical Whig thought or that their rich neighbors ever really feared them. Even at the fever pitch of America's revolutionary struggle, what the American poor wanted was no more than their "fair" share of the existing system. America stayed on a middle path. No loyalist civilian was ever put to death by legally sanctioned process for a civil offense. Thousands of loyalists were bullied, tarred and feathered, or otherwise humiliated. America was undeniably a brutal land: for example, a woman who had helped English soldiers was imprisoned and stripped— "exposing her," as she explained, "to many Thousands of People Naked."[10] But there was no American Reign of Terror. Jefferson in his *Notes on Virginia* proudly wrote that "not a single execution for treason" had occurred in revolutionary Virginia.[11]

A wide range of reasons can be brought forward to explain the persistence of social solidarity and constitutional legality in America at this decisive turn of European and American history. The issue here is to account for the nonappearance in the United States of the new, popular class consciousness which was to be in France the motor that first drove the sansculottes to insurrection and then, by reaction, led the Jacobin bourgeoisie to engage in hyperbolic universalist rhetoric and repressive illegality.

The War of American Independence was not fought in an institutional void as was the French Revolution. In the dispute between the loyalist governor of Massachusetts and the Massachusetts General Court, it was Hutchinson who fled and the "rebel" legislators who remained, albeit in the suburbs instead of Boston. More trivially but no less typically, when the British postal system ceased to function, its place was assumed by a homegrown system that had been created in Baltimore when the British dismissed Benjamin Franklin as postmaster general on the eve of the Revolution. In France, a collapsing Old Regime pulled down with it an ancient and fragile web of social and political institutions. In America, the effect of revolution was to strengthen local institutional forms.

America's working institutions had been grounded in its social life for more than a century, and the Revolution affected them only tangentially. Provincial charters were changed during the Revolution, but there was no legal or administrative holocaust. The secular British tradition of common law was not put aside by the Revolution, but retained its provincial particularities throught the war as well as during the early federal period. American civil laws were not rewritten—or, for that matter, even written, since few legal compendia existed at the time. Cautious propertied patriots were well aware of the social consequences of institutional disorder and rushed in to fill whatever institutional or legal void appeared: the Massachusetts Provincial Congress, for example, urged the Continental Congress to recommend the immediate creation of new civil authorities because "there are in many parts of the colony alarming symptoms of the abatement of the sense in the minds of some people of the sacredness of private property, which is plainly assignable to the want of civil government."[12]

Social continuity likewise remained the stabilizing backdrop of law and order. In France, the Le Chapelier law of 1791 radically transformed the social landscape by abolishing guilds and making liberal individualism, defined in terms of property rights, the first law of the land. No such social-legal upheaval took place in America. Ravage there was, but it was of a straightforward, material kind. France in 1789 was set adrift by the destruction of both its political and corporate social structures. Nothing even remotely approaching this occurred in revolutionary America.

Of equal importance was the unusual ideological density and consistency of the Radical Whig world view, which in the late 1770s was still used to voice America's larger political goals. Before the Revolution the doctrine had shown extraordinary specificity: in the colonies it was an immutable cultural legacy, separated from both society and local politics. It also remained essentially intractable for a time after 1776. Before the Revolution, local politicians had spoken in the language of Whig thought and acted as they pleased; during the Revolution, a similar if transformed disjunction existed between the stable Whig rhetoric of revolutionary discourse and the widespread material effects of war. Radical Whig theory with its myth of a virtuous people neither moved forward toward a novel and more transformative idea of a virtuous and exploited class, nor did it move backward in order to give the loyalists the reasoned defense of a genuine corporate tradition. In the words of a self-styled "True Patriot" writing in New Jersey in 1779

> there are two extremes in republican governments, which it be-hooves us carefully to avoid. The one is, that *noble birth, or wealth and riches,* should be considered as an hereditary title to the govern-ment of the republic . . . The other extreme is, that the government can be managed by the *promiscuous multitude of the community,* as in some of the States of ancient Greece . . . The happy medium is, where the people at large have the sole power of annually electing such officers of the state as are to be entrusted with the *most invalu-able rights, liberties and properties* of the people.[13]

One is tempted to say that American radical ideology remained almost miraculously poised between the True Patriot's two ex-tremes. Thomas Paine wrote of republicanism and not of democ-racy, or—heaven forbid—social democracy. Paine did go some small distance beyond ordinary Commonwealth theory: monarchy, as he saw it, was not merely bad but useless. On balance, however, his egalitarianism was very restrained. An extension of material equality was in his scheme of things, but as the natural effect of republican prosperity. His extraordinarily popular pamphlet *Com-mon Sense* radicalized Whig ideology but did not transcend it. Paine's defense of private property was unconditional. His politics was basically inclusive and conservative. After the Fort Wilson episode he remarked, ecumenically, that "the difference is exceed-ingly great, between not being in favor and being considered an enemy."[14]

So it was that the state constitution of Vermont in 1777 and of Massachusetts in 1780 specifically associated the confiscation of property with the hated principle of taxation without representa-tion. Gracchus Babeuf in 1795 lamented the fate of what he called propertyless "impropriétaires," but property in America remained in the eyes of the public the means to freedom. As Jefferson—who hated debt—explained in his *Notes on Virginia,* "dependence begets subservience and venality, suffocates the germ of virtue, and pre-pares fit tools for the designs of ambition."[15] The American revo-lutionaries inverted the thought of the Parisian sansculottes, who assumed as a matter of course that custom and the state should regulate the proper use of property. John Adams and his friends thought it self-evident that individual property rights could never be infringed.

The absence of a corporatist social past was another important factor which made impossible in America a leftist kind of dérapage, slipping toward either a universalist ideology or popular class consciousness. The structures of American social life had for more than a century been individualistic to a remarkable extent. Even if some more determining definition of communitarian solidarity had, by happenstance, emerged in revolutionary America in the late 1770s, it could not have found an anti-individualist ambience in which to thrive. In France, Jacobin universalism harbored the secular suspicion of individualism that had been nurtured during the course of the eighteenth century by the incomplete transformations of French society. Revolutionary sansculottism as a social and political force had two root systems: a highly radicalized version of the bourgeois Jacobins' classical egalitarianism, on the one hand, and, on the other hand, secular traditions of popular and corporate action. Both elements were missing in America. This initial deficiency, more than any other factor, made the transition to a society of classes impossible.

At the formative moment of American politics, in the years when the traditions of the American Republic took shape, urban crowds existed, but only to uphold a Radical Whig ideology that was not particular to themselves. This ideology, unlike Jacobinism, placed inalienable individual rights at the center of the new politics. Neither Boston nor Philadelphia—not to speak of New York—had an urban tradition of corporate social life. Socially, the hegemony of individualist forms meant that in revolutionary Philadelphia it was hard to maintain politically dysfunctional, communitarian social action. American artisans, for example, soon tired of price controls. Trade, some of them wrote in July 1779, "should be as free as air, uninterrupted as the tide,"[16] an idea that would have been utterly unthinkable in revolutionary Paris after 1792.

The unusual hegemony of unchanging Whiggish ways of thinking was a factor everywhere in America: on the left, on the right, and in the center. Just as the poor, on the left, did not become a class, so did the American possessing elite, its "bourgeoisie," in the center of politics, remain impervious to the sibylline charms of radical rhetoric. Josiah Quincy wrote anxiously to his son-in-law that in his politics, and with his *"darling Liberty,"* the "Man of *Substance* [will be] reduced to a Level, with those who have none . . . What is to become of your Property?"[17] But as it happened, Quincy's fears were misplaced.

The foremost characteristic of the French Revolution was the bourgeoisie's inability to resist the classical, Spartan mirage of moral equality. The universalist-minded Jacobins drifted steadily leftward after 1789 toward a counterproductive alliance with the plebs. After 1791 especially, the bourgeois Jacobins tried to resolve their problems by injecting into their politics a massive dose of symbolic equality: in dress, forms of address, speech, and political ritual. In 1793 they went so far as to give tepid and brief material embodiment to this universalist rhetoric of equality through the government's partial control of the economy and the punitive if desultory enforcement of the use of paper money.

By late 1793 the French bourgeoisie had gone much further than they had dreamed possible five years before, and the German philosopher Fichte praised the Jacobins for that very reason: thanks to revolutionary praxis, he wrote as early as 1795, the French Jacobins had discovered that the assertion of individualism in modern life required a massively communitarian program of statist social regulation. Practical necessity, he rejoiced, had triggered for the Jacobins a social epiphany.

The propertied merchants, lawyers, and planters assembled at Philadelphia had no such cathartic revelation. Their curtailment of private and property rights was cautious to a degree. The rhetoric of classical virtue never led them to think the poor were either more virtuous or more deserving than they themselves were. Their own property rights, they consistently assumed, were embedded in law and nature: "What does Mr. Roberdeau mean," wrote an irate correspondent to Benjamin Rush in 1779, "when he says that 'there is no Law to prevent Regulations of prices being made.' Is it not part of your Constitution that no man shall be molested in his Person or Property fined or imprisoned, not by the Judgment of his Peers and the Law of the Land?"[18]

On what we might today call the political right, reactionary loyalists in America were no more able to transcend the principles of Radical Whiggism than were the middle-class revolutionaries of the left or the center. On the left, the essential nonevent was the nonappearance in Philadelphia and other cities of a "working class"; on the right, the comparable factor was intellectual paralysis of those people who should have been most hostile to Radical Whig thought, the loyalists.

How many Americans were hostile to independence is not known, but it could have been as many as a third of the population. In some parts of the backcountry, especially in South Carolina where the western area was underrepresented in government, pre-revolutionary social conflicts that had opposed poor-white Regulators to eastern planters were carried over into the new era. Hundreds of thousands of Americans, especially in New York, Pennsylvania, and northern New Jersey, were fence sitters who only rallied to independence in 1780–81, when they concluded from the very length of the conflict that the British would never be victorious. (In a way, all that General Washington had to do to win was to hold his shifting ground: time more than reason, mused Paine wistfully, ordinarily determines the choices that men make.) Twenty-five thousand Americans served in British armies or militias; and sixty to eighty thousand fled, sometimes to Great Britain but more commonly to Canada, where they pined for America. The size of the loyalist migration in proportion to America's population was twenty times greater than in revolutionary France, a disproportion that speaks for the representative nature of the loyalist party. Most loyalists were poor. Four out of five of them were artisans or farmers. By 1787 most of those who received pensions from the British government pleaded destitution. In short, loyalists were typical, native-born, colonial Americans, and only a minority of them were Anglicans.

Paradoxically, their very representativeness crippled them politically. A comparison can be made in this respect between the American crowd and American loyalists. The loyalists were unable to formulate a genuinely traditionalist ideology because they too subscribed to the dominant Radical Whig, neo-Puritan colonial ethic. The strident calls of Jonathan Boucher, an Anglican traditionalist, a

Filmerite—a very recent immigrant and, like Paine, an ideologue, though of a very different stripe—fell leadenly deadborn from his pulpit. Most loyalists presented themselves as true Whigs, defenders of English liberties. William Smith, an Anglican and a Philadelphian antagonist of Tom Paine, signed his seven denunciatory letters of April 1776 with the telling pseudonym of Cato. The archetypal loyalist, Thomas Hutchinson, governor of Massachusetts (whose brother-in-law and social equal, Richard Mather, was a staunch patriot), proposed not the abolition but merely the suspension of "what are called English liberties." Rebels and patriots were quite close in all respects but one. As independence neared, Samuel Quincy, a loyalist, wrote to his brother Josiah, a patriot: "*Our* Notions both of Government and Religion may be variant, but perhaps are not altogeher discordant . . . I hope [there] cannot fairly be imputed to either of us . . . a defect of Conscience or Uprightness of Intention.[19]

Because they were ideologically impotent, loyalists had to fall back on mundane arguments: Britain, they said, had not yet violated American liberties but might well do so after winning what was a civil war. They reminded merchants that Americans could not defend their commerce without the help of the British navy. Following another tack, the loyalists simply turned the Whig conspiratorial argument upside down and claimed that the rebellion was manipulated by scheming, ambitious men. In the early 1770s the loyalists denounced the rebels as false Whigs and covert republicans. They reminded their fellow Americans that, according to their own doctrine, republicanism could not work in so vast a country. Their most efficacious metaphor was familial: rebellious Americans were ungrateful children.

Sociologically speaking, one of the most suggestive facts about the loyalists is that in Massachusetts the patriot leadership was on the average seven years younger than its loyalist counterpart, a point which may imply that loyalists basically were Radical Whigs who were set in their ways and were therefore unable to respond to the changing climate of the times. Loyalism was more a matter of temperament than of principle, and temperament is a product of experience, age, and habit. Rebellion was a kind of family quarrel. Virginian loyalists who worked for Britian but stayed behind—and remained in some ultimate sense loyal to America—were punished financially far less severely than their political companions who said very little that was legally punishable but left their families and abandoned their native country. This same absence of an ideological split between the American left and right made postwar reconciliation relatively easy. In France during the late 1790s, besieged centrist republicans, though worried about leftist attacks on property, continued to perceive rightist traditionalists as irreconcilable enemies, and rightly so: returning French émigré were deeply embittered men, as were their descendants for more than a century. In America, by contrast, after independence returning loyalists faded effortlessly into the new political scenery. The southern provinces were something of an exception to this rule, but even there General Greene largely succeeded in healing the breach between planters and backwoodsmen.

The *dérapage* of the American Revolution did not last very long or go very far. Even before the war's end, the drift began toward a renewed conservative defense of property and hierarchy. In this rightist ebb, as had been true during the preceding radical flow, the evolution of institutions was broadly indicative of the new mood of politics. In the constitution which the Massachusetts voters finally accepted in 1780, the governor was once again endowed with broad powers. Pennsylvania, Vermont, and Georgia took on a senate. The electoral franchise was tightened. The College of Philadelphia and King's College in New York, whose charters had been confiscated, were reprivatized. The scope of the courts was broadened at the expense of elected legislatures. In a surprising judgment, a tribunal in the state of New York found in favor of a loyalist who had argued that international law took precedence over popularly sanctioned local jurisprudence. In 1787 Benjamin Rush wrote to Richard Price that "the same enthusiasm now pervades all classes in favor of government that actuated us in favor of liberty in the years 1774 and 1775."

THE FIRST ASPECT of America's ideological history during the War of Independence was thus the stability of Radical Whig thought, which at that time allowed neither progressivist class consciousness nor organicist reaction. The main thrust of the same history after independence was quite different. Independence, once achieved, allowed Americans to reconsider their ideological situation and to move in a direction that widened the scope of individualism as a social value.

Before the 1770s, in the prewar Radical Whig scheme of things, the power of Parliament was not feared because it protected an oppressed people from an oppressive monarch. The separation of powers, which the Whigs ordinarily acclaimed, was thought to guarantee the power of the legislature, representing the people as a whole, against the monarchic executive. In a sovereign popular state, that argument no longer applied. The object of politics shifted dramatically. The new goal of constitution makers was to protect the people's liberty against the people's own penchant for communitarian abuse. "An elective despotism," wrote Jefferson in 1782–83, "was not the government we fought for, but one which should . . . be founded on free principles . . . in which the powers of government should be so divided and balanced among several bodies of magistracy, as that no one could transcend their legal limits, without being effectually checked and restrained by the others." The separation of powers was much praised; and it was guaranteed by an intricate system of checks and balances which paradoxically allowed each branch of the government to poach on the territory of its neighbors,—a system that differed diametrically from the pattern of revolutionary republicanism in France, where in 1793–94 a single committee, more or less empowered by a dazed national Convention, monopolized all types of judicial and legislative prerogatives, including even the power of execution.

That concentration of might was reversed in America, whose distinctive institutional departure was the growing independence of the judiciary. Although the prerogatives of the courts were temporarily curtailed in the early 1780s, after 1800 the American judiciary became increasingly influential in the business of government. This basic development became in the second half of the nineteenth century what it still is today, a cardinal axiom of American constitutional practice. The American state is weak, but its courts are strong.

In 1789 Sieyès explicitly denied that the end of the state could be anything but "a unity of purpose and a concert of means." He rejected the notion that the state could become the theater of competing interests. At much the same time, Americans suddenly reversed that judgment. For many citizens of the newly independent nation, the first purpose of a vigorous national state was to defend the rights of individual citizens against the state, rather than to assert the claims of the people against injustice, whether social or political. From one end of the new country to the other, Americans dared to sing the therapeutic praise of individualism of all kinds. Washington's secretary of war, the Federalist general Henry Knox, wisely opined that Indians would not prosper until they developed "a love for exclusive property." Theoreticians of punishment reflected on the individual's responsibility for self-improvement and on the obvious merits of solitary confinement. The Puritan fathers, like Jean-Jacques Rousseau, had despised the theater. But entertainment rather than the politics of the common Good now seemed a natural outlet for American restlessness. In answer to his own question "What had been the deep cause of Shays's Rebellion?" a Philadelphian journalist replied in 1787, in a vein at once trivial and profound: "The want of theaters, dances, shows, and other public amusements."[20] The definition of virtue had changed. In the words of a recent historian of the epoch, it "more often referred to a private quality, a man's capacity to look out for himself and his dependents—almost the opposite of classical virtue."[21]

From the late 1780s on, a new and indigenous American political system pulled itself together. Its most obvious principle was nationalistic zeal, but its most important feature was the novel and ideological defense of pluralism, deeply rooted, not in theory, but in the practice and secular experience of American social life. The spirit of the Constitution of 1787 was much better aligned with the secularized and individualist genius of American culture than had been the spirit of 1776, with its socially anomalous emphasis on conspiracy, virtue, and a united people. This coming together, after independence, of cultural, social, and political principles—that is, of an individualism that was at once transcendental and materialistic, or of nationalism and pluralism—became the durable foundation of America's new civil religion and political system.

Two sets of comparisons can be made here: first, the comparison between independent America and nineteenth-century nationalistic

Europe; second, that between the new United States and the prenational, prerevolutionary American colonies.

From the beginning of the eighteenth to the middle of the nineteenth century the different peoples of Europe "nationalized" their
old dynastic and traditional loyalties. After 1789 monarchic Europe
was reshaped into an assemblage of nation-states; and in every
instance the realization of national longings was connected to some
particular form of domestic political change.

For Britain (England, Scotland, Wales, and for some time colonial America also), parliamentary liberties were an irreducible element of nationhood; the heroine of one of Mozart's operas is made
to exclaim: "Ich bin eine Engländerin zur Freiheit geboren."

Revolutionary French Jacobinism was likewise a nationalist and
a political statement. That political message was clouded because
the relationship of Jacobinism to parlimentary forms was sadly
tortured. But it did exist: Jacobinism, despite its ideological intolerance and social rigidity, uncompromisingly asserted the inalienable rights of equal individuals before the law.

German national consciousness, by contrast, was from the beginning more intrinsically conservative and corporatist than was the
French. In that profoundly religious Lutheran culture, where suspicion of Enlightenment values was already strong, national feeling
arose after 1800 in reaction to a conquering, foreign, revolutionary
nationalism. Because that hated French occupation justified itself by
reference to 1789, with its popular sovereignty, rule of reason, and
individualism in social life, these same principles became, by un-
derstandable reaction, suspect to the romantic and organicist apologists of German nationhood. In Germany, parliamentarianism,
which was indigenous to Britain and could not be ignored in
France, became a foreign artifact.

In Russian politics and culture, ephemeral and uncertain late-
nineteenth-century urban world views were stamped with a nostalgia for peasant communitarianism and a longing to recreate in
another register the ancient and Orthodox ideological fusion of
church and state.

Although every national political culture had its own variant on
the relationship between nationalist fulfillment and political
changes, that theme was constant and important. In the 1860s and

1870s a Germany without Bismarck might well have veered away from its own antiparliamentarian *Sonderweg* toward an Anglo-French model of liberal politics, but it is still true that nationalism ordinarily amplified and multiplied some other fundamental political principle, even if the results could, with luck, be appealed.

Marx gave theoretical consistency to this synthetic principle of political and national symbiosis in his appreciation of the Franco-Prussian War of 1870–71. He hoped for a German victory, which would expand the audience for Marxist doctrine at the expense of French petit-bourgeois Proudhonism. More critically and theoretically, the unification of the German state would, he thought, further German working-class consciousness, because only national independence could release its pent-up force. Political union, he argued, makes possible the crystallization of social and political principles whose preconditions have long existed but which cannot come into their own unaided.

To turn to the second comparison: in prerevolutionary America, nascent nationalism had given rare consistency to the Radical Whig ideology, while in postrevolutionary America a strengthened nationalism gave consistency to the inverse, new, indigenous, pluralist solution of the late 1780s. American nationalism deployed the particularities of the American definitions of the self and of what society should be. For the better (politically), and perhaps also for the worse (socially)—a liability that ought not to be ignored—America's new conception of what it had politically become made it possible for Americans to reconcile the various strands of their past, of self and other, in a way which the French revolutionaries were never able to achieve.

The history of eighteenth-century American politics was thus doubly ideological. In 1818 John Adams remarked that "the revolution was effected before the war commenced. The revolution was in the minds and hearts of the people." Radical Whig ideology, in other words, had predisposed Americans to revolt. In a second phase, during the 1780s, maieutic nationalism furthered yet another new politics, pluralistic but still messianic and exemplary. From first to last, during this formative period of America's modern history, ideology was the Ariadne's thread of politics.

To understand America's postwar trajectory, one must therefore

keep in mind the rapid growth of American national sentiment after
1776. Britain, which had been a mother, became a malicious step-
mother; and the king became a failed father. Britain's loss was
America's great gain: Americans were moral, and the British were
immoral and corrupt. Independence further widened that happy
perception. In the mid-1770s, Washington the Virginian wrote
home that Yankees were "an exceeding dirty and nasty people." In
the 1780s, Washington the American would not have written anything of the kind. The common experience of the war against
Britain was crucial: the officer corps of Washington's Continental
army sustained that same sense of revolutionary fraternity (sharpened no doubt by the indifference and greed of many American
civilians) which was to be an important feature of French revolutionary sensibility. Of the fifty-five delegates who met at Philadelphia to draft the Constitution of the United States, twenty-one had
been officers during the War of Independence. With surprising
speed Americans after 1776 acquired that growing sense of nation
which soon became notorious and offensive to many Europeans
and Latin Americans. Contemporary American histories of the period reveal this new self-awareness in their very method: the explanation of events is given no longer in terms of providence but of
fate. Though much influenced by both Renaissance Palladianism
and modern French architecture, Jefferson designed Monticello less
as an aristocratic villa than as a monumental farmhouse worthy of
America's democratic greatness.[22] In a similar fashion, but quite
tragically, the parallel war which Americans of British origin fought
against Britain's allies, the American Indians, also became a formative, nationalizing experience: it is bitterly ironic that the creation of
American nationhood presupposed the physical destruction of native American peoples. Countless massacres, ranging from the defeat inflicted by the Pilgrims on the Pequots in 1637 to the Battle of
Fallen Timbers in 1795, parallel the development of a specifically
Anglo-American consciousness.

Having acquired a dramatic new sense of self, Americans, in John
Adams's words, could envisage the course of their country's recent
history as "the history of mankind during that epoch." Their renewed vision enabled them to modulate their country's previously
dominant political ideology. Now they could take into ideological

account those material realities and possibilities of American social and economic life which as a colonial people they had steadfastly ignored. Although war had not been able to affect the imperviousness of Radical Whig ideology, independence easily did so.

Americans who had in theory been persistently suspicious of trade and commerce discovered that these modern forms, which had of course been a part of their day-to-day lives for more than a century, were not so conceptually detestable as they had once supposed. While the French Jacobins remained adamant ruralists, hostile to finance and industry, even learned American gentlemen gradually accepted after 1780 the prospect of deep-seated material and social change. "At the expiration of twenty five years hence," explained Madison in 1788, "I conceive that, in every part of the United States, there will be so great a population as there is now in the settled parts. We see, already, that, in the most populous parts of the Union, and where there is but a medium, manufactures are beginning to be established."

Americans also pondered in a different light the eighteenth-century topos of aging societies, present in works as varied as those of Adam Smith and Jean-Jacques Rousseau. Nations, like individuals, they knew, aged and changed. But America, they now suddenly understood, was growing and not declining. America, which had been a nation of virtuous farmers, was about to become an unprecedentedly virtuous and commercial republic, which was surely no disgrace. Rural prosperity required an expansion of America's role in world trade. The Radical Whigs and the Puritan fathers had—in theory—despised commerce because it quickened greed, as many of them no doubt knew from firsthand experience: John Adams had reflected in 1776 that "the spirit of commerce corrupts the morals of families."[23] In the late 1780s, however, commerce was much more often praised. Developed and complex industry, the growth of which implied the same division of labor whose consequences the benevolent Adam Smith had feared, was still redoubtable; but domestic industries were wholly different: "[To] the fair daughters of Columbia," a gallant and practical orator called out to the citizenesses of Petersburg, Virginia, on the Fourth of July 1809, "may their manufactures (if possible) exceed their beauty." New times, it seemed, required strikingly new thoughts. Just as the ideology of the prerevolutionary Radical Whigs had adjusted to obvious need and taken account of British political corruption, so did American republicans in the 1780s come to grips with the maturation of their own society. Proximate equality of condition as a social goal was transmuted into individualist equality of opportunity. In the realm of rhetoric, satire (which appeals to shared norms) gave way to invective, a medium that was more appropriate to the needs of a vigorous and individuated culture.

Even Jefferson in the years to come would reverse "the priorities implicit in the classical tradition"[24]—or some of them, at any rate. In 1776 Jefferson had been a Lockean of a kind, but like many other slave-owning Virginian planters he was also in those early years a "moral sentimentalist" whose first concern was sociability and republican fraternity (for whites). Where Sieyès was to find in Adam Smith's views on the division of labor a justification of the separation between the passive voters and their active elected officials, Jefferson had found in Smith an apologist of republican and martial virtue. In 1790 Jefferson thought better of Locke: "[His] little book on government," he remarked (somewhat ambiguously, it is true), "is perfect as far as it goes."[25] Jefferson's economic views also shifted in later years: his continued advocacy of yeoman farming was in the ideological tradition of Radical Whig thinking; but his frank acceptance of western expansionism (which he ought to have disliked since it empowered the nation rather than its constituent states) and his endorsement of commercialized agriculture were novel. Jefferson looked forward to higher standards of living for everyone, in both America and Europe. The new wealth of richer American farmers would trickle down and increase the wealth of European artisans as well. Rising food prices would not make Americans more corrupt but more prosperous and more cultivated. A new, evolutionary view of economic and social forms justified these shifts, whose profound cause was a desire to adapt ideological stance to practical reality.

THE DEBATE ON the ratification of the Constitution can be fruitfully considered in this same context of unfolding political and cultural logics. Among its elements are the particularly American and changing definitions of the self and of the rights of others. Its conclusion elaborated a new compromise between those two statements, an unprecedented synthesis that was greatly furthered by a soaring American sense of nation.

The Articles of Confederation that had been drafted between 1777 and 1781 were in terms of structure, obsolete at the moment of conception. Because they had been drawn up in reaction to the centralism of the British Empire, the Articles were incompletely nationalistic—less the charter of a national government than (in its own words) "a firm league of friendship" among sovereign partners, where ultimate authority remained vested in the individual states. The national Congress had little to say about either taxation or the regulation of commerce. Ratification of the founding text, like the modification of its parts, required the unanimous approval of the states. Without an executive, without the power to raise taxes or an army, without even a fixed capital as it wandered, unloved, from Philadelphia to Princeton, Annapolis, Trenton, or New York, the Congress could not do much. It simply watched as crop prices fell and international trade stagnated. In some states, creditors did all they could to avoid their debtors, understandably eager to pay them back in depreciated paper currency. Unpaid army officers considered the merits of a military coup. Local factionalism seemed to be the essence of local politics. Economic nationalists, such as Robert Morris, who tried to restore payments in gold and who urged Congress to charter a national bank, decided that these material goals could not be reached in the fragmented context of confederation. Even such a defender of states rights as Madison concluded that local sovereignties and civil liberties could only be durably maintained within the larger context of a national and federated state. In effect, as nearly everyone agreed, the Articles of Confederation needed to be revised.

These practical shortcomings grated less because of their intrinsic nature, however, than because they appeared as affronts to the American vision of a "natural" political order and as insults to the new nation's sense of self. For some Americans at least, the Articles of Confederation were an embarrassing national statement that could no longer be allowed. Americans were deeply anxious on this score. Even such a manifestly social travail as Shays's Rebellion was interpreted as a sign of national decadence. Real institutional and

economic problems did exist between 1781 and 1787 as they had in
the early 1770s, but they loomed particularly large in men's minds
because they were given new currency by changing perceptions of
nation and of politics.

Charles Beard, in one of the most celebrated books on American
history, argued in 1913 that the constitution of 1787 was a betrayal of
the principles of independence. In a *marxisant* and materialist mode,
Beard explained that the achievement of 1787—as against that of
1776 —was the handiwork of rich, antidemocratic men, their pockets stuffed with federal notes to be redeemed at a high price.

On the face of it, Beard was right to argue that federalists (mis-
named, since the federalists were actually the nationalistic advocates
of a stronger, if federal, central government) were often rich and
antifederalist states' righters were often poor. In the larger sense,
however, his argument was off the mark. Plain greed mattered much
less than the logic of America's new and ongoing political culture in
its relationship to new and commercialized social forms. Everywhere
in the North Atlantic world, the drift of political and economic
change in the late eighteenth century was toward the construction of
new and centralized nation-states that would guarantee the assertion
of individualism in political and economic life. As Hamilton wrote
in *Federalist* 8, the industrious habits of contemporaries, absorbed "in
the pursuits of gain and devoted to the improvements of agriculture
and commerce, are incompatible with the condition of a nation of
soldiers, which was the true condition of the people [of the ancient
republics of Greece]." National parliaments that expressed popular
sovereignty, like national free-trade zones that facilitated capitalist
economic growth, went hand in hand with individualistic statements
on the rights of men. Beard's economic explanation is not incorrect,
but it is too literal and narrow to be entirely correct.

Revealingly, the grass-roots opponents of the new federal system
were often self-sufficient farmers not heavily engaged in a market
economy. The strongest supporters of the new arrangements were
city merchants and professionals. The more that Americans were
involved in what can be described as a typically American economic
and social situation, the more they favored change toward a more
nationalistic and more pluralistic state. It is certainly relevant that
such people were richer than their opponents. Nonetheless, per-

sonal wealth, like place of residence (most antifederalists lived inland), was less specifically determining than was involvement in a modern sociological and cultural context of commercial exchange.

Judging by their rate of absenteeism at the polls, most Americans were indifferent to the whole issue. Among those who did care and who were ideologically articulate, federalism easily won the day. The new politics, however, was quite hard on those whose place in the market economy was weak: in 1786 the rebellion of Shays's two thousand indebted and embattled farmers in eastern Massachusetts revealed the extent of that unease. But ultimately, because antifederalism could not invoke counterprinciples other than those of pure and obsolescent Radical Whig ideology, Shays's Rebellion, like the protests of rebellious Pennsylvania whiskey distillers or the efforts of the antifederalists generally, could not be sustained. The transformative capacity of the new federalist ethos was awesome: Samuel Adams (much admired by Brissot), a voluntarily poor man, an American Robespierre who prided himself on his innocence and virtue, had no patience with Shays's men and may even have wanted them to be hung.

The historical task of the federalists in 1787 was to adapt the general impulses of a capitalistic age—more or less as Beard suggested—to the varied particularities of America's cultural past and present. "In a large Society," wrote Madison, "the people are broken into so many interests and parties, that a common sentiment is less likely to be felt, and the requisite concert less likely to be formed by a majority of the whole." The problem of politics, he concluded, was to accept this fact—which, as it happens, had been true in America for nearly a century—and to work from it toward the creation of a republican consensus that would not deny America's communitarian antecedents.

The true originality, and the real source, of the secular resilience of the federalist solution was that this futuristic "bourgeois" doctrine did not ignore America's prenational, Whig, and religiously visionary past. The nationalists withdrew a proposal that would have enabled Congress to veto the legislation of the states. The new arrangements did not betray America's tradition of grass-roots government. The aim of the Republic ultimately proved to be, in Madison's words, to "support a due supremacy of national authority, and leave in force the local authorities so far as they can be subordinately useful." John Jay rightly presented the new national state as no more than another element in a long chain of governance. It would stand in relation to the thirteen states "in the same light in which counties stand to the State, of which they are a part, viz., merely as districts to facilitate the purposes of domestic order and good government." The federalists accepted the idea that each state would send two delegates to the Senate, regardless of size or population, a striking concession to localism that was wrongly taken by the nationalists to be a catastrophic defeat. Thanks to that supposed reverse, American republicanism became a broader umbrella and a more popular "universe of discourse," an open-ended populist myth rather than a prescriptive, abstract, and centralizing faith, as was true to French Jacobinism. What the nationalists thought to be the American Constitution's theoretical weakness proved to be its strength in practice, whether considered from their own nationalist perspective or from that of the democratic, localist antifederalists. Localists also misread initially what was to be their greatest asset, namely, that their popular base in the states could henceforth find a more convincing political embodiment at the higher and more universalist level of the nation.

In the late 1780s the antifederalists, fixated as they were on the political culture of the Old Whigs, found themselves hanging in a void. Pathetically, they invoked the reality of localism and the Whiggish image of a golden past. Their case had undeniable American relevance. As one antifederalist put it, why should Americans who had fought against "the iron yoke of British bondage" be so foolish as to bend their "necks to as heavy a one of our own make." Cato was even more explicit: we Americans had not thrown "off the yoke of Britain and called ourselves independent [to] let the rich and insolent be our rulers." But in the new context of nationalistic, cultural independence, localistic antifederalism was no longer a viable political principle. Great men who had risen to fame in the earlier rhetorical context of Radical Whig thinking found it hard to transcend the words that had brought them to prominence ten years before. This difficulty is easily understood: after more than half a century of ideological immobility, it was difficult for them to understand that after independence change had finally become the rule of American public culture, as it had been the rule of its social and economic life for more than a hundred years. John Dickinson, who had been a hero in 1768, fell from public favor when he timorously refused a few years later to sign the Declaration of Independence; and he fell out of step a second time in 1786 as a belated devotee of states' rights. He ought to have pondered more deeply the message of his own words: "Experience must be our only guide. Reason may mislead us." The vagaries of personal biographies had great relevance to the evolution—or immobility—of political postures. Foresighted men such as Madison understood that in the changing context of the time their goals could not be fixed things. Less subtle minds were unable to make the turn.

The new American federal political system was Janus-faced. Though basically modern, since it welcomed the individuating and commercial forms typical of the nineteenth century, it also subsumed important aspects of America's ideological legacies. This blend of old and new did not occur as the architects of the new regime expected. Madison, the chief author of the *Federalist Papers*,[26] still hoped to assert solidarity as a social and political principle. Because he feared the selfish, local factionalism of state governments, Madison reasoned, with striking originality, that in a large nation the petty passions of the states would necessarily cancel each other out. But the new regime, he also thought, would bring to the fore enlightened men who did not care about themselves but who loved the public good and had "the most attractive merit and most diffusive and established character." Hamilton likewise hoped that the professions might be a breeding ground for disinterested umpires who would rise above the fray of sectarian interests and fly the flag of higher values. He also failed to understand the connection between the rights of the individual and the rights of the American nation-state. It is a striking anomaly that a bill of (individual) rights saw the light of day only as an addition to the (national) Constitution rather than as a constituent part of it. It took vision to understand the new structuring categories of society and politics that were only then coming into being. Their initial incomprehensibility reveals that the inner logic of American politics was by no means obvious, even to those who most desired its fulfillment. History has many ruses.

And just as individualism and nationalism were unanticipatedly convergent, so did communitarian sensibilities survive in unexpected ways. The new political system was consensual rather than confrontational. This implied that the poor would have some right to be heard. The public good might be achieved in various ways: by good men in the Madisonian calm of their book-lined studies; or by cynical politicians in smoke-filled rooms; or, intermediately, by rich and calculating men, such as the celebrated John Hancock, who decided to use their wealth—or their flamboyant signatures—to secure visible public fame. It would in any case be a freely accepted social value that was to be above bitter factional desires.

Americans were to be one people united by common devotion to a single moral and political principle rather than by their place of residence, religion, or material interest. Popular sovereignty and direct representation—the two key concepts which structured the North Atlantic republican myth at that historic moment—were irrevocably inscribed in the American Constitution. As James Wilson explained, the Constitution was "in its principle . . . purely democratical," and he compared America with a pyramid (which still appears on a one dollar bill) whose stability depended on the breadth of its foundation.

The concept of popular, national sovereignty had many effects in America. In Britain, even for liberals, the shape of government referred to what Milton had called the "known rules of ancient liberty." In America, the spirit of politics and the text of the Constitution referred to the people's changing will rather than to some fixed historicist tradition. Jefferson ingeniously calculated that laws should lapse every nineteen years, when a new generation of citizens came into its own. The transformed and "revolutionized" practice of American politics was also maintained: politicians thought it normal to refer their decisions to the people, and "out-of-doors" politics become a way of life. The first decades of national independence also witnessed a great burst of state-sponsored economic projects, many of them carried out in the name of the public good. Typical, finally, of the blend of "virtue" and capitalism was the fate of proposed restrictions on the actions of legislators during the recasting of state constitutions: restraints on the economic activity of legislators were rejected, but plural officeholding was successfully curtailed.[27] In many concrete ways, the agenda of American republicanism remained democratically significant. American government, in the words of Lincoln, was "dedicated to a proposition." The intent of the founders was to redefine republican liberty in terms of personal autonomy. Their goal was not to license abuse. The Constitution asserted the principle of an American citizenship, which the Articles of Confederation had not developed. The Radical Whig's minimalist definition of the state, though not abandoned, was changed. The new federal state was an active, supraregional entity, the likes of which the signers of the Declaration of Independence had certainly not envisaged. Unlike colonial governors, the elected president of the new Republic was not hobbled by a council of notables. Members of the cabinet held their places at his pleasure. The president was an elected official, chosen by the people, albeit indirectly. His term of office was brief. Foreign titles were not recognized by American republican law, a derisory detail today but an important point at the time, as Napoleon realized when he relegalized the use of titles in France, a practice that the French republics of the nineteenth century did not dare to undo.

It has also been suggested that Madison and Jefferson were content to create a system of institutions designed basically to check the despotic side of popular sovereignty because they tacitly assumed that civic republicanism was deeply embedded in American civil society. They were seemingly unconcerned about creating institutions that would enable their audience of supposedly republican yeoman to reshape civil society through politics, because they did not think this was their first task. They presumably assumed, in the words spoken by some New England ministers in 1787, that "the spirit of true republican government may universally pervade the citizens of the United States."[28] Hostility to government of any kind was, after all, a historically sanctioned attitude for a formerly colonialized people, and one which Americans shared with another British and provincial nation, that of the Scots. For Madison it was enough, therefore, to reassert the principle of national popular sovereignty rather than to spell out the way in which it would be applied. The limiting case of this conjectural type of argument is to propose that the founders did not discuss the problem of slavery, which we know they despised, because they knew that they could do nothing to put an end to it.

In the context of the times—as the founders fully understood— the democratic, popular, and egalitarian aspects of American pluralism were anomalously striking. We cannot judge eighteenth-century Americans merely by the standards of equality and justice that prevail in our own time. What matters more is that, in 1787, most Russians were still serfs to be bought and sold; that Louis XVI still ruled by divine right in a country where Protestants had just acquired the legal right to worship publicly; and that most Englishmen were disenfranchised both politically, in the name of an inherited constitution, and economically, by market forces that were no longer checked by law.

In short, the republican spirit of 1776 was transformed but not abandoned. Many of the founders—including Madison—were directly or indirectly familiar with Hume's empirical theory of morals. In that view, virtue was a mere label attached by moralizing mankind to satisfying rules. But the founders understood that startling and empirical message democratically. Federalist republicans took up Hume's mechanistic challenge and strove to elaborate a systemic set of rules which would allow the blossoming of public virtues in the uncertain soil of modern times. For the founders, a thirst for vainglorious fame might have virtuous results if properly framed by an appropriate constitution.

We can safely assume that most Americans had not read Hume. But the blend of old and new, of transcendence and materialism, which the more learned founders understood in terms derived from high culture—and in ways that have fascinated many historians of the period—was apprehended no less efficaciously by many humbler Americans who experienced it in their daily work and thoughts.

THE TRIUMPH OF AMERICA'S national federalism was soon complete. Within months, public opinion rallied to a document that had been elaborated by delegates who had labored and argued for months without a clear mandate, in closed (and almost concealed) session. Though public debates on the proposed Constitution had initially been fierce, opposition to the new system essentially fell away. It was "a miracle," wrote Washington in January 1790, "that there should have been so much unanimity, in points of such importance, among such a number of citizens, so widely scattered and so different in their interests." In 1794 the Federalists gave thought to running as their candidate for the presidency Patrick Henry, perhaps the most notorious of the antifederalists of 1787, a man who had refused to attend the Philadelphia convention because he had "smelt a rat."

By contrast, the personal success of the Federalist statesmen within the new institutional arrangement of their own creation was ephemeral. Rates of incumbency for elected politicians were lower after the Revolution than they had been in the decades that preceded it. Embedded as it was in an imaginative definition of popular sovereignty, the new American cultural and political system evolved ceaselessly, surprising one entrenched group after another. The Federalists had naively assumed that ensconced hierarchies of talent and wealth might subsist unchanged. This was to misread the restless dimension of the American self, tempered now by the universalist principles of the new Republic. The Federalists were shocked when the principles of nationalistic, Republican individualism which they had used against antifederalists were invoked against them in turn. The relentless flow of American culture and society required once more in the 1790s, as it had in the 1780s, an agility and capacity for adaptation which many men could not summon.

In 1800 the American political system was still incomplete. The informal institutionalization of competing political parties remained to be accomplished. One formal institutional task was also unfinished, namely, the elevation of the judiciary as the balancing mechanism of the new arrangement, but this denouement was already fated at the time of Jefferson's inauguration (to that president's ensuing dismay). Though this was not yet completely apparent, the strength of the American governmental system and of popular sovereignty would not rest in an appointed, centralized, national bureaucracy, such as Robert Morris had hoped for in the 1780s, but more informally in a national system of courts that were at once hierarchized and decentralized, powerful though not elected, but mindful also of local and minority interests. By accepting the federalist and national context of politics, Jeffersonian Republicans were able to complete the edifice of the American state. This was their first historical achievement.

Jefferson's second historical assignment was to bring together, in theory at least, the full possibilities of this new American synthesis by grounding the variously Whiggish, enlightened, democratic, naturalistic, and heretofore revolutionary egalitarianism on a more modest but firmer and more indigenous foundation. In the late 1790s the Republicans outflanked the Federalists on the left, just as the Radical Whigs had been short-circuited on the right by the Federalists ten years before. Although the Jeffersonians were required to function within an individualist and pluralist system that was not of their creation, they were by 1800 better situated than their Federalist rivals to use it to the full. The Jeffersonian Republicans proved more mindful of America's localist and communitarian past than the Federalists—and more pragmatic as well. Where Washington—backward-looking in this respect at least—denounced the "self-created societies" which, he thought, were behind the Whiskey Rebellion, Jeffersonian democrats found in themselves the desire to invoke the new principles of the federal Constitution which they had recently opposed: "Are not all private associations established on the foundation of their authority," they asked, "an authority sanctioned by the first principles of social life and guaranteed by the spirit of laws?"[29]

The self-conscious imitations of French republicanism (trivially done by using "fellow citizen" as a term of address, or by dating letters from "the eighteenth year of American Independence") were soon abandoned. But there was no stopping the ideological assertion of egalitarian individualism and of the frontiersman's populist rejection of established wealth. A Jeffersonian and republican sensibility, at once localist and universalist, become a permanent feature of the American political landscape. Republican virtue paradoxically became the handmaiden of democratic, individualist meritocracy. With great ups and downs, to be sure, that mixed spirit has survived as an essential part of America's vigorous political and civic culture.

It is that same republican principle, albeit ceaselessly transformed, whose continued acceptance explains the enthusiasm that Lincoln would arouse in intellectuals like Whitman and Emerson, and, less certainly, in us today. The American system of the 1780s remained in the mid-nineteenth century a genuinely transformative force that harnessed private energies for public good. At a time roughly contemporaneous with the destruction of the Paris Commune, the abolition of slavery, during the bloodiest conflict in the nineteenth-century north Atlantic world, was proof of America's sustained democratic vitality.

The federalist solution of 1787, democratized by Jeffersonian Republicans, in 1801 brought to its political conclusion the revolutionary denouement of America's first 150 years. A unique political culture came into being whose roots were simultaneously in America's savagely privatist, localist economic past and in its republican, universalist and neo-religious yearning to be an exemplary social and political community as well.

As compared with America, the gap in France, during the years from 1789 to 1794, would be much wider between the narrowly defined possessive individualism of the elite and the demanding communitarian sensibility of the poor, whose culture had been structured by centuries of corporate existence. In America, a transcendental vision of the self, whose origin lay in dissenting Protestant and Puritan thinking, easily took into account the notion that the self might find fulfillment in the larger social whole: "Ambition in a Republic," John Adams wrote prophetically in 1777, "is but another Name for . . . Virtue."

At the same time, the American definitions of both private and public good had—and still have—many troubling implications. The temptation of political stasis in America was very strong. A more realistic appreciation of economic fact could easily lead to the resigned acceptance of whatever social forms uncontrolled economic and technological change might produce. More crippling yet, the nationalist and secularized vision of God's chosen people blessed with a manifest destiny could easily lead Americans, corrupted by economic good fortune, to suppose that their fortuitous social forms were ideologically and even religiously immanent. Protestants of the Jacksonian industrializing era were particularly prone to confuse national purpose with national religion and to see the American nation in its current social form as the first agent of God's will for mankind. Radicals might sometimes find an audience when they argued that America's social forms should remain fraternal and worthy of its exemplary past; but this same secularized neo-religious sense, compounded by revolutionary Americans' sense of their exceptional political destiny, could just as easily be twisted to some immobilist, self-satisfied purpose. It was tempting for Federalists after 1787 and Republicans after 1801 to suppose that their society was, in the main, organically mature in its current forms. Jefferson's Republicans were quick to suppose that the fears of decadence which they had previously entertained could be avoided if American society moved not toward corruption through time but through space toward ever more abundant and uncorrupting western farm lands. Nearly from the first, America's Puritan-born identity had Pharisaic and aggressive implications. Slavery was accepted by Jefferson's Republicans as a temporarily inevitable fact of American social life: the sustained public and private incoherence of John Randolph of Roanoke, magnified by a revived religiosity, bore witness to the southern planters' anguished desire to reconcile a legacy of Republican virtue with the continued practice of slavery in an epoch when the principle of slavery had everywhere become the antithesis of virtue.

A simultaneously gratifying and ominous contrast can be drawn between politics in the France of Napoleon and politics in the Republic of President Jefferson, between French and American patterns of thought as they had been engendered by revolution and had become embedded in the political cultures of the two countries.

Ostensibly, Bonaparte's politics was infinitely vicious: the emperor was obsessed by the problem of political manipulation. To that end, he bribed the poor in Paris with cheap food, the rich with titles and decorations, and the nation as a whole with military conquests. His legal, educational, religious, and administrative systems were invariably concerned with the maintenance of undisputed hierarchic order. His legal code—vestigially extant today in Louisiana, which became an American possession only in 1804—associated women with minors and employees, whose social existence was defined in terms of property, a reduction that was an unwitting parody of the already constraining, misogynist individualism of the Jacobins. Incessant war was for the emperor a method of social control that allowed the perpetuation of a repressive governance which the French possessing class increasingly resented. As Mme de Staël so aptly put it, Napoleon was Robespierre on horseback.

Jefferson inverted the patterns of Napoleonic rule. His goal as president was ostensibly the pacific empowerment of the simple man. Where Napoleon provoked all of his neighbors in turn, and finally all of them at once, Jefferson's Republicans seriously considered the abolition of America's rather ephemeral military establishment. The more fundamental implication of America's republican political culture as Jefferson practiced it, however, was far less encouraging. Implicit in Napoleon's statecraft was the principle, fundamental to French political culture, that politics could reshape social forms. Politics in Jefferson's New World was by contrast an end in itself rather than a means for social change. The election of 1800 aroused consternation in New England and New York, but ultimately Jefferson's politics came to very little. Ironically, even Hamilton had a more positive view of the role of government. Both Madison and Saint-Just had called for a drastic reduction in the number of laws, but only in America was this principle applied. It may even be supposed that the reconciliation of America's two divergent traditions of government, republican communitarianism and Lockean individualistic liberalism, required that they be set in the larger context of minimalist Jeffersonian and Jacksonian government. The practical conclusion of Jefferson's empowered, moralistic, and republican rhetoric was not the greater enfranchisement of the poor, but social stasis and the sad beginning of the American spoils system, the "thirst for offices." It was not as an agency for democratic social change that the Democratic Tammany Society of New York was to find its niche in historical lore.

Republican democrats after Jefferson reacted passively to the abuses of industrialism, as their predecessors had reacted passively to the emergence of commercialism in the 1790s and 1800s. During the 1790s many prominent members of the Democratic-Republican societies had been abolitionists, but during the administration of Jefferson, who genuinely detested the "peculiar institution," slavery was left essentially untouched, even if the importation of new slaves was declared illegal. Jefferson's reflections on the natural inferiority of blacks make for painful reading.

His great governmental aim proved to be no more than the suppression of supposed Federalist "monarchic conspiracies," as Jackson's aim would be to overcome the supposed "politics of privilege."[30] "The path we have to pursue is so quiet," wrote Jefferson to one of his correspondents in 1802, " that we have nothing scarcely to propose to our Legislature . . . If we can prevent the government from wasting the labors of the people under the pretence of taking care of them, they must become happy." Jacksonian thought did not innovate when it presented as self-evident the natural connection between this kind of nongovernment and popular democracy. The repressive effects of French Jacobinism are easy to perceive. Those of American republicanism are harder to identify, but they should not be ignored.

SOME RECENT HISTORIANS of eighteenth-century colonial America have been even more pessimistic in their appraisal of America's Jeffersonian tradition. Their argument has focused less on the limits of America's exceptionalist, republican-individualist tradition than on the supposed existence of a more popular alternative to that system. On the hidden agenda of these neo-Marxist historians was a compelling and presentist purpose inspired by the work of E. P. Thompson. Their aim, at once learned and political, was to establish the existence of a subterranean thread that would link a pre-industrial revolutionary social consciousness to some modern force that would in turn lever transformative change in America today.

Without doubt, their radical inquiries have been fruitful in a material sense: it is now clear that in eighteenth-century America the gap between the rich and the poor was greater than had been thought; that poor whites despised eastern planters; that farmers in western Massachusetts bitterly resented the institutional and fiscal advantages of wealthy merchants both before and after the Revolution. But the neo-Marxist historians have not succeeded in making generally valid statements that prove the existence, in either colonial or revolutionary America, of a consciousness of class, of a particularist sense of solidarity which might be politicized. They have not shown that the rich had acquired a sense of class which legitimized, even in their own eyes, some right to rule, or that the poor had acquired the ideological ability to assert their existence as a separate class in the body social.

Implied in this double failure is a reminder that American political culture as it emerged in the crucible of its Revolution was decidedly consensual. America's democratic legacy, as is still the case today, only allows frustratingly *limited* transformations of society through politics, and those, only if the call for them is set within a national framework that ignores and at times vigorously *denies* the concept of social class. "The American genius," wrote the despairing and perspicacious Orestes Brownson, "is republican as opposed to monarchical, but it is not democratic." American radicalism has not fluctuated with the ebb and tide of class consciousness. It is the limited strength of America's republican nostalgia that feeds its capacity for social justice. American reformism moves with the uncertain imagination of the American scholar and the American worker, with the intensity of the nation's secularized, neo-religious, and moralized civil anger, both learned and populist.

Because America's revolutionary and communitarian ideological past was a living memory, its thirst for betterment might suddenly be stirred: "Tho' obscured," wrote the optimistic William Blake about America, "this is the form of the Angelic land." At the same time, an intensely troubling paradox underscores American political culture, a paradox rooted in the genesis of the new American political system which came to life in the last decades of the eighteenth century. The organicist perception of American nationhood, of postrevolutionary America's sense of self, often neutralizes the republican nostalgia, civil and political, which too was America's birthright. American democracy as defined by the Founding Fathers, by Madison and Jefferson and their democratic successors— here the myth of Lincoln again comes to mind—has been a powerful but uncertain weapon.

6

Possessive Individualism or Determining Community in the French Revolution

THE STANDARD HISTORICAL periodization of the French Revolution follows the rhythm of the revolutionary days, the Parisian insurrections—most of them popular in origin—that successively toppled "absolute" monarchy in the summer of 1789, constitutional monarchy on 10 August 1792, constitutional Girondin republicanism in May-June 1793, and dictatorial republicanism in July 1794, with Robespierre's execution. In the second phase, from 1794 to 1799, the story ordinarily focuses on the apparent consolidation and eventual collapse amid general indifference of the centrist republican regime commonly associated with the name of Sieyès. The key events are thought to be the unsuccessful coup of the Babouvist "communist" left in 1796, followed by the two momentarily successful coups staged by the centrists themselves, first against the right-wing republicans in September 1797 and next against the left-wing republicans in 1799. The story ends with General Bonaparte's overthrow of all parliamentary groups on 18 brumaire (November 1799).

Thematically, however, the history of the Revolution is best divided in a different way. The first and least complicated phase of this drama centers on the collapse of the corporatist and organicist ancien régime between 1786 and 1789. The storming of the Bastille on July 14, 1789, was its high point. Second, from 1789 to late 1793, comes the ever more unstable politics of a basically individualist-minded possessing elite that was nonetheless ideologically universalist and, as such, eager to rule for and with the people. After 1790 especially, these were the years of the Jacobins, whose universalism, sincerely expressed at first, gradually became a mask for their self-serving defense of private property. This period concluded with Robespierre's change of course and his subjugation of the popular movement between November 1793 and March 1794—a critical change of heart that deserves more attention than many historians have given it. The triumph of the Mountain (or left-wing Jacobins) over the Gironde (or right-wing Jacobins), thanks to the help of the Paris crowd, in May-June 1793 was the high point of this second wave.

The third period, from 1794 onward, exacerbated the growing contradictions of the previous phase. The Directory (1795-1799) was in fact the tool of a consciously and even aggressively propertied and falsely universalist elite. These friends of Sieyès were, it is true, vestigially and rhetorically progressive in their ideology. But because their fear of the poor had made them stridently conservative in their social practice, these men were without any illusions about their ability to govern popularly, in any sense of that word. The Jacobins of the earlier 1789–1794 period had intended—at first, at least—to reconcile their particularist defense of property with the universalist and popular principle of revolutionary republicanism. But the universalism of the Directory was soon understood to be a sham. The words of Sieyès in 1799 were the same as those he had spoken in 1789, yet their social meaning was completely different. Though the Directory has been relatively little studied, it is a highly interesting political system which must be understood as the culmination rather than the negation of the revolutionary Jacobinism of 1793–94.

THE POLITICS OF the pre-Revolution began in the summer of 1786, when the minister of finance explained to the monarch that the French state could no longer pay its way. Though appointed as a court favorite, Charles de Calonne understood that no alternative existed to a major institutional overhaul. In February 1787 he called together an appointed Assembly of Notables that would, he hoped, support his program of enlightened despotism, that is to say, of reform from above. The stakes were high. In the short run, Calonne's aim was to raise state revenue, as a result of the voluntary abolition of traditional fiscal and corporate privilege. Over the long run, Calonne's decision implied that the monarchy would henceforth govern with the consent or at least the advice of the possessing and enlightened elite that included rich bourgeois and politically liberal aristocrats.

What shape this program would have in practice, no one knew. It was generally agreed that some consultative mechanism would emerge, but no one solution seemed obvious either to the crown and its servants or to enlightened opinion. After the failure of Turgot in 1776, an absolutist solution of the Prussian kind was no longer feasible. (It was only the failure of the French Revolution that made Napoleonic rule possible.) A revived corporatist state also seemed out of the question in the 1780s, so discredited were the extant corporate structures. The historical choice of the French before the Revolution was between a determining, universalist, or even egalitarian state embodying Rousseau's ideas and a mixed system, based on the English model, combining monarchic prerogative and individualist, capitalist, and parliamentary principles. Support for the first of these two options was at first very narrow, even though the prestige of the second (English parliamentary institutions) was lower in the 1780s than it had been before.

In any event, the Assembly of Notables soon foundered, partly because of Calonne's overbearing mannner. The privileged deputies refused to do much. Having little sense that the ancien régime of which they were a part was coming to an end, they spoke fair words but stood their privileged ground. They referred to a deceptive pamphlet written by Necker, the former minister of finance, who claimed that the government's financial situation was not so bad as all that; and they refused to pay. What was to be done? Propertied public opinion, both noble and non-noble, rallied to the idea of calling together the Estates General, an assembly that was archaically organized on the traditionalist principle of corporate representation but was the closest thing to a deliberative body that could be found in the unwritten "constitution" of the French ancien régime.

Judging from the contents of some of the sixty thousand cahiers de doléances, or grievance books, which were completed in preparation for the meeting of the estates by corps of all kinds, ranging from women's economic corporations to provincial assemblies of churchmen and nobles, some arrangement ought to have been possible between the crown and the elite. Many of the noble cahiers were politically more open-ended than those of the Third Estate. Most nobles supported voting by head in the meeting of the three estates (the politically liberal solution) as against voting by estates (the conservatives' great hope). Aristocratic cahiers regularly condemned royal and ministerial "absolutism." Many of them demanded the abolition of the lettres de cachet, or orders of arbitrary detention. Censorship was widely and bitterly criticized. Nobles and royal functionaries alike, it seemed, understood by 1787–88 that the need to institutionalize meritocratic individualism was real. Similarly, most non-noble spokesmen saw the need for compromise, even if the thin end of a politically intolerant and excluding wedge was already embedded in their constitutionalist and parliamentary pronouncements. In 1789 the possessing "bourgeois" elite still deferred to the monarchy, and for some months Louis XVI, the "restorer of French liberties," was wildly popular. Not a single cahier of the Third Estate suggested that France might do without a nobility, and everyone agreed to the desirability of nobility when taken as an honorific order.

The crown, had it availed itself of this era of good feelings, might have avoided institutional chaos if it had resolutely embraced a policy of parliamentary and constitutional monarchy. Louis and Necker might have turned the corner had they revived, in a more flexible context, Turgot's economic and social program of possessive individualism and rationalist reform. Louis could not go on as an absolute monarch, but he might have survived as a "patriot king."

It was urgent that the monarchy should act. Even in these halcyon days, consensus was far from general. Although everyone agreed that the nobles' fiscal exemptions would have to stop, disagreement soon followed. There was much noble foot-dragging on how many deputies each estate would have. Not surprisingly, the aristocratic Paris parlement recommended in September 1788 that the assembled estates should vote separately and that each estate should have as many deputies as it had had in 1614, when the Estates General had last been called. Each non-noble would be matched by one noble and one cleric. In consequence of this reactionary, self-seeking ruling, the popularity that the aristocratic, parlementaires, in their deceptive guise as opponents of "ministerial despotism," had secured during the preceding half century vanished overnight.

Unfortunately, when the estates met in May 1789, these issues of representation had not yet been conclusively arbitrated by Necker, once again in power as the replacement for the discredited Calonne. Necker decided to allow the Third Estate as many deputies as the first two orders combined, but voting would still be by Estates. This was a bastard solution that made no sense at all and was politically dangerous. Implicit in its various clauses was the defense of traditional rules as well as the subversive acceptance of the eventual fusion of the three estates into a single assembly where the deputies of the Third Estate would dominate those of the first two orders. Although Necker was basically a conservative monarchist, his choice pointed more to the embodiment of a single, determining general will than to the creation of a modern constitutional monarchy with two consultative chambers on the English model.

From mid-1787 on, it become increasingly clear that the French monarchy could not continue as the arbiter of a traditionalist, corporatist society which existed in name only. The crown's only hope was to find an alternate solution that would allow it to go on in an updated, parliamentary mode. Yet the monarch and his first minister showed no initiative and allowed their vestigial powers to slip away: "I think, " wrote Jefferson to Adams in late 1787, "that in the course of three months the royal authority has lost, and the rights of the nation gained, as much ground, by a revolution of public opinion only, as England gained in all her civil wars under the Stuarts." Gradually, the crown lost its claim to political legitimacy. Sovereignty and the concept of an indivisible French nation which had been embodied for centuries in the sacralized person of the monarch fell into the hands of whatever figures or institutions might claim to represent the revolutionary and sovereign will of the French people. In these last weeks of the ancien régime, the crown proved unable to manage even its own demise: Louis XVI failed again as an absolute monarch between 1787 and 1789, just as he had failed in 1776 and would fail later as a constitutional sovereign.

THE ESTATES GENERAL were convoked in May 1789. Matters did not proceed smoothly. Though politically liberal minorities existed in both the first and second orders, most churchmen and most nobles refused the invitation of the non-noble deputies to make all the delegates the members of a single National Assembly. The conservative clerical and noble majorities dug in their heels and refused to work toward the construction of a representative but still monarchic state. Opinions suddenly polarized on the right and on the left. Most privileged deputies would have accepted a coup by the monarchy against the Third Estate in the first two weeks of July 1789 if it had been seriously intended. Conversely, the bourgeois deputies, when threatened by the king, accepted with some relief the extra-legal help of the Parisian crowds which attacked the Bastille on 14 July 1789 and broke the monarchy's desultory will to resist. And yet, despite those reservations on both the left and the right and also despite the hesitation and incompetence of the crown, a restructuring of the elite along the lines of individualistic rationality was the central theme of the first years of the French Revolution, just as it had been the central theme of late monarchic politics in the 1770s and 1780s.

Many threads link the revolutionary liberalism of 1789 to the revolutionary authoritarianism of 1794. The propertied French Revolutionaries of 1789 believed in the undivided sovereignty of the people. They detested "factions." To put it in Marxist terms, this "bourgeois" elite, like other social groups that have suddenly come to power, presented its case for dominance in universalist terms. As ardent nationalists they were uninterested in the representation of interests. They had no use for a system of checks and balances. The disciples of both Rousseau and the Physiocrats could agree on that score. The virtues of a monocameral government seemed to them self-evident. Because they did not distinguish between the people and the state, they did not see the need for a strong executive which could set its will against defiant legislative bodies.

These were destabilizing liabilities, but in 1789 many members of the elite, both noble and bourgeois, also understood that constitutional monarchy was, practically speaking, the best institutional expression of the social system that they currently desired. They believed that the king, whose capacity for resistance they did not suspect, would agree to their reshaping of his role. They thought that the divinely ordained King of France would agree to become the King of the French by the will of the people.

After the initial confusion of June and July 1789, it seemed that this new arrangement might in fact work. By participating in the celebration, held on July 14, 1790, of the fall of the Bastille the year before, the king seemed to have made his peace with the Revolution. Most nobles, it also appeared, had agreed to play their role in a new universalist state that was to be governed by a meritocratic elite of which they would be an important part.

This compliance was shown during the celebrated night of August 1789, when one aristocrat or churchman after another rose to sacrifice some hereditary or corporate privilege on the altar of revolutionary fraternity. In the first lines of his *Social Contract*, Rousseau had explained that man, though everywhere born free, was in chains. The members of the Estates General, both noble and non-noble, resolved to set him free. This wave of privileged self-sacrifice was due in no small part ad hoc calculation: many noble deputies did not own feudal dues; some of them, in fact, owned precious little property of any kind. Everyone felt the pressing need to make concessions that would stop the waves of peasant insurrection which were shaking the countryside in July and August 1789. Nonetheless, the motives of the noble delegates were anything but sordid. Many of them were lucid observers of their times. Thousands of them were sincere in accepting the end of feudalism "in its entirety." Some of them, one year later, accepted the abolition of nobility as a distinctive order, either because they thought it desirable or because they thought it could not be helped. In a mood that may well have been typical of the day, one noble deputy, the Marquis de Ferrières, concluded in a note to his wife that France would soon have a government "more or less like that of England. Nobility will then be here what it is in that island, a purely honorary distinction."[1] More relevant, perhaps, than such words is the fact that hundreds—perhaps thousands—of nobles bought up confiscated church lands which were sold as national properties (the *biens nationaux*). Many nobles also took on positions in the new decentralized, elective administration which had sprung up after the collapse of the ancien régime.

In short, even if many nobles regretted the demise of the Old Regime, many of them accepted the inevitability of the Revolution. Similarly, the elite of the Third Estate accepted liberal and repentant conservative nobles as social partners in the new politics. These victorious deputies did pass a rash of aggressively anti-aristocratic measures. Equality of taxation became a fact. All Frenchmen were declared to be equal citizens before the law. Careers were "open to talent," an individualistic but also a revolutionary step, since at that time hierarchies of talents were taken (somewhat strangely from our modernist and more egalitarian point of view) to be the perfect antithesis of hierarchies of birth. Corporate orders or estates were declared nonexistent. In the late summer of 1790 the parlements were abolished.[2]

It is important to see, however, that these anti-noble bourgeois gestures were not aimed at the nobles as private persons. They were directed against the principle of nobility, that is, against the concept of corporate traditionalism. The deputies of the Third Estate did not aim to humiliate or even diminish individual nobles. Third Estate political figures, many of whom, including the Marquis de Mirabeau, were of noble birth, went out of their way in 1789–90 to welcome former aristocrats who as private persons had acepted their new place in a reconstructed elite based on a mix of talent, prestige, and property. Even Sieyès, the archetypal foe of aristocratic privilege and the author of the immensely popular pamphlet, *What Is the Third Estate?* (a question he answered by saying that it was nothing and should be everything), acknowledged that it was the nobles who had been "the first defenders of justice and humanity." In the second half of 1789, Sieyès warned that nobles and priests had collaborated in the making of the French constitution and that it would be foolish to snub them now: "Every one senses today," he wrote, "the need to build social unity from the debris of the estates and of the large corporations."[3]

The goal of the bourgeois revolutionaries in 1789 was not to reorganize the ownership of property. They did not aim to confiscate noble lands or to deny the social preeminence of former nobles. It was the ideological and institutional structure of French society and of the French state that obsessed them. Inherited corporate and public privilege was anathema to these universalistically minded men. No intermediary body of any kind, they thought, could stand between the sovereign state and the private citizen. At the same time, it was invariably accepted by the deputies of the Third Estate, the *Constituants*—as the members of the former estates were now called because they were drafting a new constitution—that some citizens, many of them former nobles, were more talented and richer than other citizens and might, as such, find their superior niche in the new order. The reborn nation would accept all of its children, including both those who had dominated the older society of estates and those whom it had formerly excluded. Politically, the situations of nobles and Jews in France between 1789 and 1791 were curiously symmetrical. One could have applied to the former holder of privilege the message which a liberal noble had for Jews: "The Jews as a nation [within France] must be denied everything. But as individuals they must receive every thing. They must become citizens . . . Some say that they do not wish to be French citizens. If that is so, they must be banished. There can be no nation within the nation."[4] Some enlightened and dedicatedly universalist elitists like Condorcet, who was more interested in the dictates of reason than in those of nature, were bold enough to think that propertied women might become politically enfranchised citizens.

Gradually, however, the social and parliamentary program of elitist and constitutional monarchy fell apart. Just as the monarchic state had failed to reform itself when Maupeou and Turgot had acted on *behalf* of the elite, but without the *help* of the elite in the 1770s, so did constitutional monarchy fail to pull itself together *with* the help of the elite between 1789 and 1791. The complicated marriage of monarchic traditionalism and bourgeois, universalist meritocracy did not succeed; and in retrospect, it is tempting to conclude that it bore within itself the seeds of its own destruction. The program of the elite was too vast. The *Constituants* expected to reconcile not just nobles and non-nobles, or the king and his people, but possessive individualism and popular communitarian sensibility generally. In the past, man's true and positive nature had manifested itself occasionally in the lives and thoughts of self-sacrificing heroes such as Socrates, Cato, Phocion, Marcus Aurelius, and Belisarius. In their new world, all French men and women would be personally heroic and socially docile. Their aim was to institutionalize the fissiparous and self-defeating individualist-universalist myth of the late 1780s. The *fête de la fédération* on 14 July 1790, when delegations thronged to Paris from the four corners of the kingdom, marked the zenith of their popularity. The fruitless pursuit of their ill-fated mythic goal gave a historical dimension and pathos to their failed attempt.

Although the elitist deputies of 1789 wished to make the rights of private property absolute, they deferred to universalist principle in many ways—even ominously so. They were intensely nationalistic. "The Nation," explained Sieyès in *What Is the Third Estate?* "exists before all things . . . Nations on earth must be conceived as individuals outside the social bond . . . The exercise of their will is free and independent of all civil forms." The revolutionaries prided themselves on being patriots, defenders of a common, transcendental fatherland. The nation-state was for them the institutional expression of the underlying natural unity of all French men if not women. All male citizens were in their eyes equal and alike despite apparent differences of social rank and wealth.

For the monarchists, each patriarchal French family had replicated in civil society the political authority of the king. The Jacobins would soon imagine themselves to be members of a large public family which expressed the unspoken needs of the Grande Nation, itself a much vaster but still familial cell. France for the first time in its history was endowed with a national flag, which shrank and sandwiched the royal white between one blue and one red stripe, the colors of the Parisian capital. Provinces that had existed since ancient times were broken up into dozens of small departments, uniform in size if not in population. Every citizen could walk in a day from his home to the administrative capital of his district, to take an active part in the political business of the community.

Unlike the American Constitution of 1787 with its prudent checks and balances and its recognition of divergent interests, the French Constitution of 1791 was monocameral and holistic: in Brissot's words, no political reunion could be deemed valid unless it assumed "unity of interests [and] truth in its principles." The French people could have but a single national will. In 1794 Mary Wollstonecraft in her account of the French Revolution commented approvingly on the monocameralism of the French system: "Then deputies who opposed the upper chamber did it from a belief that it would be *the asylum of a new aristocracy*." John Adams, a reluctant pluralist but an enthusiastic pessimist, commented dryly in his copy of her book:

"So it ought to be." It would take about a century for the propertied and liberal French elite to see his point.

MANY OF THE problems that brought down the elitist, individualist-universalist program of enlightened reform were not of the meritocrats' own making. It may be argued, as Tocqueville did after the Revolution of 1848 (and as Gouverneur Morris had done episodically during the French Revolution itself), that the French at the end of the eighteenth century were incapable of any kind of self-government. The matrices of public life before 1789 had bred bad habits: in the professional guilds the French, who were a litigious people, had learned to argue rather than to compose their differences. In their aristocratic culture, compromise was tantamount to weakness. In the cities especially the institutions of local self-government had become a cipher. An obscurantist and absolutist state had taught even liberals to be covertly intransigent and obstinate.

The first immediate problem was that the constitutional monarchists ran out of money. This could hardly have been helped: 77 percent of the cahiers had demanded lower taxes, and it would have been difficult to explain to the nation at large that the first effect of a successful revolution would be the very reverse of what had been intended. Attempts to raise new loans failed. Nor did the members of the new National Assembly, the Constituants, think that they could balance their budget by simply abolishing the royal debt. Many of them, including Mirabeau, had close links to Parisian debtholders. Government bonds were, after all, a form of property; and respect for private, individual property ran deep. That fetish was in fact the most durable part of the deputies' worldview. So great was the hegemony of bourgeois thought on this issue that even the Paris plebs assumed in 1789 that the owners of the royal debt deserved to be paid in full. In view of these constraints, the Constituants decided they had no choice but to manufacture paper currency.

New enemies were made when the legislators decided to seize the vast holdings of the church (nearly 10 percent of national landed wealth) in order to provide backing for this new money, the assignats. In March 1790 they voted after intense debate to create 400 millions' worth of these notes (45 billions' worth were eventually printed). The deputies generously decided that expropriated clerics would receive handsome government stipends. But then, perhaps following the principle which holds that whoever pays the piper calls the tune, the Constituants in July 1790 ungenerously decided to take in hand all clerical appointments. In the past, bishops had been named by the sovereign king; now the sovereign people would choose them. In November priests were required to take an oath of allegiance to the new religious and political system. Only seven out of 169 bishops agreed to do so. Since religious dogma was not at stake, the Constituants fancied that the bishops would fall into line once the pope decided to give his consent to the new "civil constitution" of the clergy; but after some hesitation, he did not. The king then refused as a private person to accept the new state religion, though under pressure he did, as a monarch, agree to sanction its creation. The anticlericalism of many deputies blinded them to what they should have been able to predict: in a fit of ideological self-indulgence, they had pushed not just the church but thousands of parish priests into the camp of their social enemies.

But some financial difficulties were to be expected, and money, in any case, was the catalyst of political catastrophe rather than its first cause. (This same relationship of economics to politics runs through the entire history of the Revolution.) More relevant was the excessive zeal of the individualistic, rationalist elite. As Burke pointed out at once, they were too ambitious, too destructive, and too contemptuous of France's ancient religious and corporatist habits and institutions. The gap was too wide, as has been said, between their narrow, negativist individualism and the sensibility of the nation at large. This significant subject must be considered conjecturally, since it has elicited only sparse historical research.

Many disorders were attributable to that very institutional breakdown which the deputies of the Third Estate had encouraged and, in places, decreed. In America, the rebels had retained their local institutions: British royal authority had been more ignored and replaced than destroyed. The French Constituants wanted to throw everything down all at once, and this was all the more serious because, over the years and centuries, so much had already fallen down of its own accord. Lacking esteem for prerevolutionary corporate and representative institutions, the deputies gave free rein to their ideological imagination: the antique majesty of the ancien régime—of kings, bishops, and nobles—had been so great, and their triumph over it so complete! In this moral and institutional climate, the collection of taxes and the conduct of government business became impossible.

Provincial and corporate institutions were ruthlessly abolished, often to the horror of local bourgeois lawyers and officials whose lives had been enmeshed in these arrangements. Systems of weights and measures were to be changed and improved. Government officials (including bishops) were to be elected, not appointed. It was decided that hierarchy would no longer apply as an administrative principle—a dangerous step for a country which had had little experience in self-government. The older courts were abolished and the emphasis of the new jurisprudence was placed on fraternal, universalist reconciliation and arbitration rather than on authoritarian judgment handed down from above. "The French calamities," warned Britain's sententious if observant ambassador to Paris in 1791, "afford the best lesson against the Abstraction of Politics."

Nor did the Constituants in the new National Assembly limit themselves to political, religious, and institutional engineering. The new individualistic world order was extended from politics to social life; here was the second great cause of their undoing. The American revolutionaries had been very conservative in their alterations of customary law, but in France the Constituants were very bold. Legislation on younger children's right to inherit and on the dissolution of marriage was radically tilted in 1790 and 1792 toward individuals and against the family as a unit. But the most drastic step was the Constituent or National Assembly's destruction of feudalism and corporatism. Between 1789 and 1791 the victorious elite did not hesitate to impose their meritocratic program on a people who had very little use for it, and the consequences of that decision, at once foolish and seemingly fated, were soon felt.

At first, the enactment of this individualistic part of the monarchic constitutionalist program proceeded almost uneventfully, as far as rural feudalism was concerned. Transformations were extensive.

After the feudal holocaust of the night of 4 August 1789, when feudalism was declared abolished "in its entirety," the deputies, somewhat chastened, did backtrack a good deal on the practical application of their edict. They tried to distinguish between transformed contractual obligation and matters of personal servitude: between honorific feudal rights, which were suppressed, and banal or economic rights, which were to be redeemed by the peasantry. But these distinctions the peasants studiously ignored. Excitement ran high in the countryside from the spring of 1789 right up to 1792. The harvest of 1788 had been the poorest one since 1712; the winter of 1788–89 had been very cold; hailstorms in the spring of 1789 had destroyed many crops. In the town of Sézanne, near Rheims, the price of grain reached an all-time high, in a few months rising from sixteen francs a quintal to forty-six francs (or more than nine gold dollars) by July 1789. Peasants were not about to back off. For them the Revolution was a unique chance to stop paying anything, whether feudal dues or taxes. They were not uninterested in bourgeois notions of representative government, but they also had their own concerns. Though some feudal dues were salvaged at law by their owners, who were able particularly after 1795 to include them in readjusted land rents, notably in western France (much as they had done with the clerical tithe when it had been abolished in 1790), most feudal dues simply lapsed. Few Frenchmen paid much attention when all feudal dues, without exception, were formally abolished in 1792 and 1793.

On balance, the revolutionary land settlement was a conditional success. At the top of society, nearly all noble landlords resigned themselves to the new arrangements. Prudent owners of reclaimable feudal dues did little to assert their vestigial legal rights. The sale of church lands, the biens nationaux, most of which were bought up by bourgeois and noble landlords for less than half of their true worth, was for the rich adequate compensation for what they had had to give up elsewhere. Many peasants, it is true, were less pleased. In some parts of France, such as the Vendée, their bitterness at having been excluded by bourgeois revolutionaries from purchasing the biens nationaux drove them, logically enough, to counterrevolution. But most French peasants were less demanding, or less able to demand, so that the more common pattern of rural politics was one of gradual conciliation, at least from 1789 onward.

In the short run, the tactical alliance of peasants and bourgeois may, paradoxically, have destabilized the Revolution. Because they had benefited from the revolutionary settlement and feared a return to the ancien régime, many otherwise conservative peasants would support any universalist government that held sway in Paris, however extreme it might be. If the choice was between Robespierre and a return to 1788, many propertied owners of the biens nationaux —large or small—felt they had no choice. Bonaparte in particular capitalized on that fear. In the long run, however, the revolutionary land settlement with its propeasant abolition of most feudal dues bound the peasantry and the bourgeoisie together in France as it did nowhere else. The abolition of feudalism by the landowning elite on terms favorable to the peasants gave to bourgeois republican French politicians a popular audience that was unrivaled in Europe.

Far more dangerous was the second, urban facet of the liberal-monarchist, or Feuillant, program (the name "Feuillant," like the term "Jacobin," came from a clerical house that had become the site of a political club). At stake was the meritocratic abolition of urban corporatism and the spread of monetized relationships. In their attack on *rural* feudalism, the deputies left the village communities untouched; besides, their laws on the division of village common lands in September 1791 went generally unenforced. By contrast, the abolition of *urban* corporatism was a truly destructive and revolutionary act that affected the lives of countless city dwellers. In 1791 the Allarde and Le Chapelier laws completed the attack on the urban corps initiated by Turgot in 1776 and implied if not stated during the night of August 4 when feudalism was destroyed "in its entirety." In 1791 all trade unions were explicitly abolished. Workers, as individuals, were required to sell their labor to employers who, as individuals, were forbidden to form associations or cartels. This radical institutionalization of a narrow and possessive type of individualism was a drastic step, the likes of which English entrepreneurs did not attempt to legislate until the next century. Even if the architects of the Le Chapelier law did not fully realize what they were doing, and even if many of them were moved by an immediate issue (the recent wave of strikes by carpenters, woodworkers, hatters, and typographers), their act set the stage for a parting of the ways between the elite and the Parisian masses who had helped bring down the ancien régime in 1789 and whose sensibility the elite now completely ignored.

Two world views were in conflict. For the urban poor, economic relations were part of the fabric of social life. For the elite, money was the absolute point of reference. The monarchist Calonne had endeavored in 1787 to set an official parity between the prices of silver and gold because he considered all coins to be primarily units of accounting. In 1790 the bourgeois revolutionaries entrusted that monetary relationship to the market: the state would define its unit of accounting in relation to a set quantity of gold, and then it would once again become monetarily invisible.[5]

How unhappy the urban poor actually were in 1791 is hard to say. The current state of research does not allow historians to consider this momentous question in all of its details. It may even be that the investigations which would further historical understanding cannot be achieved in the context of social history as it is strictly defined. Because the old institutions of popular sensibility had been destroyed and new ones were not yet in being, and because the leaders of the masses were momentarily seduced by the shallow individualism of the propertied Constituants, the anxieties of the urban masses could not find suitable (and therefore, eventually, archival) expression.

One possible lead is to consider the sudden burst of political and popular radicalism in June and July 1791, which was occasioned by the flight of the king, as a parasocial protest whose profound causes even participants in the movement could not fully understand. It is surely significant that nearly all of the 250 men and women who were arrested by the Feuillant authorities as political enemies in the summer of 1791 resurfaced within months as militant sansculottes. This kind of historical judgment is, however, some distance removed from saying that such social anxieties definitely existed. Supposing that the disorientations of the suddenly "decorporatized" urban poor could not have found their way into the kinds of documents that archivists store and historians read does not necessarily imply that these anxieties, anyway, must have been felt. What the poor thought between 1789 and 1791 about the Constituants' social program remains, unfortunately, a matter of inference rather than proof.

THE BREAKDOWN OF constitutional monarchy in 1791 was in part an accident. A more conciliatory monarch might have made the system work. But the failure of the "liberal universalists" can also be understood as a predictable reaction of the French public to a kind of individualist statement that went much further than French society could allow.

On the right, the reorganization of the French Church was bound to offend, as did the abolition of the nobility, even as an honorific order in June 1790. In addition, the drastic limitations placed on the king's powers and the curtailment of his ceremonial role were more than he could stand. In June 1791 he fled, in disguise, from Paris in a cumbersome and conspicuous stagecoach. His poorly planned, arrested flight to Varennes on the way to Austrian-controlled territory, from which he had hoped to lead a counterrevolution, marked the beginning of the end for the program of constitutional monarchy. The desertion of the father king not only destroyed the vestigial prestige of the crown but also dealt a grievous blow to the constitutional monarchists, who had depended on the king far more than they realized.

More ominous yet for the Feuillants and their most intelligent leader, Antoine Barnave, a Protestant lawyer whose mother was a noblewoman, was their program's lack of appeal on the left—to the peasants and to the urban working people, particularly in Paris. The rise in food prices had put wage earners on edge. French society's technological inability to produce, compounded by extreme inequalities in the distribution of wealth, meant that most Frenchmen used most of their daily income to buy their daily bread. Fear of hunger and starvation obsessed countless people who staggered through life from one uncertain meal to the next. Throughout the revolutionary period this fear of dearth was the invariable first goal to popular political action, as well as, sadly, to popular calls for violence and blood. It had not helped, therefore, when in August 1789 the assembly had ratified another key element of the Physiocratic program by decreeing internal free trade in grain. So keen was the assembly's devotion to the abstract principles of possessive individualism that the deputies often went against the interests of their own propertied audience. In March 1791, for example, they rejected a Lyons silk manufacturer's plea for a high and frankly protectionist tariff.

The play of ideology was yet another dimension of the popular puzzle. As dissatisfactions materialized, the contradictory principles and self-destructive nature of the elite's joint program of possessive individualism and nationalist, universalist unity became more and more evident. The revolutionary elite's rhetoric, their words of liberty and fraternity, radicalized an urban crowd which the Constituants had done very little to please and much to antagonize. In 1788-89 a radicalized crowd had worked to the advantage of the propertied deputies, who had not yet overcome the monarchy. It was thanks to the insurgent crowd that the deputies of the Third Estate and their politically liberal and aristocratic friends had managed to topple the ancien régime and take control of the state. But from 1791 onward, the crowd began to move beyond possessive liberalism as the Constituants had defined it; and the poor were abetted in this unprecedented and leftward drift by the Jacobins— the communitarian, civic-minded, and ideological left wing of the propertied elite.

Popular consciousness was increasingly influenced by the Jacobins' radical discourse, which presented an extreme version of the Feuillants' principles and was often couched in terms borrowed from Rousseau, whose life and thought were much admired. Significantly, Rousseau's political works were much better known than they had been earlier; the *Social Contract,* for example, was republished thirty-two times between 1789 and 1799. Echoes of Rousseau's thought found their way into countless popular statements, many of them drawn up by men and women who were barely literate. Indeed, radical words were of such importance, especially in 1793–94, that economic circumstances seem to have mattered principally because they spurred on a leftist political drift that basically had other causes.

Between 1789 and 1791 the insertion of the elite's individualist message into the context of ideological universalism had inclined the poor to accept their basically capitalist program. In 1791–92 that same universalist phraseology began to have an inverse effect on the elite's relationship to the poor. At the very moment when the newly conservative constitutional monarchists began to lose their grip on politics, their moralizing universalist principles provided their popular enemies with ideological ammunition. The Paris crowd (roughly representative of the city's quarter of a million artisans, servants, and workers, employed or unemployed) was not only better organized and more aggressive, but it was becoming increasingly politicized. By the summer of 1793, thanks in part to a government subsidy, Hébert's newspaper, the *Père Duchesne,* much favored by the sansculottes, would reach an unprecedented circulation of 80,000 issues (as against 10,000 for other Paris newsletters) and would have as many as 200,000 readers.

These changes enabled the sansculottes (as the popular revolutionaries were now being called because they did not wear breeches or silk stockings) to demand curtailment of individualism in economic life. They wanted the state to return to the economic and social sphere. They wanted to be fed. In April 1789, during an attack on a manufacturer named Réveillon, the Paris crowd had still invoked the name of the king-father. But in July 1789 the attack on the Bastille had a more complex inspiration, including the classic fear that the crown intended to starve the capital into submission, as well as a new sense of hostility to the monarchy as a political institution. This popular radicalization proceeded inexorably. The Feuillants' attack on corporate communitarianism after 1789 further unsettled the urban crowd and helped make them a ready audience for radical politicians such as Marat, who had launched his celebrated newspaper, *L'Ami du Peuple,* in September 1789. In October 1789 the crowd, of its own accord and without elitist prompting or bribery, had marched off to Versailles to bring the king back to Paris and to secure cheap food. In February 1791 a thousand men from the eastern faubourgs of Paris marched to Vincennes in the hope of capturing the fortress there. In May and June of that year the cessation of a program of public works sparked off more street riots in the capital. In July a crowd numbering in the thousands gathered to sign a petition calling for the abolition of the monarchy. By late 1791 it had become clear that the individualist and universalist program did not have sufficient appeal to seduce either tradition-alist Catholics or the common people of France. Louis XVI's attempt to run away made matters even worse for the constitu-tional monarchists, who found that they had neither a king to work with nor a popular audience. Their situation was little short of desperate.

In retrospect, what should seem surprising is not the defeat of the Feuillants but their earlier audacity. They had dared to attack not only the ancien régime but the very fabric of French corporatist sensibility, which had guaranteed their social dominance. How easily they had struck down all the ancient institutions that might in altered form have sustained their drive for power! Perhaps, like the physiocrats and philosophes before the Revolution, they thought that their utterances—their books and speeches—registered the voice of some nationwide and cross-class "public opinion." In the administrative and social void caused by the collapse of the ancien régime, the Feuillants mistook the echo of their own words for the voice of the assembled nation.

The history of France in these years is fascinating in its represen-tativity. All western countries have traveled one of the paths from gemeinschaft to gesellschaft, as the French did between 1789 and 1791. But no country, including our own, had done so with such brutality and in so short a time. In Prussian Germany this same evolution ran from the beginning of monarchic bureaucracy in the mid-seventeenth century until the abolition of the guilds in the 1860s. The transition was very slow, and the triumph of possessive liberalism was very short.

Between 1789 and 1791 the French constitutional elite compressed two centuries of German history into two years; and the materials at their disposal were drastically inadequate to their task. When the Feuillants found themselves at the most important social crossroad of modern history, they failed completely. Their definition of indi-vidualism was too narrow, and its social appeal was too shallow. The claims of the poor, whose corporate sensibility remained very strong, were bound to emerge again. There the contrast with Amer-ica is striking. The Founding Fathers did not have to fear the class consciousness of the urban mass, which had no traditionalist cor-porate bedrock on which to re-form itself. And the founders' American, neo-religious view of the self was more flexible and more attractive, even to those whose social disabilities made it improbable that their hopes of empowerment would ever be realized.

The Feuillants were ill served by the social and cultural history of the ancien régime, and especially by the weakness in prerevolutionary France of the capitalist impulse, which formed the material backdrop for the anti-individualist evolution of revolutionary politics. Their story has genuine pathos and perhaps a dimension of collective tragedy: in 1790-91, when they thought themselves most free, the members of this meritocratic elite were on the verge of being engulfed by the results of their own poor judgment.

WITH THE GROWING FAILURE in the summer of 1791 of their hybrid individualist-universalist program, the French political elite faced two choices. They could choose to emphasize either half of the individualist-universalist synthesis, either going forward toward republicanism and trying to bind the people to that universalist idea, or reneging and making an agreement with the king. In a celebrated speech, Barnave, the most lucid of the newly conservative Feuillant wing of the revolutionary party, opted for the second choice. In July 1791 he pronounced his instantly famous words: "La Révolution est finie" (the French Revolution is over). In ironic consequence of that Feuillant judgment, Louis XVI was put back on his throne with strengthened power by Barnave's uncertain allies, the Lameth brothers, former favorites of the queen, and General Lafayette, an unsuccessful and ultimately uncertain demagogue. The electoral franchise was curtailed. The distinction between active (tax-paying) and passive (landless) citizens was given greater political meaning. It was rumored that the decree abolishing the nobility would soon be repealed. This policy did not succeed, however, and late in 1791 the revolutionary elite split into two rival factions. Barnave, for his part, would be executed in the fall of 1793, after having written (in prison) the first sociological explanation of the French Revolution.

The immediate cause of Barnave's failure was the king and queen's refusal to work with him. The royal pair had decided that matters would have to get worse before they could be improved. The radicalization of the Revolution which was to take them to the guillotine seemed a passing storm which they would have to endure before returning to the normative calm of absolute power. Louis, though he did not hesitate to lie and deceive in order to further his principles, was also a Christian gentleman who could never bring himself to order his troops to fire upon the crowd: his grievous political miscalculations compounded by his innate decency allowed the Revolution to lurch ever leftward.

The root source of Barnave's failure, however, was less the monarch than a change in attitude, on the part of the elite, toward their own individualist-universalist myth. In 1792 the communitarian, universal aspect of that myth, gradually captured the imagination of the more active members of the elite. A large wing of the propertied bourgeoisie began to drift away from individualism toward more determining, communitarian, and Jacobin rhetorical forms. As the "patriotic party" fell into two warring parts, Barnave and the right center (the Feuillants) were outmatched by Brissot and the Girondins on the center left. At the same time, Barnave and those of his chastened colleagues who wanted to stop the Revolution lost control of the newly organized and powerful network of left-wing Jacobin clubs: by 1793 there would be at least five thousand such associations with half a million members. Over the whole of France during a few weeks in the summer and fall of 1791, these active and interfering local societies, which in the past year had risen up like mushrooms after a summer rain, fell in behind the leftist Girondins, or Brissotins, who wanted to push the Revolution further by relying more overtly on the people, of whose sovereign and universal will they presumed themselves to be the natural spokesmen. (Women, incidentally, were not allowed to join the clubs, though some parallel middle-class female Jacobin societies did come into being.) The individualist and universalist party split between those who would save private property directly by siding with the king and those who would try to preserve it more precariously within the context of a militantly universalist, Rousseauistic state.

Barnave's conservative-liberal option was the right one to follow in one sense: eventually, after the Revolution was over and Napoleon had fallen, it would attract the loyalties of a French possessing class, finally mindful both of popular, revolutionary "excess" and of Bonapartist, militarist oppression. By the middle decades of the nineteenth century, Barnave's rejection of a popular solution to the problem of postcorporatist politics would become standard bourgeois fare. Indeed, during the revolutionary decade the leftist Girondins would get cold feet about following the people in the fall of 1792—as Robespierre would in the fall of 1793 and the spring of 1794. In the fall of 1791, however, Barnave was unable to hold his propertied but ideologically radical audience. At this historical juncture at the dawn of contemporary history, the French possessing class did not or could not understand what was implied by an alliance with the people, who were gradually becoming a distinct social class. The incomplete nature of capitalist development in eighteenth-century France made the French propertied elite unable to understand the alienating effect on the poor of its narrow, negative world view. The first political effect of this blindness was Barnave's failure in the fall of 1791 to consolidate a party of property.

AFTER BARNAVE, who withdrew to his native Grenoble, came the Girondins, who ruled on and off in Paris from 1792 to the late spring of 1793. In regard to social and economic matters, the Girondins (or Jacobins, as they would continue to be called until they too lost control of the Jacobin clubs in the fall of 1792) had no particular plan. For them, economic concerns had lost theoretical importance when in 1789 individuals of varying wealth had become the equal citizens of a universalist state. But when it proved difficult to continue in this mode, the Girondins showed themselves, in practice if not in words, nearly as conservative as the Feuillants had been. Their economic reforms were very restrained, but they did give way somewhat on rural issues, and in April 1792 the law on the abolition of feudal dues was changed to the advantage of the peasants. In the past, peasants had been required to repurchase their former dues or to show that traditionally collected dues were usurpations that were not sanctioned by legal documents. Now the process was reversed: it was up to the landlords to show that their claims to repayment were fully justified.

In the cities the Girondins, despite their demagogic, Rousseauistic words, did even less to undo the socially individualistic program of 1789–1791. Partly as a consequence of that official indifference, conditions of life steadily worsened in Paris. The assignats, first issued as interest-bearing bonds of large denominations, became everyday fiat currency whose value steadily declined. Because merchants were not required by law (until the spring of 1793) to accept depreciated paper currency, urban wage earners were increasingly squeezed. Unemployment rose as rich and frightened patrons of the artisan crafts went abroad or, if they stayed at home, hoarded their gold. Peasants, too, became increasingly reluctant to trade produce for paper currency of questionable worth. The Girondins did practically nothing to arrest this decay. They refused to act in order to guarantee the Parisians' food supply; the all-important Le Chapelier law that had declared artisanal corporations illegal was not repealed; strikes were still forbidden. One of the more theoretically minded Girondins, Roland, soon to be minister of the interior, reasserted his support for the internal free trade of grain: "Wheat," he wrote in March 1792, "belongs to those who have bought it." Condorcet likewise opined that complete freedom of trade was the only way to stabilize the price of essential commodities. In March 1792 the Girondins voted to celebrate with great pomp the funeral of a small-town mayor named Simonneau who had been lynched by a mob during a food riot.

Instead of genuine social reform, what the Girondins—or "Brissotinis," as some derisive Englishmen called them—proposed was to radicalize the Revolution ideologically by stepping up the campaign against dissidents (whether runaway priests or noble émigrés) by broadening the electoral franchise and by hounding the nonjuring Catholic clergy—those who had refused to accept the new religious settlement. Revolutionary image mattered more than revolutionary action to the Gironde, who then dominated the Jacobin party. Theirs was a resolutely universalist program, but an increasingly calculating and deceptive one.

The first effect of the Girondin conjunction of radical word and cautious deed was a broad flowering of revolutionary symbolism in both the high art of the academies and the more popular genres. Iconography, furniture, playing cards, pottery, clothing, speech, and song were transformed. Americans had, initially at least, relied on the ancient and historicist vocabularies of the Radical Whigs; American revolutionary songs and plays were rare. The French, by contrast, thrived on innovations and rituals of all sorts. The Girondins welcomed the imagery of the "citizen armed for libertarian struggle": the pike, which for the Parisian sansculottes was a symbol of applied sovereignty, appealed to them, as did the Phrygian bonnet, or liberty cap, the premier symbol of liberty and an essential part of the revolutionary sartorial persona. On July 5, 1792, French men and women were required to wear the blue, white, and red cockade. (In the more constraining days of the Directory, foreigners and women would be forbidden to wear it.) Liberty trees were planted all over France in elaborate, ritualized, neo-religious ceremonies. To make sure that all Frenchmen communed in the new public and universalist spirit, the Girondins proposed to make attendance at republican schools compulsory, although, interestingly, some of the more radical Montagnards (members of the leftist Mountain faction that would soon dominate the Jacobin clubs) balked at that violation of private rights. Similarly, the proposed Girondins constitution of 1793 (drafted in part by Condorcet and Tom Paine) was—in its wording—as democratic as could be hoped. While it did provide for indirect elections, it also included a mechanism of popular control. Although there was not to be a board of censors in Paris as in Philadelphia, Condorcet's text included a clause entitled "On the right of petition and on the censorship by the people of their representatives' decisions."

The crux of the Girondin program of ideological radicalism was its orchestrated plan of nationalist and libertarian aggression. In 1788 Brissot, surely the first European to think of a provincial New England academy in terms of world history, had mused, while watching Commencement Day exercises at Harvard, that "in a free country everything ought to bear the stamp of patriotism." In 1792 he decided to apply this maxim more directly: in April, at his behest, war was declared against the Habsburg monarch, the pillar of European traditionalism, who happened also to be Queen Marie Antoinette's older brother. A quick little successful war (it would actually last for twenty-three years), thought the Girondins, would surely bind the people to the revolutionary regime. In a typical and outrageous statement, Condorcet, the enlightened, noble-born philosophe turned Girondin politician, explained that "if Frenchman do not declare war [on Austria] our disunion will persist, the depreciation of our paper currency will continue. An ebullient spirit which might have been usefully redirected against the enemy will be turned against us . . . All of the dangers that we face will vanish with the first cannon shot."[6]

To his credit, Robespierre, on the far left of the Jacobin bourgeois party, opposed the war. More suspicious of the military and more honest than the Girondins, whose personal antecedents, like those of Brissot (a former police spy), were often disreputable, Robespierre insisted that the true foes of the universalist Revolution were inside France and not abroad: "Set your own house in order before you decide to bring liberty to your neighbors."[7] More bluntly still, Marat wrote that the only hope was civil war, "provided that the people can be victorious." For the bourgeois left— that is, for Robespierre, Marat, and the other, less calculating Montagnard Jacobins—the issue was not yet to fool the people, as it had increasingly become for the Girondins, but to cut down the surprisingly numerous and unexpected domestic enemies of revolutionary, universalist, but nonetheless bourgeois democracy.

By late 1791–92 revolutionary France had reached a point of no return. On the left, the Paris crowd was very radical and more sure of itself than it had ever been. The king, for his part, was outraged by the high-handed tactics of the meretricious Girondin politicians who wanted to reduce him to a cipher and who threatened him with armed revolt. In March 1792 he agreed to rule with Girondin ministers, but he soon dismissed them. On June 20, 1792, when Parisian sansculottes invaded the royal palace, Pétion, the Girondin mayor of Paris, did little to help the king. Matters became very tense. Then, late in July 1792, an extravagant manifesto written by an obscure French extremist émigré but signed by the Duke of Brunswick, commander in chief of the Prussian army, threatened Parisians with physical annihilation if harm should come to the king. This irresponsible declaration brought the whole French political arrangement down. Brunswick's foolish message convinced the crowd in Paris that the king was a traitor to the Revolution, which, as it happens, he was, though that could not be proved at the time. The Girondins would have to choose between the monarch and the crowd.

At the last minute the Girondins lost their nerve. Though eager to humiliate the king, they were afraid of having to rule without

him. Their hesitations were to no effect: other Jacobin revolutionaries to their left (the Montagnards) were willing to go further with
the people. Marat turned on the pusillanimous Girondins, and
especially on his erstwhile friend and political fellow traveler, Brissot, whom he inamicably described as "apprenticed to chicanery . . .
a scandal-sheet writer, an apprentice philosopher, a fraudulent speculator, a crook, a prince's valet, a government clerk, a police spy,
publicist, municipal inquisitor, legislative senator, a faithless representative of the people, the abettor of ministerial faction and . . . the
henchman of the despot."[8]

The Montagnards were prepared to carry forward, without the
Gironde if need be, the old Girondin universalist policy of "no
enemies to the left." On August 10, 1792, with the Montagnards'
complicity, the people of Paris and some of their provincial allies
(many of them from Marseilles: hence the *Marseillaise*) attacked the
mini-army that defended the royal palace, the Tuileries. Characteristically, Louis ordered the defenders to put down their arms almost
as soon as the fighting began. After some confusion most of the
royal garrison, including the Swiss guards, were murdered by their
assailants. Three hundred Parisians were also killed—by treachery,
the people were convinced. The French Revolution lurched forward again.

IN THE SUMMER and early fall of 1792, French politics moved very
quickly. The monarchy fell on August 10. On September 2, assassins
claiming to rule in the name of the people of Paris attacked the city's
prisons and massacred more than eleven hundred prisoners—a few
of them political detainees, some of them priests and nobles, most
of them common criminals and prostitutes. On September 22, a
ramshackle French army stood its ground, surprisingly, in eastern
France at Valmy, and this victory ended the Prussian army's march
toward Paris. Goethe, who had come along with the invading
troops as a tourist, rightly wrote that a new phase of world history
had begun that day. The French Revolution might self-destruct,
but reactionary foreigners would not manage to overcome it. In
Paris a new assembly, the Convention, which took its name from
American precedent, met and proclaimed a republic.

Because the Girondins had in the end sided with the monarchy,

the radicalized Paris crowd turned against them. During the September massacres some of them narrowly escaped with their lives:
many of them would surely have been killed if the Paris Commune
had ordered their arrest, as Robespierre had advocated on September 1 or 2. All of this made Girondins think. Like Barnave a year
before, they decided in the fall of 1792 that the Revolution was over.
At first, some confused Girondin journalists had praised the mur-
ders of the September days as patriotic acts; within weeks, however,
they changed their minds and tried unsuccessfully to have the murderers brought to trial.

   After the popular movement turned against them, the Girondins
did everything they could to stop the leftward drift of the Revolution, which they themselves had favored when they had been out of
power, and whose universalist principles they still continued to
proclaim. They dismantled the apparatus of incipient legalistic terrorism whose foundation they had laid earlier in the year. They also
worked hard to postpone the trial of Louis XVI; and when the
discovery of his secret correspondence with the enemy made judgment and condemnation inevitable, most of them voted against the
death penalty. In economics, they stuck to their earlier conservative
line: any infringement of individual property rights would be
blocked, a point that dovetailed neatly with their decision to resist
the Paris crowd. By all of these decisions, the Girondins widened
the gap between themselves and the Montagnards, who became the
spearhead of universalist, bourgeois Jacobinism.

   The struggle between the Girondins and the Montagnards is a set
piece in the revolutionary drama. The most common interpretation
of their rivalry follows the Marxist class analysis labeled by Alfred
Cobban as the *Social Interpretation of the French Revolution*. In the
Marxist view, the Gironde represents the upper-middle, commercial
class, with headquarters in the trading seaport of Bordeaux, in the
department of the Gironde. The leftist Mountain represents the
middle or the lower-middle class allied to the popular masses against
the rich (represented by the Gironde). (The terms "left" and "right"
as shorthand notations for political progressives and conservatives
originated at this time.) In Marx's own words, the Terror of 1793–
94 was a "plebeian" continuation by other means of the middle
class's legalistic effort to uproot feudalism. Faced by a threat

from adamant reactionaries, the Mountain (wrote Marx) unleashed the people.

This materialist, class interpretation of Jacobinism, which goes hand in hand with a functionalist explanation of the Terror as a reaction of practical self-defense, cannot be sustained. Many of the problems which the Terror was supposed to cure (like the vestigial resistance of Vendéan peasants in 1794) were themselves caused by terroristic measures. Moreover, it is difficult to identify the Girondins and the Montagnards with certainty because they did not form parties in the modern sense; but it is reasonably clear that the Girondins were *not* richer then the Montagnards. They were often poorer and usually less respectable. The basic ideological principles of Girondins and Montagnards were quite similar. Contrary to what is often supposed, the Girondins were not deistic Voltaireans and the Montagnards were not all theistic Rousseauists. The ties between the Girondin and the prorevolutionary, primitivist wing of the Catholic clergy were very close. The Girondins were not strict parliamentarians: during their rise to power in the spring of 1792, they often threatened the constitutional monarch with popular insurrection. Nor was capitalism at issue here: at a time when the Gironde hoped to manipulate the crowd, which was hostile to free trade, some Girondins were favorable to price controls. In 1789–90 some of them, such as the Abbé Fauchet, attacked all forms of property, in stark contrast to Robespierre, who was still opposed in the spring of 1793 to any governmental interference in economic life. The principal difference between the Gironde and the Mountain was that the Girondins, many of whom had known each other before the Revolution, were quicker than the Montagnards to ensconce themselves in the interstices of power by manipulating the Paris crowd—and quicker, once they had reached their goal, to move away from the popular movement for which they had initially had universalist sympathy and which they had used to secure their own goals.

It was tactics rather than principle or social origins which divided the two Jacobin factions. Although there is little doubt about the sincerity of the universalist, populist claims that were being made at the time by the Montagnards, it still seems true that in 1793 the Girondins and Montagnards differed less over social and cultural principles than over what each faction stood to gain (or lose) by yielding to the growing demands of the plebs. From the fall of 1791 until 1799, the issue that faced all the bourgeois Jacobin leaders in turn (Barnave at first, and then Brissot and Robespierre), even though they formulated their problems differently at different times, was always the same: how far should the propertied revolutionaries, incited by universalist rhetoric (more or less sincerely felt) and in desperate need of allies, agree to travel in tandem with the people? The answer given at different times by different Jacobins was largely a function of their varying places in the day-to-day business of politics. The urgency of finding some practical application of a commonly shared universalist world view varied with the relationship to power. In late 1791 future Girondins and Montagnards—all of them out of power at the time—had agreed on what was to be done. In the fall of 1792, when the Girondins held power and the Montagnards did not, the same problem was differently perceived.

In the fall of 1791 the revolutionary elite, led by the Gironde, had set off on a very dangerous course of consciously desired political and ideological radicalization. Once launched, the drift to the left was hard to arrest, mainly because the urban crowds in Paris—but also in such cities as Marseilles, Toulouse, and Orléans, where prisoners were also massacred in September 1792—were very different from their American counterparts. In the thirteen colonies the poor had been socialized since 1700 to think that economic individualism was unavoidable. They might dislike their place at the bottom of that social order. They could at times riot or even lynch. But they were unable to reconceptualize their situation. The development of popular class consciousness during America's revolutionary struggle for independence was crippled by the lack of a communitarian past and ethos. Americans, imbued by a nationalist ideology of a secularized religious origin, then thought—and often still think—of their nation as an immanent and organic social order.

To the French, by contrast, a communitarian, corporate feeling was second nature, particularly in Paris. Guilds, corporations, and the corporatist spirit had been for centuries the kernel of urban life. Between 1789 and 1791, when the ancient institutions of French corporatism were discredited, the poor had at first given passive acceptance to economic and social individualism: few complaints were made when economic corporatism was dissolved in those early years. But the more durable effect of revolutionary politics after 1791 was the blending of two principles in the minds of the Parisian poor and some of their spokesmen: a traditionalist yearning for communitarian action, and the new universalist ideology borrowed from the bourgeois revolutionaries.

Concerning the practical applicability of universalist rhetoric, the people and the Jacobins thought very differently. For the bourgeois Jacobins (for the Gironde in 1792 and the Montagnards in 1794) the ideology of universalism became not an instrument of social change but an alternative to it, however sincere had been their earlier desire to bridge the gap between property and community. For the sansculottes, by contrast, and especially for the more radical *enragés* (both male and female), ideological universalism, which they expressed in myths of civic virtue and of the nation in arms, was the catalyst for the fusion of a new fraternity. It conveyed to the sansculottes a powerful vision of what day-to-day social relations might become. In thought and action, in their choice of words and goals, they grafted modern, bourgeois ideology onto the hoary trunk of corporate tradition. The history of the "popular movement" during the Revolution centers on the gradual drift of the crowd toward a modern social and political consciousness of class, a consciousness which blended old and new.

In 1792 and 1793 the tempo of this popular radicalization quickened dramatically, as did politics in general. At first this change developed under the protection of the Girondins, who were still out of power and hoped to use the crowd for their own ends. Excited to indignation by revolutionary ideology, the urban poor were all becoming sansculottes. It was Parisians who invaded the Tuileries palace in June 1792 and publicly humiliated the king by forcing him to put on a Phrygian cap. It was primarily the Parisian poor who overthrew the monarchy on August 10 and then in early September invaded the prisons to carry out slaughter in the name of popular justice. In the spring of 1793 the popular political fever rose even higher. With the execution of the king in January 1793 the popular movement took firmer shape and its leaders grew more self-assertive. Sansculottes militants took over most of the forty-eight sections, or administrative units, of Paris that they did not already control. They managed to secure a vote from the Convention to subsidize attendance at the section meetings by the poor, who were paid forty sous for being there. They insisted on public debate, and did not hesitate to override adverse votes when it suited their interests. They created popular societies as forums for discussion and mobilization.

Of relevance to their radicalization, of course, was the economic situation, which took an abrupt turn for the worse. In the poorer parts of Paris—the Faubourg Saint-Antoine on the right bank and the Faubourg Saint-Marcel on the left bank—one-third of the population was destitute. In a few weeks the revolutionary paper money (the assignats) lost a quarter of its value, more than it had lost in the previous two years. The conscription of hundreds of thousands of fighting men created unprecedented competition for food, and Parisians often came out second-best. In the economy of eighteenth-century France a slight decrease in the supply of food could cause a sudden and brutal increase in the price of bread. Shortages were compounded as traditional channels of distribution were thrown into disarray by the abolition of dues and tithes, which had often been paid in kind and had been a source of the cities' food supply. The insurrection of blacks in Haiti in August 1791 affected the flow of colonial staples as well.

In February 1793 Parisian housewives rioted to bring down the prices of soap and sugar. In the summer popular pressure grew for state control of prices and for the enforced circulation of paper money. Enragés such as Jacques Roux acquired a considerable audience in Paris for a popular program of this kind. Jacobin universalism might no longer convince the possessing elite, but its echoes dignified the sansculottes' secular fear of dearth. The Paris crowd inched toward what Marx would later call a world-historical consciousness of class "for itself." "Liberty," wrote Roux on June 25, 1793, "is no more than a phantom if one class of men can with impunity starve out another class of men. Equality is a mere phantom when the rich, with his monopolies, has a right of life and death over his fellow man."

In terms of method (though obviously not of content) the mutation of Parisian popular consciousness in 1793 was reminis-

cent of what had occurred to the American Whigs in the late
1780s. Then, too, unforeseen political circumstance had engendered new ideological formulations. But in Paris the pattern
worked to a very different end. In the politics of American pluralism, a new universalism reinforced by independence was
grafted onto a durable and modern social substratum of economic
and social individualism. In France, with the collapse of constitutional monarchy, the crowds blended the Jacobins' universalist
and increasingly forced rhetoric with an ancient communitarian
sensibility. The result in Paris was a unique popular movement
that looked both forward and backward. The sansculottes were
the first embryonic manifestation of a modern working class. But
they were also tradition-minded in many ways. They were hostile
to machines and money: they had no sense of the inevitability of
economic change. Often drunk with violence, they were rough,
hard-drinking people who easily succumbed to bloodlust. It was
common for them to rip their victims' bodies apart. And when
their passions were satisfied, they were hard to mobilize. Though
eager to use the state in order to secure their ends, they remained
incapable of sustained political action—as Babeuf, the theoretical
communist, came to realize late in 1795. The violent oratory of the
sansculottes and the phantasmagoric nature of their iconographi-
cal preferences expressed their mixed inspiration, simultaneously
prophetic and archaic.

Violent at the bottom, schizophrenic or at least incoherent at the
top, French revolutionary politics, forever wavering, contrasted
strikingly with the politics of revolutionary America, where the
dérapage of institutions and opinions had been easily contained.
French bourgeois radicals sensed that they had to move either
backward toward monarchic authority, as Barnave and the Feuillants had wanted to do in the fall of 1791, or forward toward the
unknown, as did the Gironde in early 1792 and the Montagnards in
mid-1793. In this frenzied setting the most action-minded Jacobins
continually rose to the fore of the "patriotic party." Insiders who
had already come to power within the revolutionary state naturally
opted for stability or even reaction, as the Gironde did in the
summer of 1792. But outsiders were equally and often sincerely
convinced that only a further realization of the universalist program

could save the Revolution. Determined and hyperactive minorities invariably carried the day from the fall of 1791 to the Terror. Their statements were hard to refute because their radical rhetoric today was identical to what their excluded opponents had argued yesterday. The reasoning that the Mountain used against the Gironde in late 1792 was like that which the Gironde had used against the Feuillants in the previous year.

Socially conservative but deeply ideological, the Jacobins were forever straining toward the left between 1791 and 1793, partly because they could not bring themselves to see that their program no longer made practical sense, but also because they hoped that their rhetoric would calm the crowds. Their mix of practical conservatism and demagogic universalism, of sincerity and self-deception, was irresistible in the short run but would eventually become self-destructive. Though intended to neutralize the popular revolution, in effect it helped the isolated poor to become an ever more aggressive and determined social class. Jacobinism was a mix of miscalculating opportunism and sincere self-delusion.

It would be difficult to apply a similar equation to revolutionary America, where crowds were more supine and politicians far more prudent. In the New World, where economic individualism was woven into the fabric of social life, a policy of communitarian drift could hardly seduce the likes of John Adams. In France, universalist rhetoric had a drug-like effect on many Jacobins: hiding from the police in early 1794, the noble-born and radical philosophe Condorcet, who was writing his *Sketch for a Historical Tableau of the Progress of the Human Spirit,* criticized the Americans' recourse (in their Constitution of 1787) to a pluralist system of checks and balances, because it "disfigures their simplicity." And why, he asked, had Americans refused to pursue an "identity of interests"? Sometime later an irate John Adams, pluralist republican that he had become, commented angrily in a marginal note to Condorcet's text: "Is it possible that a philosopher, who understood human nature, had read history, and knew anything of government, free or arbitrary, should have written this? What is his idea of an identity of interests? An equality of rights? Is an equality of rights anywhere more explicitly asserted than in the American Constitution?"[9] But what seemed absurd in Amer-

ica seemed self-evidently true to most Jacobins in 1792 and
1793.

DURING THE SPRING OF 1793 , the Girondins, who had formed
the left-wing opposition earlier, felt a desperate rightist desire to
stop the Revolution; but the Montagnards were equally determined
to save the Revolution by moving forward once again, in line with
the people of Paris. The accord of the popular revolutionaries and
the leftist bourgeois deputies gelled when another political crisis
occurred. The effects of popular riots and bad news from the eastern front were compounded in February 1793 by the outbreak of
war with Britain (at Brissot's prompting once again) and by civil
war in the Vendée in western France, where insurgent Catholic
peasants were able to perceive the Revolution for what it, sadly, had
become: a bourgeois machine for social and propertied self-aggrandizement in the name of enlightened principle but sustained at the
expense of the poor.

For some months before April 1793, Robespierre had hoped that
the Mountain could rise to power legally. Like Cromwell, Robespierre was a convinced parliamentarian and a reluctant terrorist.
He hoped at first to sway the moderate deputies who sat between
the Gironde and the Mountain in the Convention—the members of
the Plain (or the Swamp, to those who did not like them). The
deputies of the Plain were socially conservative, but they were
determined not to let the Revolution founder. Many of them had
bought biens nationaux. The Plain, thought Robespierre, would
understand that the Revolution could be saved only by energetic
radicals like himself.

In large part, events unfolded precisely as Robespierre intended.
In January 1793 the king's immediate execution was voted by a small
majority which included the king's own cousin, the former Duc
d'Orléans. Some uncertain Girondins voted to kill the king, others
to save him. Their hesitation on this score did a great deal to
discredit them in the eyes of their fellow deputies in the Convention. In the first week of April the commander in chief of the
embattled army, General Dumouriez, a friend of the Girondins,
went over to the Austrian army, just as General Lafayette had done
a little less than a year before when *his* friends, the Feuillants, had

been excluded from power. Thus the Girondins were further disgraced.

At this point Robespierre and the Mountain escalated their demands. They concluded that it would not be enough simply to secure a majority, with the help of the Plain, over the Gironde in the Convention. They looked forward to the actual expulsion of the Girondin deputies from the legislature. In the late spring of 1793, Robespierre opted to allow a popular insurrection against the Convention. On May 31 and June 2, 1793, armed Parisians surrounded the assembly and demanded that a core group of Girondin deputies be expelled. Most of them were placed under house arrest, and in October 1793 they were tried and executed. The alliance of Montagnards and sansculottes became even closer a month later, in mid-July 1793, when "federalist" (that is, rightist and pro-Girondin) insurrections broke out in different parts of France. Marat's assassination by Charlotte Corday on July 13, 1793, worked to the same end. "Every one of us," said Robespierre at the Jacobin Club in his eulogy of this gutter journalist of genius whom he personally loathed, "must forget himself, if only for a few moments, in order to embrace the Republic and devote himself without reserve to its interests."

This universalist accord between the Montagnard bourgeois Jacobins and the Parisian popular movement in the spring of 1793 forced on the Mountain a partial reconsideration of the Parisian sansculottes' "program." First came more ideological revolutionary acts, which many bourgeois radicals wanted in any case. The Montagnards decided to create a new revolutionary tribunal. The government in Paris was reorganized. Pressure on priests, émigrés, and nobles was stepped up: although noble-born officers were not excluded from the army, as the sansculottes wanted, the army was purged to some degree. Then with great reluctance the Mountain about-faced on the issue of economic individualism, which had been until then a cardinal principle of theirs, as of the Gironde and the Feuillants. As late as February 1793, Robespierre had chastised the people of Paris for rioting about food prices; their minds, he said, should be set on higher things. But in the late spring of 1793 the Mountain, pressured by the people, suddenly accepted the necessity of state interference in economic life: on June 27 the Paris stock exchange was shut down, and on July 26 the Convention decreed the death penalty for hoarding. The bourgeois program of unrestrained economic individualism was momentarily set aside.

On these new terms a powerful alliance was formed between the plebeian sansculottes, a quintessentially Parisian group anchored in the local Parisian quartiers, whose populist world view was being gradually transformed to resemble what Marx would later describe as class consciousness, and the possessing, revolutionary, and doctrinal Jacobin elite, forced for the moment to legislate against its own fundamental interests. "The Mountain needs the people," said Robespierre. "The people rely on the Mountain." In private, Robespierre was even more explicit: "Internal threats are caused by the bourgeois," he wrote. "In order to defeat the bourgeois, we must rally the people." In the first weeks of March 1793, the Girondin Pierre Vergniaud had explained that social equality could only be applied in the realm of rights: "There can be no equality of wealth, talent, industry, and work."[10] But on March 26, 1793, Jean Bon Saint-André, a Protestant minister and a prominent Montagnard, had concluded quite differently in a speech to the Convention: "It is imperative for us to enable the poor to live if we want to carry the Revolution through."

The difficulty was, of course, that the people of Paris, once they had enabled the Mountain to dominate the Convention, were not content to be silent partners in the new coalition. Concessions here and there were not enough for them. In many ways their new perception of the world owed a great deal to Jacobin thinking. Ultimately, however, Robespierre and his friends, including even Marat, had no intention of restructuring society or sharing power with either the real sansculottes, such as enragés, or the false sansculottes, such as the journalist Hébert, who edited the sansculottes' favorite newspaper, the *Père Duchesne*.

The sansculottes did not understand the basic weakness of their situation. It was difficult for them to react when the Mountain began to betray their trust. In 1789 they had accepted as natural the social dominance of wealth; in 1793–94 they accepted as natural the supremacy of parliamentary, bourgeois, universalist rule. When on September 5, 1793, they invaded the Convention hall, it was not to coerce but to convince. The Montagnards complied at first, but they were deeply shocked. It was one thing for them to praise the people and to use the sansculottes against the Gironde; it was quite another thing for them to be told what to do.

The Mountain's reaction to the escalation of popular claims in the fall of 1793 was a mix of conciliation, resistance, and ideological escapism. Once again they met some of the sansculottes' concrete demands. In August 1793 the Convention had already agreed to create "granaries of abundance," which were reminiscent of the prerevolutionary institutions that had bought grain in good times when it was cheap and redistributed it in times of dearth. On September 29, 1793, the Convention voted the enactment of price controls, in the form of a "general maximum" on prices and wages. The Feuillant separation of the civil and the political (which Marx was to hail as the first principle of the bourgeois revolution) was reversed. The state reentered the economic field from which it had been excluded between 1789 and 1791. The circulation of paper money was rigorously enforced, and the value of paper money actually did go up for some months. Robespierre and the bourgeois Jacobins also authorized the creation of the *armées révolutionnaires,* paramilitary organizations staffed by sansculottes from the cities. These urban bands joined hands with local or even rural Hébertists and sansculottes—who were often more hostile to property than were the Parisians—and set about coercing peasants into selling or giving up their hoarded foodstuffs.

Jacobin concessions to the plebs were soon followed by threatening and aggressive measures against them. The Mountain dramatically strengthened its institutional hold on the government and the government's hold on the country. On October 10, 1793, the Committee of Public Safety, dominated by the Mountain, outlined the future shape of their reinvigorated revolutionary state. In November and December the Convention vigorously reasserted its right to rule. Simultaneously the sansculottes' campaign of forced de-Christianization was abruptly halted. In Paris and many other parts of France—perhaps under the guidance of the armée révolutionnaire and of Parisian sansculottes and militants—priests, including the prorevolutionary constitutional bishop of Paris, Gobel, had been forced publicly to abjure their religious belief, often in humiliating ways. In the last weeks of 1793, Robespierre brought this anticlerical populist endeavor to a sudden end. Sansculottes atheists were humiliated in their turn. Roux, the enragé leader who had been arrested and quickly released in the summer of 1793, was arrested again. The women's popular revolutionary movement was dismantled, and here was another turning point, since the Revolution had witnessed the first instance of women organizing women's political associations, and the female leaders of these popular societies (some of whom were friends of the enragés) had achieved real influence by August and September 1793. In October 1793 the most radical of their number, Claire Lacombe, a woman of principle who had dared to condemn both the populist September massacres and the Jacobin's arbitrary arrest of nobles, was herself arrested. She was soon released, only to be arrested again in the spring of 1794. All of these events amounted to a radical turn to the right in the history of the Revolution, comparable in importance to the elite's radical turn to the left in the fall of 1791.

The Mountain's sansculottes allies were everywhere brought to heel, both in Paris and in the provinces; on February 10 1794, Roux committed suicide in prison. The arrests of merchants ceased. Under the aegis of Carnot, who "organized victory" and managed to feed and supply a revolutionary army of nearly one million men, large sectors of the economy were nationalized. The war office was cleared of the many sansculottes who had infiltrated it in 1793. The French bureaucracy grew fivefold, and the number of officials in Paris rose from five hundred in 1790 to more than sixty-five hundred in 1793–94. Vast state-owned armament works were set up, and conditions of work in them were very closely regulated. This ownership by the state of the "means of production" signaled a tightening of discipline in the work place; and the sansculottes discovered, no doubt to their surprise, that the Jacobins' grudging alternative to private property did not mean greater freedom for the poor.

Finally, the Jacobins' last means of government was ideological escapism, a solution that developed as contradictions increased between Jacobinisms other goals. Because it was difficult simultaneously to conciliate and repress the popular movement, false ideology acquired a very wide sphere indeed. In late 1793 and early 1794, the Jacobins picked up, if in a different and more urgent register, the Girondins' earlier demagogic substitutes for social reform.

By the end of 1793, Jacobinism showed increasing signs of strain. The problem was no longer that the revolutionary French state could not rule with authority or that it was incapable of managing the nation's defense: by the spring of 1794, counterrevolutionary forces, whether royalist in the west or Girondin and royalist at Lyons, were in retreat. France's premier Mediterranean naval base, Toulon, which had been handed over to the British by local royalists, was recaptured in December 1793, thanks to a young Corsican artillery officer with an odd name, Napoleone de Buonaparte, a protégé of Robespierre's younger brother. In that same month the Vendéan peasantry and their often reluctant noble and royalist officers were decimated; their *armée catholique et royale* broke up into small and inefficacious bands. In the northeast, the Austrians' advance was checked in the fall of 1793 and rolled back in the spring of 1794. On June 26, 1794, the Austrians were roundly defeated at Fleurus, and the French once again occupied the whole of Belgium. The tide of battle, which had nearly swamped the revolutionary government in the early summer of 1792 and again in the summer of 1793, had now been completely and definitively turned around.

The problem of Jacobinism lay elsewhere. Jacobinism could not be sustained because its fundamental goals were so contradictory and so different from those of the Parisian poor, without whose help the country could not be ruled. The spokesman of the sansculottes expressed in his individual demands the yearnings of his popular supporters, varyingly defined as the inhabitants of his quartiers, as all Frenchmen, as all right-thinking men and women, or as humanity in general. For the sansculottes, the leader owed his place to his typicality. For Robespierre, in revealing contrast, the "great legislator" was a lonely figure, forever misunderstood, and fated to die by his own hand. His was the typical stance of the accused bourgeois revolutionary leader, an attitude which focused on the presentation of private and arbitrary acts as universally valid, natural, and rational. Robespierre's self-centered conception of individualism was irreconcilable even with his own universalist principles, not to speak of the goals of the sansculottes. His Rousseauist and narcissist self-projection did echo the Jacobins' similarly narcissist

adoration of their own supposed selves in the fancied image of a
sovereign people. But the two Robespierrist and Jacobin visions,
the one private and the other public, were far removed not only
from the popular fraternity of the Paris crowd but also from the
republican fraternity of the French nation's ragtag but seemingly
invincible revolutionary armies. Gradually Jacobinism both alienated the poor and ceased to convince even its own natural audience,
the revolutionary landowning and professional class.

In the spring of 1794 Jacobin politics began to unravel. As might
have been expected, the first effect of the nation's armed successes
on the propertied revolutionary elite was to reinforce their feeling
that the popular movement—no longer as necessary as it had been
—should be even further restrained. To this the Committee of
Public Safety could readily agree: in early March 1794 it decided to
tighten the noose on popular politics once again. It decreed the
arrest of the Hébertists, the self-styled leaders of the sansculottes
who had sporadically attacked the Mountain from the left. In February 1794 unauthorized placards had gone up in Paris urging the
sansculottes to rebel. In response, on March 24, Hébert, his closest
allies, and about twenty militant Parisian sansculottes were executed. The Paris Commune was purged of Hébertists and placed in
the hands of Robespierre's agents. The last of the armées révolutionnaires was liquidated. Many sansculotte popular societies were
dissolved. Since late 1793 bourgeois revolutionism and the revolutionary popular movement earnestly ground each other down, just
as monarchic absolutism and the corporatist parlements had done
from 1771 to 1789.

At this juncture, however, in the spring of 1794, Robespierre's
first problem was no longer the popular left, but the right wing of
his own Jacobin "party." The liquidation of the leftist Hébertists led
to a more difficult challenge from the more conservative Montagnards headed by a great orator and opportunist, Danton. This
corrupt Montagnard, who had come to the fore as an early hero of
the Paris sansculottes and had almost surely accepted royal bribes,
wanted to do more than just execute the Hébertists. He and his
allies, including the young journalist Camille Desmoulins, a personal friend of Robespierre, dared to suggest in print that the
Terror had gone too far. The Dantonists not only wished to defend

property; they also wished to deradicalize the Revolution generally. Their goal was to strengthen social, judicial, and economic individualism at the expense of universalist values and terrorist practices. This was to renew—but more dramatically, given the circumstances of the time—Barnave's turnabout of late 1791 and the Gironde's of late 1792.

Robespierre and the hard-core Jacobins were in a quandary. Robespierre agreed that the sansculottes should be subdued: he himself had switched from movement to resistance in the late fall of 1793 when he had stopped their campaign of de-Christianization. In the spring of 1794, however, although Robespierre no longer wished to rule *with* the people, he did still want to rule *for* them. It was this vestigial universalism that set him apart from the corrupt or cynical Dantonists of 1794 and the Directorials of 1795-1799. For Robespierre and the mainstream Jacobins, ideological radicalism was still the essence of revolutionary politics. The Dantonists' about-face was too much for Robespierre: they too were executed on April 5, 1794.

By now, Robespierre's program of social repression and ideological progressivism was churning in a void. On the right, property owners, even when they were Jacobins, feared that Robespierre's brand of universalist rhetoric would soon lead to social universalism and would unwittingly bring about the forced despoliation of the rich by the poor. In April 1793 the local administration of the Hérault department in southern France had initiated the practice of imposing forced loans on the rich. (The "granaries of abundance" had been funded in that way.) The nationalization of foreign trade and weapons manufacturing was an ominous portent as well. The Robespierrist decrees of Ventôse (26 February and 3 March 1794), which the Convention passed on the basis of a proposal made by Saint-Just and which provided the legal means for the easy expropriation of persons who had been denounced, even anonymously, as counter-revolutionary aristocrats, fed these propertied anxieties. Before his election to the Convention, Saint-Just had been vocal in his sympathy for the peasants of his district. It could be supposed that his were not idle words, though it is now known that most Robespierrists did not really intend to apply these decrees. On the far left at the same time, the genuinely communitarian sansculottes felt cheated by the execution of their leaders, by the abolition of the armées révolutionnaires, and by the imposition of a new maximum, or ceiling, on wages. That measure made sense to the bourgeois Robespierrists: having regulated prices, they would regulate wages accordingly. But the ceiling on wages made no human sense at all to the sansculottes. They were disappointed and exhausted. Their hearts grew heavy; they had become the shock troops of the Revolution, in the Vendée and on the eastern border, and their wounds were deep.

In the late spring of 1794, Robespierre had few friends left, and as they too fell away his ideological and institutional escapism became more fevered. The Terror gained in intensity at the very moment when the practical need to maintain it in order to galvanize the nation against foreign invasion lessened. Unable to secure the loyalty of either the plebs or the possessing class, Robespierre had no choice but to tyrannize everyone. "Virtue," Samuel Adams had written in 1775, "is the surest means of securing the public liberty." But in Robespierre's Republic, virtue had become empty rhetoric and a poor compensation for social stasis and the *loss* of liberty. In 1789 the elite had assumed that the administration of France could be decentralized and its bureaucracy elected because the state was coterminous with the united and sovereign nation. By 1794 the terms of the problem had been inverted. Society was within the state.[11] In the spring of 1794, the practical effect of universalist fraternity was to justify blind terror: the Revolution, like Saturn, devoured its own firstborns.

Unable to mold French society to their wishes, the remaining Jacobins drifted toward a compensatory restructuring of culture— language, literature, and history. Classic plays were rewritten to suit the needs of the moment. Symbols of all sorts were used, both to express escapist desires and to convince the masses that Jacobinism could relate to their lives, appearances notwithstanding. All over France, Jacobinism in 1793 and early 1794 spawned a welter of symbolic images. The signs whose use the Girondins had already encouraged were multiplied a hundredfold, often to the point of laughable extravagance. Linguistic excess became commonplace, even though Jacobins had prided themselves at first on the laconic and heroic plainness of their "anti-rhetoric." In public fetes, a generously female Marianne was sometimes made to stand for the Republic, as was, at other times, a splendidly masculine Hercules, wielder of an expressive mace that was the dread of aristocrats. Sexual metaphors readily came to the minds of those who were desperate to create the illusion of social complementarity. The great neoclassical artist, Louis David, orchestrated vast fetes whose leitmotiv was the harmonious, universalist blending of opposites: men and women, the young and the aged, Parisians and provincials, Frenchmen and foreigners, word and music, sight and sound. Much energy was devoted to the purification and simplification of French syntax and spelling so that the French language might become a universal idiom, equally accessible to men and women of all nations and social classes: "France has received from America the example of legislative regeneration," wrote Antoine Tournon, author of a *Grammaire des sans-culottes* (who was soon to be executed), "let us give to all nations the example of linguistic regeneration."[12]

To complete their moral restructuring of the world, the Jacobins chose to reshape space and time. Here was a yearning typical of a revolutionary age: Jefferson himself had toyed with the idea of computing all of America's weights and measures in terms of some Newtonian unit called the "ryttenhouse," but his friend David Rittenhouse had quickly demonstrated the impracticability of the scheme.[13] In France, the new computations became an affair of state: a new republican calendar, invented by a corrupt Montagnard (soon to be executed as well) contained thirty-six weeks, each ten days long, with five extra *sans-culottides*.) Diligent watchmakers produced the decimal clocks that divided the days into twenty rather than twenty-four hours. Thousands of towns were renamed for revolutionary heroes, especially if they had borne the name of a local saint. (Only two instances of this revolutionary nomenclature survived into the following century.) Hundreds of thousands of citizens, male and female, were drawn into active or passive participation in public celebrations. All were the objects of unrelenting, occasionally convincing, Jacobin propaganda: in Paris alone, three hundred children were given the first name of Brutus in 1793–94.[14]

In this climate of revolutionary and republican unanimity, dissent of any kind became traitorous, a conspiratorial insult to the majesty of popular sovereignty. Before the Revolution, Necker had eulogized "public opinion," which brought together the sum of varied individual and enlightened opinions. The Jacobins preferred to think in terms of a single, self-evident "esprit public"; and, as Mona Ozouf has pointed out, Saint-Just went one step farther to the "conscience publique." Politically, the world of the Jacobins was divided into two parts: an ever shrinking band of pure patriots regenerated by the Revolution (many of them on government pay), who were committed to defend a Jacobin and universalist Republic of selfless virtue; and an ever growing number of counterrevolutionary "aristocrats" who perversely cultivated in themselves the dark side of human nature. In the camp of humanity were the Jacobin *clubistes,* who, in Dijon for example, defined themselves as "the purest extract of the people, a body of intrepid and zealous men, armed with force, prudence, and, above all, public opinion, which is superior to all other powers."[15] On the other side stood the imagined enemies of the people, so corrupt and malevolent that they hardly deserved the semblance of a trial: "Nothing is more difficult," wrote a member of the Committee of Public Safety, "than to prove the crimes of conspirators. They work in darkness; their crimes are reflected acts; material proof of their deeds is nearly always missing. Unless they actually succeed, no evidence of their malevolence is to be found. As far as they are concerned, condemnation must be based on the conviction of guilt alone."[16]

DURING THE LAST WEEKS of the Terror, after June 1794, the rule of law was suspended in both theory and practice. The rhythm of execution, modest by twentieth-century standards, was stepped up. The social origins of victims were more varied than before. Because the Republic of Virtue thrived on the persecution of weak and "immoral" groups (such as prostitutes, nuns, or noblewomen), many of its victims (for example, the speakers of local dialects) may have been chosen not in spite of their marginality but as a result of it. Unable to address the true social problems of the age, the Robespierrist Terrorists made up for their powerlessness by the persecution of defenceless people who belonged to social groups whose principles they did not like. The effect of their universalism, which had in 1789 celebrated the dawn of a new age, had become the reverse of what it was supposed to be.

The Terror is a critical moment in the history of Western culture. Looking forward, it points to the totalitarian terrorism of the twentieth century and to the senseless extermination of innocents, carried out in the name of ideological truth by professional revolutionaries who are indifferent to the concerns of ordinary men and women. Looking backward, it reminds one of the fundamental structures of French culture and society before the Revolution. Explanations of the phenomenon relate to many different issues contemporaneous with or antecedent to the events of 1793–94, such as the self-righteousness of Enlightenment thought, which fancied itself embedded in Nature and Reason, or the constraints of war, or social envy, bloodlust, and personal revenge. Terror, once set in motion, became its own justification: it generated enemies who then had to be terrorized.

In many important respects, the Jacobins' ability to impose ideological escapism and terrorism as a solution to their political impasse bears witness to the social and institutional disorganization of French life after the individualist dérapage of the 1789–1791 period, and to its antecedent, the ambiguous conditions of French social life during the last decades of the ancien régime. In a more structured, individualist, and economically advanced society, the Jacobins could hardly have succeeded as they did. The roots of the Terror, embedded to a large extent in politics, also point to the shapelessness of French culture and society *before* the Revolution; to the shallow implantation of individualism which after 1789 made possible the invocation of communitarian virtue; and to the disintegration of traditional, institutionalized corporatism, a decay which made the social yearning for community a loose cannon on the decks of French politics and society.

Like Girondism in 1792, Montagnard Jacobinism in 1794 was an unstable doctrine. It presupposed the reconciliation of irreconcilable opposites. In its last phase, after October 1793, Terrorism was for some months a tactically useful alternative to genuine consensus, but France soon sickened of the bloodshed. In the Convention, even the most radical feared for their lives. In a celebrated passage Saint-Just, on the eve of Robespierre's collapse, reflected on what the Revolution had become: "The use of terror has jaded us, just as the palate is jaded by strong liquors . . . The Revolution is a frozen thing. Principles have weakened. Liberty caps worn by intriguers are all that is left."

In these circumstances, a continuation of terroristic Jacobinism after the spring of 1794 would have been nothing less than suicidal: it is significant that such prominent Jacobin revolutionaries as Saint-Just and Robespierre constantly invoked the great classical suicides, Seneca, Brutus, Cato, and Socrates, as victims of their devotion to the public good. On Ninth Thermidor (27 July 1794), a conspiracy inside the Convention brought the whole rickety system crashing down. Robespierre and Saint-Just and some dozens of their friends were executed the next day. The people of Paris did little to save them.

THE HISTORY OF French politics in the six years following the fall of Robespierre is conceptually a single era, even though it includes the last year of the Convention (whose members had supported Robespierre in early 1794) and the five years of the Directory, a governing body elected under a new constitution adopted in 1795, whose architects were obsessed by their detestation of Robespierre.

The essence of the Directorial (or Thermidorean) program was quite simple: the sanculottes movement was to be violently brought to heel. The political rights of the poor were explicitly curtailed, a step which Tom Paine correctly gauged to be the end of France's "civic empire." But hypocritically, the individualist-universalist myth (reinterpreted conservatively, of course) remained in theory the cardinal principle of the regime.

In some isolated domains this balance was still convincing: the regime's devotion to the Enlightenment was successfully displayed in the legendary creation of another set of state-run Grandes Ecoles (the Ecole Polytechnique in 1794–95 and the Ecole Normale in 1794). These institutions revealed both the intellectualism of the regime and its defense of individualism, since the graduates were not guaranteed employment and the professions remained open to all with talent, including those who did not have state-awarded degrees to prove it. Generally, however, the contradiction between the regime's ideological goals, at once universalist and individualist, which had been concealed in 1789 but made evident in 1794, became painfully obvious after 1795.

Of course, many Directorials had private motives for wanting to further the progressive ideology of the regime. As private persons, they would otherwise have had much to lose. Many of them had voted for the death of the king, or had themselves been Jacobin Terrorists, including the former viscount from Provence, Barras, who had betrayed Robespierre in Thermidor and was now an eminent political personage—the patron of the young Corsican, Bonaparte, who would soon gratefully inherit Barras's discarded mistress, Joséphine de Beauharnais, the Caribbean-born widow of a noble, prorevolutionary general executed in 1794. Many people had a complicated past. But the Directorials' program went beyond their private situations. They still hoped to ensconce possessive individualism in a context of illusive revolutionary ideology. Their obsession on this score shows the persistent strength in France after 1794 of an empty communitarian rhetoric, now ennobled by the memory of civil strife and sacrifice.

In 1798 a republican journalist sympathetic to the Directorial regime presented his self-serving view of what France would be like in a hundred years. Most important, the five-man executive Directory was still there. Priests and churches, however, had vanished. "Thanks to a general abundance, and to an approximate equality of material condition, due to the effect of partible inheritance and to the weight of taxation rather than to a violent redistribution of landed property, great inequalities of wealth are no more. Criminality, born as it was of extreme need and extreme wealth, is extinct."[17] These were by no means ignoble aims, but the Directorials' hopes were nonetheless increasingly trivial because, unlike the earlier Jacobins, the Thermidoreans of the late 1790s had no use whatever for the popular movement. The difference between them and Robespierre was that Robespierre had always hoped to combine his universalist principles and bourgeois practices in a way that the sansculottes might accept. The Directorials, despite their words, hoped instead to secure their own ends for and by themselves. It is that ruthless collective egotism which makes their continued reference to republican universalist ideology ring false.

Jacobinism after the fall of Robespierre split into three different currents. The motivations of the rightist *réacteurs* are easiest to understand. In spite of their revolutionary past, or perhaps because of it, these unscrupulous and reactionary ex-Jacobins were ready to do nearly anything in order to guarantee the social order and their personal place in it. They were not much troubled in 1795 by the wholesale murder, in the provinces, of former sansculottes and Robespierrists by royalist and Catholic bands, which the police and judiciary did very little to control. To them, left-wing radicalism in all its forms was anathema. Many of these réacteur Thermidoreans would welcome Napoleon's rise to power. The former terrorist, Fouché, one of their leading lights, played an important role after 1800 as the emperor's ennobled and very efficient minister of police.

On the other side, on the left of acceptable Directorial politics, were the réacteurs' opposite numbers, the members of the Crest, or the *Crêtois*. They had supported the Mountain during Robespierre's Reign of Virtue, and they still thought of themselves as virtuous Jacobins. Many of these deputies had accepted Robespierre's fall with some relief, not because they disapproved of his ideological radicalism but because they wrongly assumed that the universalism of 1789 could still be sustained in 1794 without terror. The Crêtois were not communists, though some of them, under the pressure of events, eventually drifted into an alliance with the enemies of private property. Generally the Crêtois believed, as had Robespierre, that economic individualism and broad universalism could be reconciled in a virtuous Republic.

The Crêtois who, unlike the Girondins, were men of principle, soon regretted that they had abandoned Robespierre. In the spring of 1795, when the sansculottes invaded the Convention for the last time, the Crêtois took their side. The majority of the ex-Jacobins were willing to forgive the Crêtois devotion to the cause of the people and to radical, Jacobin principle, provided that these matters were safely quarantined in the realm of high abstraction. But when the Crêtois tried to give substance to their words and allied themselves with the sansculottes, their furious colleagues turned on them and had them arrested and tried. As proof of their devotion to the cause of the people, these Martyrs of Prairial decided to die in an exemplary, Catonian way: many of them stabbed themselves to death in the courtroom when their sentences were read out, passing the fatal knife to one another in a last gesture of self-assertion and self-sacrifice.

The more typical path of the erstwhile Jacobins was an intermediate course between the rightist réacteurs and the leftist Crest. The former abbé, Sieyès, was the leading thinker of these middling republicans. He and the other mainstream Directorials loudly proclaimed the principles of communitarian and universalist citizenship, but they had no intention whatever of putting them into practice. Economic individualism was their first concern. "Civil equality," explained one of Sieyès's closest allies, the Protestant Boissy d'Anglas, "no sensible man can ask for more."[18] As was to be expected, the regime (like that of the Girondins in 1792 and of the Montagnards in 1794) developed a very complex symbolism that expressed its commitment to unsubstantiated republican values. Deputies adopted Roman dress. The use of the pronoun "tu" (as against the more formal "vous") was required in official correspondence. The regime insisted that the revolutionary calendar and new place names be used. The Catholic Church was persecuted more vigorously in 1797 and 1798 than it had been in 1794. The regime more or less sponsored a counterreligious, civil cult called Theophilanthropy, which, incidentally, the anticlerical Tom Paine welcomed with some eagerness. The Directory also used foreign policy as a buttress against internal stresses: wars of rapine and conquest were one of the Directory's principle sources of income. In 1794 David had staged vast public holidays to celebrate the unanimity of a revolutionary people. The Directory continued this practice of public fetes, but theirs became stiff, pedagogic rites, some of them circus-like performances.

In these conditions of hostile neglect, the material life of the urban poor worsened dramatically. Late in 1794 conditions were particularly bad. The winter was very cold. The harvest had been poor. The war, paper money, and the state's organization of victory had disrupted traditional methods of supplying food. The institutional disengagement of the Directory, its decision to withdraw from the economic sphere, was followed by the complete collapse of the assignats, a circumstance that allowed the rich, nationwide, to buy another set of biens nationaux that were put up for sale for as little as 5 percent of their real worth. In that same winter the very poor, both destitute and inadequately clothed, literally froze or starved to death. The incidence of prostitution rose sharply. In the spring of 1795 the sansculottes, many of them women, rose up once more, first in April and again in May, in the name of "bread and the constitution of 1793." After lynching a deputy whose head they paraded around the Convention on a pike, they were overcome. At least four thousand of them were arrested by the army at the prompting of the socially conservative, ex-Jacobins, many of whom had, in their former, supposedly radical incarnation, spoken quite lyrically about the constitution of 1793.

The failure of these spontaneous sansculotte insurrections in April and May 1795 had a world-historical effect: they convinced Gracchus Babeuf, the first revolutionary communist, that the popular movement should be rethought in both theory and practice. The people, who had formerly served the Jacobin bourgeoisie, would have to find their own way. To the earlier liberal vision of pluralist social harmony, Babeuf opposed the prospect of all-out class war. That was his basic strategy. But Babeuf also concluded that spontaneous popular insurrection would not be enough to overthrow the system. He looked forward to a Leninist type of conspiracy of civilians and soldiers that would seize power and rule dictatorially and terroristically on behalf of the people, for a short time at least. Propertied politicians would be overpowered and, if need be, murdered. Strategically and conceptually, Babeuf went well beyond the sansculottes' classic insurrectionary demand for cheap bread. His goal was not just the reentry of the state into economics through suspension of the laws of the market, such as Robespierre had reluctantly accepted, but the abolition of all private property.

Obviously, the distance that had been traveled by the popular movement is of major importance. In 1789 French working people had accepted the propertied elite's scheme of economic and social individualism. Although only 41 of the 943 grievance books drawn up before the Revolution by urban corporate groups had requested the abolition of guilds, the abolition in 1791 of corporatism itself had not elicited much explicit protest. Marat alone had criticized the Le Chapelier law, but he had done so for political reasons, without understanding what that liberal, narrowly individualist document implied. Before 1789 this foreign-born ne'er-do-well had yearned to join the state-sponsored Academy of Science and to pass himself off as the scion of a noble Spanish family. (His father was in fact an Italian convert to Protestantism who made a poor living as an apothecary in a small Swiss town.) By 1792, however, Marat had gone some distance from that starting point. He had become a polemicist of genius, a French (and a much more radical) Tom Paine. His thought was closer to modern, insurrectionary socialism than to the Radical Whig principles he had espoused in his youth.

Marat was murdered in July 1793, nine days after damning Roux for his excessive egalitarianism. But in 1796 Babeuf pushed forward the process of popular ideological radicalization that Marat had exemplified. Private property, he decided, was an abomination. Men were born equal (some Babouvists were sympathetic to the rights of women; others not) and should remain so, as members of an egalitarian community rather than as worshipers of false individualism. All distinctions were bad, wrote Babeuf: "The supposed superiority of talents and intelligence is a pipe dream ... The importance we set on intelligence is born of opinion, not fact. We really should consider if physical, natural strength isn't just as important." Thanks to Babeuf's theorizing, and also because so many provincial sansculottes had fled to Paris for safety, the Babouvist conspiracy became something of a national party, more self-aware theoretically than the Parisian sansculottes had ever been between 1789 and 1795.

Because the Directory could still rely on the army in 1796, the regime had little trouble in suppressing the Babouvist plot. Most sansculotte militants were identified and arrested. But despite these tactical successes, Sieyès's government consisted in the end of no more than a self-destructive, hypocritical mouthing of Jacobin and prerevolutionary "liberal universalist" thought. The Directorials soon found themselves entrapped in a parodic version of the dilemma that the Girondins and Montagnards had faced earlier on. The Directorials' spurious emphasis on ideological radicalism, which did not convince the propertied elite, served to justify the cause of Babouvist communism: at his trial, after the failure of his insurrectionary coup, Babeuf exculpated himself by referring to the Rousseauist principles that figured in the very constitution of the government that was about to kill him. Although the regime had expected its ideology to defuse social tensions, its effect in 1796, as it had been in the early 1790s, was exactly the reverse. Directorial ideology strengthened the resolve of the communists, while weakening the desire of the propertied bourgeoisie to accept a republican form of government, however socially conservative it might be. Most propertied Frenchmen, even if they were not devout Catholics (and many of them were) were hostile to the persecution of the clergy. After a leftward lurch in September 1797, the Directory cut itself off from its base. Richard Cobb writes of France at this time: "The recognition signals had been lost, without being replaced by others, so that people groped along a narrow ledge, uncertain of the direction in which they were going or what they might meet round the corner."[19] It could be added that the signs existed but that they pointed left while the regime was actually moving to the right.

In some respects the Directory did administratively useful work. The finances of the state were gradually set in order and paper money was given up. Enclosures were encouraged. French manufactures were nurtured by the state. Trade also picked up. A new, more efficient hierarchic administration was put into place. Since harvests were good after 1796, conditions of life improved. Military recruitment was better regulated. New legislation was passed to strengthen the role of fathers and rescind the rights of illegitimate children. Yet none of these reforms or supposed improvements, however much they might please the possessing class, could make up for the basic character flaw of the regime.

Historians have varyingly accounted for the failure of the Directory. It can be plausibly supposed, for example, that the institutional structure of the regime was unusually arcane: instead of a president, the Republic's executive was a five-man Directory. Laws had to be approved by two assemblies, annually renewed in parts. The regime's economic and fiscal difficulties were consequential: because the Directory never had enough money, it was unable in 1799 to pay its own officials. It also had to allow its thieving generals a free hand in the foreign territories which they conquered, notably in Italy. Bonaparte, haloed by his spectacular victories in Italy and distant Egypt, where he had been sent by the worried Directors to conquer a road to an even more distant India, became obstreperous and later, of course, uncontrollable.

Much has been made of foreign and counterrevolutionary conspiracies. The institutional instability of the regime, it is often suggested, was compounded by insurrectionary plots. From time to time, as in September 1797, the regime was forced—it was said—to suspend due process of law in order to undo its nearly triumphant foes. Eventually, the argument ran, the regime fell victim to the ill will of its opponents on both the left and the right: to the Babouvists, the émigrés, the pretender to the throne, his English fund raisers abroad, and his counterrevolutionary, Catholic, royalist followers at home.

Such tangible factors were all of some consequence in determining the failures of the Directory. In a similar vein, inefficacy had also been in America one of the motives behind the framers' decision to bypass the Continental Congress in order to draft the new federal Constitution. But in both countries, material failings were more a catalyst than a true cause. In the New World, the reshaping of the republican state answered not just immediate circumstance, but society's need to create pluralistic institutions that would reconcile individual endeavor and the public good by setting them in a new institutional and cultural framework. In France, the root cause of the Directory's failure lay in its inability to reconcile its falsely universalist ideology with its social program and in its unwillingness to meet the deep-seated communitarian longing of French working people for a more regulated economic and social life.

In a satirical essay which he wrote shortly before his death in 1797, Edmund Burke, a friend of the American Revolution but a bitter enemy of the upheaval in France, reviewed the various constitutional possibilities which the French might adopt. The one he recommended to them—in view of the penchant that Sieyès and his allies had for declaring illegal those elections which they did not win—was a system in which the elected chose the electors. And the curious thing is that Sieyès did propose such a text to Bonaparte shortly after the coup of 18 Brumaire. The right to elect parliament was to be withdrawn from primary assemblies and transferred to a republican-minded and ideologically universalist but socially reliable "college of conservatives" that would somehow represent the nation's profound aspirations. Part of the beauty of the plan, of course, was that Sieyès himself would choose the members of that college, who would then choose the parliamentarians, who would then choose Sieyès. The scheme was pleasingly self-contained. It also contrasted strikingly with the continued assertion of popular sovereignty by propertied American Republicans in 1787, and was a good example of what French bourgeois universalism had come to mean by 1799.

Bonaparte, who returned to Egypt in October 1799 and staged his coup one month later, did not, it is true, much like this complicated plan; but he did not leave Sieyès empty-handed. To thank the former abbé for his help in overthrowing the Republic—and with it also, the Revolution which Sieyès had done so much to further in 1789—Napoleon assigned to his new client not just a large pension, but, eventually, a handsome new title as well: Count Sieyès. When Sieyès appeared in court dress at a Napoleonic function, another former revolutionary guffawed to a friend, "Have you seen Sieyès? 'What Is the Third Estate?' "

The Political and Social Effects of French and American Republicanism

ON THE EVE of 1889 the Third Republic considered the kind of monument that would be most suitable to commemorate the one hundredth anniversary of the French Revolution. Gustave Eiffel won the prize with his celebrated tower, a unique engineering feat that expressed, or so it seemed to French republicans, the innovative spirit of their doctrine. Less respectfully, a conservative wag proposed the erection of a giant guillotine.

Reactions to America's political and social history have been more subdued. Most Americans feel that their country's life history has been a political success, but many of them also understand that countless Americans have suffered grievously—and failed—in their struggle to widen their social space in that political paradise. Historical judgment bears out this double-edged, commonsense verdict.

America's political trajectory has not been without its catastrophes. Of these, the worst was the Civil War. Six hundred thousand Americans, among them the nation's first magistrate, died during that fratricidal struggle, more than ten times the fifty thousand casualties of the civil war in France in 1871. And once more, in the late nineteenth century, American society seemed to be on the verge of some great political catharsis: in 1894 seven hundred thousand workers went on strike. When the governor of Illinois, a socialist sympathizer, refused to call out the militia, President Grover Cleveland authorized the use of federal troops to break the strikes. In 1896 when the populist William Jennings Bryan, the Great Commoner, won the Democratic party nomination, many Americans feared that their country was about to fall apart. Since then, in the 1930s during the Great Depression and more recently during the Vietnam War, the fabric of American politics has been stretched very far.

Nonetheless, the basic fact of America's political biography is that its revolutionary and liberal political tradition has survived as the sustaining framework of its modern institutions. It is within this steadfast but open compass that independent America, once an isolated agricultural society of three million inhabitants, has become an industrial world power of 250 million.

French republicanism cannot lay claim to such successes. Yet French history is not so chaotic as at first appears: bureaucratic centralism underpins French politics, and the Gallic polity has not been so unstable as might be supposed from the dizzying succession of two monarchies, two empires, and five republics. "Which is preferable", it may be asked, "a politics of consensus, as in America, that breaks down occasionally, or a French politics of confrontation which ordinarily sublimates social conflict in empty and harmless rhetoric?" Nevertheless, the basic contrast between the stability of American politics and the French crises of political legitimacy cannot be denied.

The relative merits of the two countries' social histories, however, are more difficult to sort out, especially for America, where political harmony and social trauma are intricately intertwined. The effects of America's consensual republicanism have been on balance positive. The central argument of this book hinges on that assumption. But the hidden social effects of America's political consensus have been problematic.

The fundamental difference between the social trajectories of the two nations centers, of course, on the "nonappearance" of class in America as the operative principle of either social relations or national politics. This difference cannot be explained materially. The distance between rich and poor has often been greater in America than in France: during the Old Regime, noble landlords and "peasant rogues" were much closer than American planters and their black slaves. And in the late nineteenth century the divisive force of high capitalism as probably less burdensome and less violent in Saint-Etienne than it was in Pittsburgh. Conditions of life in New York's slums were hardly better than they were in Paris's "red belt."

For many reasons these significant differences in wealth have not resurfaced in America as durable differences in class, explicitly stated and consciously perceived. First among them is the celebrated safety valve of the frontier. Of consequence also are American prosperity, the dynamic character of American industrialism, and the satisfaction of seemingly insatiable private greed by America's inexhaustible cornucopia. Ethnic and racial divisions have also impeded the elaboration of broader class loyalties. So has the absence of a premodern corporate or feudal past.

These are important developments, but the crucial element behind modern American "classlessness" has been political. Paradoxically, the American Republic has simultaneously opened the door to change and made it unusually difficult for Americans to conceptualize and alter their material and social situations.

On the one hand, American republicanism, though fundamentally individualist and materialist, has had a powerful mythical, democratic, and communitarian dimension. Its premier expression has been Abraham Lincoln, an ambitious arriviste, a midwestern, petit-bourgeois, social-climbing lawyer, much derided in his time but instantly recognized upon his death as a martyr to the cause of human freedom everywhere. American republicanism, though ever mindful of property rights, has, when pressured, responded to at least some of the needs of the disenfranchised. Reform is normally thought possible in America, even by that society's most bitter critics. And in symbiotic manner, its propertied elites, culturally conditioned to understand the need for social compromise, will often yield to popular entreaty.

Power, wealth, and a sense of justice, though ordinarily at odds, are not so disassociated in America as they have been elsewhere. It was not incongruous that Lincoln's abolitionist Republican party should have soon become the vehicle of robber-baron capitalism; or, in a different mode, that Lincoln's son (a Harvard graduate) should have tried to be a railway magnate. But neither was it out of step with the American order of things for Theodore and Franklin Roosevelt, like John and Robert Kennedy later—American aristocrats of a kind, and all of them graduates of America's most privileged educational institution — to have instinctive sympathy for the socially weak and the politically disenfranchised.

American republicanism has been a socially conciliatory doctrine, often surprisingly mindful of the need for communitarian action. Moreover, the extent of its capacity for compromise has reflected its faithfulness to the spirit of America's religious and political origins. It is indeed the case, as Louis Hartz has argued, that America does not have a *feudal* past: individualism has always been the first social value. But it is wrong to think that America has had no *communitarian* past. Communitarianism appeared not only in the fabric of prerevolutionary social life but in the continued ideological perception of what American society was, and, especially after 1776, should be. Gordon Wood is right in emphasizing the Federalists' disassociation of republicanism and democracy; but he is on less certain ground when he implies that the Federalists were not interested in "the problem of virtue."[1] Though discouraged about the decline of public mores, which they saw in the populist factionalism of Confederation politics—the Federalists did not give up on republican virtue, and neither did their descendants. They sought instead to elicit it in new and different ways.

On the other hand, America, though politically stable and conceptually classless, has been unusually cruel to humble men and women whose personal destiny has fallen lamentably short of their youthful dreams. Defeated French workers blamed the bourgeois state, but defeated Americans usually blamed themselves. The American republican consensus was kind to those whom it took in, but doubly harsh to those whom it exploited and excluded. Indeed, the sense of empowerment and success which many fortunate immigrants have felt in their American incarnation may have had as its necessary counterpart the continued subjugation of historically marginalized minorities.

American republicanism did not exclude social categories as such. Americans, for example, did not for long ration their electoral franchise by wealth. But by setting itself aridly within the confines of the Constitution as it was shortsightedly thought to exist, American republicanism denied full citizenship to millions. In the name of a self-serving definition of what was "natural," American republicanism, unchallenged by a popular consciousness of class, rejected the full humanity of the very weak and betrayed the nobler ideological expectations of the founders. The contrast between the universalism of the American Republic and its physical, biological exclusiveness was greater and more cruel than that between the sham rhetoric of French Jacobinism and the more discrete and sublimated exclusion of the poor as members of a class. In France, proletarians could become bourgeois, albeit infrequently. American blacks could hardly avoid being what they were. Jefferson did not hesitate to deny the full humanity of his slaves in terms which few French traditionalists have dared to endorse. And blacks are only the most extreme case of a larger pattern: a similar exclusiveness engulfed eastern and southern European immigrants to America in the late nineteenth century; it is affecting Latin American migrants today. It must be remembered too that the American Revolution and the birth of an American nation marked a dreadful turning point in the history of native Americans.

The case of women after 1776 is also relevant. After the Revolution, American women gained new public prestige as the wives and mothers of republican heroes.[2] Their heightened sense of self was reflected in a more frequent willingness to live their lives independently. But the elaboration of this newfound public and political status coincided with a politically sanctioned and negating domestication of women as a sex. After 1790 republican mothers were perceived to be the biologically ideal vehicles of privatist religion. Their homes became a refuge from public culture rather than an extension of it. What the new American Republic gave with one hand, it easily allowed others to take away: "She has learned by the use of her Independence," wrote Tocqueville of the young American woman of his day, "to surrender it without a struggle and without a murmur, when the time comes for making the sacrifice."[3]

Americans are a pilgrim people with a promised vision of their future, but their dreams are too often denied. It is difficult to imagine that Martin Luther King's messianic and pacifist vision could had arisen in any other modern polity. But it is also true that nowhere else (outside of South Africa) has the transition from formal rights to social empowerment, for so large and disenfranchised a minority as American blacks, been so successfully resisted.

Because their totalizing vision has not been informed by a sustained judgment of their nation's social and economic structures—which they often persist in regarding as immanent creations—disenfranchised Americans have been unable to realize their visionary goals. Abraham Lincoln did come to see the need to free all the slaves; but the lands of the rebellious southern planters were not expropriated. The liberated bondsmen did not receive their "Forty acres and a mule." Poor blacks were no more empowered in 1865 to defend their newly won formal rights of citizenship than poor whites had been before them.

The social and cultural effects of French republicanism have been quite different and, in many ways, even more negative. Because it generated class war, first in inchoate form with the sansculottes of 1792–93, and then in the countervailing conceptualizations of Babeuf and his socialist successors, French republicanism ripped the nation apart. Republicanism in France failed as a doctrine of social and ideological consensus, and its failure occasioned frightful civil war. In June 1848 and May 1871 the conservative Republic slaughtered leftist workers as no monarchist regime had ever dared to do. After the bloody week that marked the end of the Paris Commune, tens of thousands of bodies were stacked in collective graves quickly dug in Baron Haussmann's new and elegant public parks. In the late 1930s many middle-class French men and women, horrified by the rise of the Popular Front, pondered the merits of international fascism. They warmed to the slogan "Better Hitler than Léon Blum." When Jews were deported by the Germans with the complicity of the Vichy regime, bourgeois French republicans did not do much to help their persecuted fellow citizens.

The popular left was rejected, as were Catholics on the other side. The bourgeois Republic of the late nineteenth century was no more gentle toward the traditionalist right than the revolutionaries had been toward the church before 1800. In the 1880s, and again in the early 1900s, the whole dynamic of the French Republic was fueled by irreligion: "Le cléricalisme," said Léon Gambetta, who had made his name as a nationalist, populist, and republican hero during the Franco-Prussian War of 1870–71, "voilà l'ennemi!"

Republican doctrine did not coalesce around a complementary blend of practical and transcendental values in France as it did in revolutionary America. In consequence, its most durable if inadvertent effect was to reinforce the strength of the centralized bureaucratic state, on whose limited omnipresence the bourgeoisie had to rely in order to repress their numerous opponents —physically, if need be. The Third French Republic, it was said, governed badly but (for a while) defended itself quite well.

These are impressive failures. But just as the success story of American politics has many shadows, so does the gloomy social history of modern France have brighter nuances. The social effects of French politics have in an obvious sense been sadly deleterious; those of American pluralism have been less so. But a comparison of the two social structures is by no means invariably to America's advantage. Confrontational politics, though it has done the French working class little material good, has had cultural merit. It may have been the persistent hope of social revolution — of "la lutte finale," of "le grand soir"—that best enabled millions of exploited French women and men to face economic subjugation and the grinding routines of daily life. Their need for solace was great. France was, with the United States, one of the last Western industrial countries to create a welfare state that guaranteed the poor and the unemployed some measure of relief. In that climate of "republican" indifference, the expectation of an imminent social Armageddon was for the weak and poor a critical psychological compensation, the analogue in France of the more ecumenical and even less precise American vision of a blessed people in a promised land. Though destitute and culturally marginalized, French workers, unlike American blacks, were never socially or politically invisible. They were buoyed by a sense of class solidarity. The hope of the poor in France was not taken away.

Nineteenth- and twentieth-century French communitarian strategies were inspired by both the insurrectionary message of Jacobinism and the sansculottes' discovery of the limits of Jacobin politics. Jacobinism, as it had developed during the Great Terror of 1793–94, with its overblown, deceptive rhetoric and its mindless bloodiness, was a quasi-pathological political ideology. But the basic schema of nineteenth-century French radicals, which made unyielding class consciousness the motor of redistributive justice (a schema engendered by the French Revolution), has had, and in many ways still has, obvious historical relevance. The Paris Commune of 1871 was a revolutionary and anarchistic regime that was hostile to many forms of abusive and speculative wealth, but it was not politically tyrannical or even vengeful. Its message is still instructive for those whose social goal is the ennoblement of all individuals in a democratic and communitarian context.

IN SUMMARIZING the political and social effects of French and American republicanism, it could be said that the vision of democratic empowerment in a context of liberal democracy in either France or America is and always has been a pipe dream. But it may be that the judgment of history is not yet in. Some joint lesson is still to be learned from combining the divergent empowering traditions that are embedded in these two national histories. The French and American political traditions are perhaps two sides of a single coin, two strategies in a single struggle.

The historical progressions of France and America should then be read together, optimistically, as complementary versions of a single story. Taken in that sense, these two histories, more than those of any other countries of the North Atlantic world, can provide a model for the inseparable claims of freedom, empowerment, and citizenship. The Sister Republics can then be imagined as a single polity, a single, powerful model, constituting—in words taken from a debate at the Democratic–Republican Society of Philadelphia in April 1794 — "the temple of Liberty, the residence of Arts, Sciences, Liberality, and Humanity, [a] Hercules in the extermination of every monster of unlawful domination."[4]

Notes

Selected Bibliography

Index

Notes

Introduction: Republicanism in France and America

1. The pamphlet was written by the conservative Austro-German publicist Friedrich von Gentz. Cited by R. R. Palmer, *The Age of Democratic Revolution: A History of Europe and America, 1760–1800* (Princeton: Princeton University Press, 1959), p. 188.
2. *The Eighteenth Brumaire of Louis Napoleon Bonaparte*, in *The Marx-Engels Reader*, ed. Robert C. Tucker (W. W. Norton: New York, 1972), p. 437.

1. Forced Community and Transcendental Individualism in America's First Colonies

1. Louis Hartz, *The Liberal Tradition in America: An Interpretation of American Political Thought since the Revolution* (New York: Harcourt, Brace, and World, 1955), p. 9. It should be pointed out that the meaning of the French term "libéral" is paradoxically close to that of the word "neoconservative" in America. Ordinarily, French "libéralisme" does not go far beyond what most "liberal" American intellectuals define as possessive or acquisitive individualism. In these pages the term "liberal," unless otherwise qualified, stands for the empowerment of the self in a cultural context of becoming that is neither politically authoritarian nor socially atomistic.
2. Hartz, *Liberal Tradition*, p. 4.
3. Ibid.
4. D. W. Meinig, *The Shaping of America: A Geographical Perspective on Five Hundred Years of History*, vol. I, *Atlantic America, 1492–1800* (New Haven: Yale University Press, 1986), p. 238.
5. Perry Miller, *The New England Mind: The Seventeenth Century* (Cambridge, Mass.: Harvard University Press, 1954), pp. 416–417.
6. Cited by Sacvan Bercovitch, *The Puritan Origins of the American Self* (New Haven: Yale University Press, 1975), p. 17.
7. William Carey MacWilliams, *The Idea of Fraternity in America* (Berkeley: University of California Press, 1973), p. 121.
8. Edmund Sears Morgan, *The Puritan Family: Religion and Domestic Relations in Seventeenth-Century New England* (New York: Harper and Row, 1944), p. 10.
9. Morgan, *Puritan Family*, p. 39.

10. See Lyle Koehler, *A Search for Power: The "Weaker Sex" in Seventeenth-Century New England* (Urbana: University of Illinois Press, 1980), p. 82.

11. Jean-Louis Flandrin, *Le Sexe et l'Occident* (Paris: Seuil, 1981), p. 259.

12. Edwin Powers, *Crime and Punishment in Early Massachusetts, 1620–1692* (Boston: Beacon Press, 1966), p. 303.

13. David Flaherty, *Privacy in Colonial New England* (Charlottesville: University of Virginia Press, 1972), p. 186.

14. Miller, *New England Mind: Seventeenth Century*, p. 298.

15. Symbolically, until the 1820s American provinces or states (with the exception of Massachusetts) were not required to offer "just compensation" for impounded and unimproved land needed to build roads, by virtue of the basic principle of common law holding that land ultimately belonged not to individuals but to the crown. See W. M. Treanor, "Origins and Significance of the Just Takings Clause of the Fifth Amendment," *Yale Law Journal*, 94 (January 1985), 694–716. I am indebted for this reference to an unpublished paper by Morton J. Horwitz.

16. Quoted by Moses Coit Tyler, *A History of American Literature* (Ithaca: Cornell University Press, 1974), p. 457.

17. Philip Johnson, *Wonder-Working Providence* (London, 1654), p. 61, cited by Sacvan Bercovitch in *Puritan New England: Essays on Religion, Society, and Culture*, ed. Alden T. Vaughan and Francis J. Brenner (New York: St. Martin's Press, 1977), p. 276.

18. John Higginson, cited by Bercovitch in Vaughan and Brenner, *Puritan New England*, p. 277.

19. Lois Carr and L. Walsh, "The Planter's Wife," in *A Heritage of Her Own: Toward a New Social History of American Women*, ed. Nancy F. Cott and Elizabeth H. Pleck (New York: Simon and Schuster, 1979), p. 25.

20. Flaherty, *Privacy in Colonial New England*, p. 186.

21. Cited by Meinig, *Shaping of America*, pp. 133–134.

22. David Hall, "Toward a History of Popular Religion in Early New England," *William and Mary Quarterly*, 41 (1984), 52.

23. For an account of this episode, see Oscar and Lilian Handlin, "Religion, Nationalism, and Revolution in America," in *Religion, Ideology and Nationalism in Europe and America: Essays Presented in Honor of Yeroshua Arieli* (Jerusalem: Historical Society of Israèl and the Zalman Shazar, 1986), p. 224.

24. Cited by Oscar and Mary Handlin, *The Dimensions of Liberty* (Boston: Atheneum, 1966), p. 71.

25. Miller, *New England Mind: Seventeenth Century*, pp. 69, 73.

26. Ibid., p. 375.

27. Susan Geib, "The Saugus Iron Works as an Example of Early Industrialism," in *New England Begins* (Boston: Museum of Fine Arts, 1982), II, 353.

28. Bernard Bailyn, *The New England Merchants in the Seventeenth Century* (Cambridge, Mass: Harvard University Press, 1979), p. 34.

29. Cited by T. H. Breen, *Puritans and Adventurers: Change and Persistence in Early America* (New York: Oxford University Press, 1980), pp. 17–18.

30. Cited ibid., p. 23.
31. Flaherty, *Privacy in Colonial New England,* p. 142.
32. Cited in Richard B. Morris, *Government and Labor in Early America* (New York: Columbia University Press, 1946), p. 139.
33. Ibid., p. 354.
34. Cited ibid., p. 147.
35. See Darrett B. and Anita H. Rutman, *A Place in Time: Middlesex County, Virginia, 1650–1750* (New York: Norton, 1984), pp. 99–100; and John B. Minor, *The Minor Family of Virginia* (Lynchburg, Va.: J. P. Bell, 1923,) p. 7.

2. The Decay of Traditionalist Corporatism in Seventeenth-Century France

1. L'abbé Sieyès, *Qu'est-ce que le Tiers Etat?* ed. Roberto Zapperi (Geneva: Droz, 1970), p. 187.
2. Cited in André Delaporte, *L'Idée d'égalité en France au XVIIIe siècle* (Paris: Presses Universitaires de France, 1987).
3. See Marcel Gauchet, "Des deux corps du roi au pouvoir sans corps: christianisme et politique," *Le Débat,* no. 14, 1981.
4. Mary Wollstonecraft, *An Historical and Moral View of the Origin and Progress of the French Revolution* (London, 1795), p. 520, in a passage entitled "Excuse for the Ferocity of the Parisians."
5. Claude Perrault, *Mémoires de ma vie,* ed. Paul Bonnefon (Paris: Renouard, 1909) p. 132.
6. Cited By C.B.A. Behrens, *The Ancien Régime* (London: Thames and Hudson, 1967), p. 100.

3. An Ideology of Virtue in Eighteenth-Century America

1. See Bettye Hobbs Pruitt, "Self-Sufficiency and the Agricultural Economy of Eighteenth-Century Massachusetts," *William and Mary Quarterly,* 51 (July 1984), 338.
2. Letter from John Adams to Mercy Warren, April 16, 1776, In *The Warren-Adams Letters,* ed. Worthington Ford, I, 222–223, cited by Stephen E. Patterson, *Political Parties in Revolutionary Massachusetts* (Madison: University of Wisconsin Press, 1973), p. 27.
3. Napoleon, who measured five feet two inches, was not much shorter than the average for Frenchmen generally, which was about five feet four inches.
4. James Henretta, "Wealth and Social Structure in Colonial America," in Jack P. Greene and J. R. Pole, *Colonial British America* (Baltimore: Johns Hopkins University Press, 1984), p. 281.
5. William Carey MacWilliams, *The Idea of Fraternity in America* (Berkeley: University of California Press, 1973), p. 169.
6. Cited in David Levin, *Cotton Mather: The Young Life of the Lord's Remembrancer, 1663–1703* (Cambridge, Mass.: Harvard University Press, 1978), p. 259.

7. See Gary B. Nash, *The Urban Crucible: Social Change, Political Consciousness, and the Origins of the American Revolution.* (Cambridge, Mass.: Harvard University Press, 1979), pp. 132–134. Nash presents these riots (inaccurately, to my mind) as proof of popular resentment against "aristocratic, wealthy, and ambitious men."

8. The unconscious aspects of the hatred of Indians are explored in Neal Salisbury, *Manitou and Providence* (Oxford: Oxford University Press, 1982).

9. Wayne Craven, *Colonial American Portraiture: The Economic, Religious, Social, Cultural, Philosophical, Scientific, and Aesthetic Foundations* (New York: Cambridge University Press, 1986), p. 55.

10. Cited by Ellen K. Rothman, *Hand and Hearts: A History of Courtship in America* (New York: Basic Books, 1984), p. 48.

11. Cited by David Flaherty, *Privacy in Colonial New England* (Charlottesville: University of Virginia Press, 1972), p. 53.

12. Cited by Bernard Bailyn, *Education in the Forming of American Society: Needs and Opportunities for Study* (Chapel Hill: University of North Carolina Press, 1960), p. 35.

13. Cited by Patterson, *Political Parties in Revolutionary Massachusetts,* p. 24.

14. Rhys Isaacs, *The Transformation of Virginia* (Chapel Hill: University of North Carolina Press, 1982), p. 119.

15. Cited by Edwin G. Burrows and Michael Wallace, "The American Revolution: The Ideology and Psychology of National Liberation," *Perspectives in American History,* 7 (1972), 191.

16. Cited by Linda Ayres, *Harvard Divided: An Exhibition Held at the Fogg Art Museum, Harvard University . . . 1976* (Cambridge, Mass.: Fogg Art Museum, 1976), p. 70.

17. Cited by Nathan O. Hatch, *The Sacred Cause of Liberty: Republican Thought on the Millennium in Revolutionary New England* (New Haven: Yale University Press, 1977), p. 45.

18. For a related interpretation, see Bernard Bailyn, *The Ideological Origins of the American Revolution* (Cambridge, Mass.: Harvard University Press, 1967), pp. 211–213.

19. Cited by Peter Shaw, *American Patriots and the Rituals of Revolution* (Cambridge, Mass.: Harvard University Press, 1981), p. 94.

4. Possessive Individualism and Universalist Illusion in Prerevolutionary France

1. Cited by Norman Hampson, *The Enlightenment: An Evaluation of Its Assumptions, Attitudes, and Values* (London: Penguin, 1982), p. 128.

2. Cited by Katherine Rogers, *Feminism in Eighteenth-Century England* (Urbana: University of Illinois Press, 1982), p. 67.

3. It rose again briefly in the 1780s and then fell steadily, by nearly half, during the nineteenth century. See D. R. Weir, "Life under Pressure: France and England, 1670–1870," *Journal of Economic History,* 44 (1984), 27–47.

4. Arthur Young, *Travels in France* (Cambridge: Cambridge University Press, 1929), p. 117.

5. Marquis de Mirabeau, *L'Ami des hommes, ou Traité de la population,* 4 vols. (Avignon, 1756), I, 275.

6. Cited by Marcel Reinhard, "Elite et noblesse dans la seconde moitié du dix-huitième siècle," *Revue d'histoire moderne et contemporaine,* 3 (January 1956), 15.

7. Rousseau, *Ecrits sur la musique* (Paris, 1838) pp. 288–289. Cited by Maynard Solomon, *Beethoven* (New York: Schirmer Books, 1977), p. 295.

8. Cited by Hampson, *Enlightenment,* p. 60.

9. Mably later urged Americans to ponder the advantages of "the same form of worship, of obedience to the same divine laws." *Remarks concerning the Government and Laws of the United States of America in Four Letters Addressed to Mr. John Adams* (Dublin, 1785), p. 120.

10. Rabaut Saint-Etienne, *Considérations sur les intérêts du Tiers Etat* (Paris, 1788), p. 50.

11. See Jeffrey Merrick's unpublished paper, "Patterns and Politics of Suicide in Late-Eighteenth-Century Paris" (Department of History, Barnard College, 1987), p. 31.

12. "By the king's will, God is not allowed to perform miracles in this place."

13. See Francois Furet and Mona Ozouf, "Deux légitimations historiques de la société française au XVIIIe siècle: Mably et Boulainvilliers," *Annales E.S.C.,* June 1979; and Yan François's forthcoming "Jansénisme et politique au XVIIIe siècle: légitimation et délégitimation de la monarchie chez G. N. Maultrot."

14. Cited by André Delaporte, *L'Idée d'égalité en France au XVIIIe siècle* (Paris: Presses Universitaires de France, 1987), p. 175.

15. *Correspondence du Marquis de Ferrières,* ed. H. Carré (Paris: A. Colin, 1922), p. 120 (10 août 1789).

16. Mme de Charrière, "Elise ou l'Université" (1795), *Oeuvres Complètes,* ed. J. D. Candoux (Geneva: Slatkine, 1979), VII, 417.

17. Menuret de Chambaud, cited by John McManners, *Death and the Enlightenment: Changing Attitudes to Death among Christians and Unbelievers in Eighteenth-Century France* (Oxford: Oxford University Press, 1981), p. 15.

18. Lafont de Saint-Yenne, *Sentiments sur quelques ouvrages de peinture, sculpture et gravure, écrits à un particulier en province* (Paris, 1754), pp. 91–92.

19. Claude Helvetius, *De l'Esprit,* ed. Guy Besse (Paris: Editions sociales, 1968), p. 154.

20. Letter from Diderot to Mme d'Epinay, *Correspondance,* vol. X (Paris: Editions de Minuit, 1963), p. 177.

21. Guillaume T. F. Raynal, *Dissertation sur les suites de la découverte de l'Amérique qui a obtenu en 1785 une mention honorable de l'Académie . . . de Lyon* (Lyon, 1787), p. 51.

22. Willi Paul Adams, "The Colonial German Language Press and the American Revolution," in *The Press and the American Revolution,* ed. Bernard Bailyn and John B. Hench (Boston: New England University Press, 1981), p. 198.

23. Cited by Adrienne Koch, *Power, Morals, and the Founding Fathers* (Ithaca: Cornell University Press, 1961), p. 89.

5. Public Good and Transcendental Self in the American Revolution

1. James A. Henretta, *The Evolution of American Society, 1700–1815: An Interdisciplinary Analysis* (Lexington, Mass.: D.C. Heath, 1973), p. 161.
2. In the same vein, more property was destroyed in London during the week of the Gordon riots in the 1780s than in Paris during the whole of the French Revolution.
3. See Patrick Thierry, "De la Révolution américaine à la Révolution francaise," *Critique*, June–July 1987, p. 484.
4. Cited by Stephan Thernstrom, *A History of the American People* (New York: Harcourt Brace Jovanovich, 1984) I, 155.
5. Cited by Carl Bridenbaugh, *The Spirit of 76: The Growth of American Patriotism before Independence* (New York: Oxford University Press, 1975), pp. 82–83.
6. Cited by Don Higginbotham, *The War of American Independence: Military Attitudes, Policies, and Practice* (New York: Macmillan, 1971), p. 266.
7. Cited in Carl Degler, *Out of Our Past: The Forces That Shaped Modern America* (New York: Harper, 1962), p. 98.
8. For Young's biography, see Pauline Maier, *The Old Revolutionaries: Political Lives in the Age of Samuel Adams* (New York: Knopf, 1980), pp. 101–138.
9. Cited by Lucien Jaume in "Le Public et le privé chez les Jacobins, 1789–1794," *Revue Française de Science Politique,* (April 1987), 242.
10. Cited in *A Heritage of Her Own: Toward a New Social History of American Women,* ed. Nancy F. Cott and Elizabeth H. Pleck (New York: Simon and Schuster, 1979), p. 145.
11. Cited by Higginbotham, *War of American Independence,* p. 280.
12. Cited by Richard B. Morris, *The American Revolution Reconsidered* (New York: Harper and Row, 1967), p. 53.
13. Cited by Willi Paul Adams, *The First American Constitutions: Republican Ideology and the Making of the State Constitutions in the Revolutionary Era,* trans. Rita and Robert Kimber (Chapel Hill: University of North Carolina Press, 1980), p. 148.
14. Cited by Eric Foner, "Tom Paine's Radical Republic," in Alfred F. Young, ed., *The American Revolution: Explorations in the History of American Radicalism* (De Kalb: Northern Illinois University Press, 1976), p. 217.
15. Jefferson, *Notes on Virginia,* Query XIX, "The present state of manufactures, commerce, interior and exterior trade."
16. Cited by Foner, "Tom Paine's Radical Republic," p. 215.
17. Cited by Joseph L. Davis, *Sectionalism in American Politics, 1774–1787* (Madison: University of Wisconsin Press, 1977), p. 8.
18. Cited by Jackson Turner Main, *Political Parties before the Revolution* (Chapel Hill: University of North Carolina Press, 1973), p. 49.

19. Cited by Linda Ayres, *Harvard Divided* (Cambridge, Mass.: Fogg Art Museum, 1976), p. 53.

20. Cited by Main, *Political Parties before the Revolution,* p. 72.

21. Joyce O. Appleby, *Capitalism and a New Social Order: The Republican Vision of the 1790s* (New York: New York University Press, 1984), p. 15.

22. See David Handlin, *American Architecture* (London: Thames and Hudson, 1985), p. 47.

23. In a letter from John Adams to Mercy Warren, April 16, 1776, in *The Warren-Adams Letters,* ed. Worthington Ford (Boston: Massachusetts Historical Society, 1917–1925), I, 222–223, cited by Stephen E. Patterson, *Political Parties in Revolutionary Massachusetts* (Madison: University of Wisconsin Press, 1973), p. 64.

24. Joyce Appleby, "What Is Still American in the Political Philosophy of Thomas Jefferson?" *William and Mary Quarterly,* 39 (April 1982), pp. 287–309.

25. Jefferson to Randolph, May 30, 1790, in *Writings of Thomas Jefferson,* ed. Andrew A. Lipscomb and Albert Ellery Bergh, VIII, 31, cited by Appleby, *What Is Still American,* p. 305.

26. The *Federalist Papers* were translated into French in 1792 by Trudaine de la Sablière, who was executed in 1794. The novel message of the papers does not appear to have raised any echo whatever in France.

27. Main, *Political Parties before the Revolution,* p. 75.

28. Cited by Nathan O. Hatch, *The Sacred Cause of Liberty: Republican Thought on the Millennium in Revolutionary New England* (New Haven: Yale University Press, 1977), p. 2.

29. Cited by Appleby, *Capitalism and a New Social Order,* p. 67.

30. Russell L. Hanson, *The Democratic Imagination in America: Conversations with Our Past* (Princeton: Princeton University Press, 1985), p. 131.

6. Possessive Individualism or Determining Community in the French Revolution

1. Marquis de Ferrières, *Correspondance inédite* (Paris: A. Colin, 1932), p. 228.

2. Marcel Garaud, *La Révolution et l'égalité civile* (Paris: Sirey, 1953), p. 96.

3. Cited by Roberto Zapperi in his introduction to Sieyès *Qu'est-ce que le Tiers Etat?* (Geneva: Droz, 1970), p. 35.

4. Cited in Patrick Girard, *Les Juifs en France, de l'émancipation à l'égalité* (Paris: Calmann Lévy, 1976), p. 51.

5. See M. Dorigny, "Les Idées économiques des Girondins," *Actes du Colloque Girondins et Montagnards,* ed. Albert Soboul (Paris: Société des Etudes Robespierristes, 1980), p. 97.

6. Cited by Georges Michon, *Robespierre et la guerre révolutionnaire* (Paris: Rivière, 1937), p. 68, n. 1.

7. Robespierre, speaking at the Jacobin Club on January 23, 1792.

8. Cited by Alfred Cobban, *A History of Modern France, 1719–1799* (New York: Penguin, 1977), p.195.

9. Cited by Zoltan Haraszti, *John Adams and the Prophets of Progress* (Cambridge, Mass.: Harvard University Press, 1952), p. 255.

10. Cited by Albert Soboul, *La Civilisation et la Révolution française* (Paris: Arthaud, 1970–1983), II, 127.

11. See Brian C. J. Singer, *Society, Theory, and the French Revolution: Studies in Revolutionary Imagery* (London: Macmillan, 1986), p. 189.

12. Cited by Jacques Guilhaumou, "Antoine Tournon et la grammaire des sans-culottes (1794): syntaxe et acte de parole à l'époque de la révolution française," *Linx*, 15 (1987), 47.

13. Garry Wills, *Inventing America: Jefferson's Declaration of Independence* (Garden City, N.Y.: Doubleday, 1978), p. 105.

14. Robert L. Herbert, *David, Voltaire, "Brutus," and the French Revolution: An Essay in Art and Politics* (London: Viking, 1972), p. 105.

15. Cited by Louis de Cardenal, *La Province pendant la Révolution: histoire des clubs jacobins, 1789–1795* (Paris: Payot, 1929), p. 239.

16. Billaud-Varennes, *Archives parlementaires*, vol. LXIX (Paris, 1906), p. 21 (le 15 juillet 1793).

17. Cited by Jeremy Popkin, "Les Journaux républicains, 1795–1799." *Revue d'Histoire Moderne et Contemporaine*, 31 (January 1984), 143.

18. Cited by Georges Lefebvre, *Les Thermidoriens* (Paris: A. Colin, 1937), p. 165.

19. Richard Cobb, *Reactions to the French Revolution* (New York: Oxford University Press, 1972), p. 115.

Epilogue: The Political and Social Effects of French and American Republicanism

1. For a critique of Wood, see Russell L. Hanson, *The Democratic Imagination in America: Conversations with Our Past* (Lawrenceville, N.J.: Princeton University Press, 1985), pp. 72–75.

2. See, for example, Mary Beth Norton, "The Evolution of White Women's Experience in Early America," *American Historical Review*, 89 (June 1984), 616.

3. Cited by Nancy F. Cott, *The Bonds of Womanhood: Women's Sphere in New England, 1780–1835* (New Haven: Yale University Press, 1977), p. 78.

4. From Philip Sheldon Foner, *The Democratic-Republican Societies, 1790–1800: A Documentary Source Book* (Westport, Conn.: Greenwood Press, 1976), cited by Joyce Appleby, *Capitalism and a New Social Order: The Republican Vision of the 1790s* (New York: New York University Press, 1984), p. 57.

Selected Bibliography

This study owes its original impetus to two major works: Bernard Bailyn's *Ideological Origins of the American Revolution,* published in 1967, and François Furet's *Penser la Révolution,* which appeared in 1978. If the two revolutions, the French and American, were originally of a kind (that is, if they were ideological in their first cause), as these two anti-Marxist authors argue, why then did their trajectories diverge so markedly?

I have also relied (albeit for my own ends and in a manner that may dismay the authors) on the revisionist work done on both sides of the Atlantic during the last two decades: in France, to emphasize the ideological origins of the French revolution; in America, by contrast, to attack the consensual and ideological theory of American politics. The French ideological exegesis is suggestive. Its American counterpart—anti-ideological neo-Marxist analysis—while it has yielded interesting evidence, is not theoretically compelling. Although I sympathize with the goals of these radical and revisionist historians, I am skeptical of their sense of American history. I have not ignored the evidence produced by such students of the period as Gary Nash, Eric Foner, Edward Countryman, Alan Kulikoff, Jesse Lemisch, and Alfred Young, who have all underscored America's prerevolutionary or revolutionary social divisions; but I have vigoroulsy rejected the conceptual system within which their very useful findings have been set.

I have also shied away from the theoretical implications of Michael Zuckerman's highly crafted book, *The Peaceable Kingdoms of Colonial New England,* and of other local studies, such as Kenneth Lockridge's work on colonial Dedham. In my view, it is as difficult to attack the essentially individualist and capitalist nature of American colonial life from the right as from the left. (The first pages of Darrett and Anita Rutman's *A Place in*

Time, describing nostalgia as the obsession of community studies, is a useful corrective here.) The American subjects of King George were neither bucolic peasant villagers nor potential members of an embryonic working class. They were very much as most historians have depicted them: embattled farmers.

I have applied a similar distinction to the facts and theory of French Marxist readings. I have relied to a broad extent on the applied work of such Marxist historians as Mathiez and Lefebvre, Soboul and Mazauric, Vovelle and Guilhaumou, but not on their "social interpretation of the French Revolution." Far more congenial to my view, obviously, have been the books of such writers as Robert Darnton, Pierre Goubert, Steven Kaplan, Mona Ozouf, Jean-François Revel, and Daniel Roche, whose message is that French society was less class-bound and less economically determined than Marxist historiography has asserted.

The following works, which are divided into two groups (those on America and those on France), are mostly modern studies that contain valuable factual and interpretative material and will also indicate the shape of my interests.

America

Adams, Willi Paul. *The First American Constitutions: Republican Ideology and the Making of the State Constitutions in the Revolutionary Era.* Trans. Rita and Robert Kimber. Chapel Hill: University of North Carolina Press, 1980.

Alexander, John K. *Render Them Submissive: Responses to Poverty in Philadelphia, 1760–1800.* Amherst: University of Massachusetts Press, 1980.

Anderson, Fred. *A People's Army: Massachusetts Soldiers and Society in the Seven Years' War.* Chapel Hill: Universtity of North Carolina Press, 1984.

Appleby, Joyce Oldham. *Capitalism and a New Social Order: The Republican Vision of the 1790s.* New York: New York University Press, 1984.

Ayres, Linda. *Harvard Divided: An Exhibition Held at the Fogg Art Museum, Harvard University, Cambridge, Mass., June 3 through October 10, 1976.* Cambridge, Mass.: Fogg Art Museum, 1976.

Bailyn, Bernard. *The England Merchants in the Seventeenth Century.* 1955. Reprint. Cambridge, Mass.: Harvard University Press, 1979.

———*Education in the Forming of American Society: Needs and Opportunities for Study.* Chapel Hill: University of North Carolina Press, 1960.

———*The Ideological Origins of the American Revolution.* Cambridge, Mass.: Belknap Press of Harvard University Press, 1967.

———*The Ordeal of Thomas Hutchinson.* Cambridge, Mass.: Belknap Press of Harvard University Press, 1974.

————ed., with Jane N. Garrett. *Pamphlets of the American Revolution, 1750–1776,* vol. I. Cambridge, Mass.: Belknap Press of Harvard University Press, 1965.

Bailyn, Bernard, David Brion Davis, David Herbert Donald, John J. Thomas, Robert Wiebe, and Gordon S. Wood. *The Great Republic: A History of the American People,* vol. I, 2nd ed. Lexington, Mass.: D. C. Heath, 1981.

Banning, Lance. *The Jeffersonian Persuasion: Evolution of a Party Ideology.* Ithaca: Cornell University Press, 1978.

Beeman, Richard, Stephen Botein, and Edward C. Carter II. *Beyond Confederation: Origins of the Constituion and American National Identity.* Chapel Hill: University of North Carolina Press, 1987.

Bender, Thomas. *Community and Social Change in America.* New Brunswick N.J.: Rutgers University Press, 1978.

Bercovitch, Sacvan. *The Puritan Origins of the American Self.* New Haven: Yale University Press, 1975.

————*The American Jeremiad.* Madison: University of Wisconsin Press, 1978.

Bonomi, Patricia U. *A Factious People: Politics and Society in Colonial New York.* New York: Columbia University Press, 1971.

————*Under the Cope of Heaven: Religion, Society, and Politics in Colonial America.* Oxford: Oxford University Press, 1987.

Boorstin, Daniel J. *The Americans: The Colonial Experience.* New York: Random House, 1958.

Bouriez-Gregg, Françoise. *Les Classes sociales aux Etats-Unis.* Paris: Armand Colin, 1954.

Boyer, Paul, and Stephen Nissenbaum. *Salem Possessed: The Social Origins of Witchcraft.* Cambridge, Mass.: Harvard University Press, 1974.

Breen, T. H. *The Character of the Good Ruler: A Study of Puritan Political Ideas in New England, 1630–1730.* New Haven: Yale University Press, 1970.

————*Puritans and Adventurers: Change and Persistence in Early America.* New York: Oxford University Press, 1980.

Bridenbaugh, Carl. *The Spirit of 76: The Growth of American Patriotism before Independence.* New York: Oxford University Press, 1975.

Brodie, Fawn. *Thomas Jefferson: An Intimate History.* New York: Norton, 1974.

Brown, Richard D. *Revolutionary Politics in Massachusetts: The Boston Committee of Correspondence and the Towns, 1772–1774.* New York: Norton, 1976.

Brown, Robert Eldon. *Middle-Class Democracy and the Revolution in Massachusetts, 1691–1780.* Ithaca: Cornell University Press, 1955.

Buel, Joy Day, and Richard Buel, Jr. *The Way of Duty: A Woman and Her Family in Revolutionary America.* New York: Norton, 1984.

Bushman, Richard L. *From Puritan to Yankee: Character and Social Order in Connecticut, 1690–1765.* Cambridge, Mass.: Harvard University Press, 1976.

Chapin, Bradley. *Criminal Justice in Colonial America, 1606–1660.* Athens, Ga.: University of Georgia Press, 1983.

Cherry, Conrad. *Nature and Religious Imagination from Edwards to Bushnell.* Philadelphia: Fortress Press, 1980.

Childs, Frances S. *French Refugee Life in the United States, 1790–1800.* Baltimore: Johns Hopkins University Press, 1940.

Chinard, Gilbert. *Jefferson et les idéologues d'après sa correspondance inédite avec Destutt de Tracy. Cabanis. J.-B. Say, et Auguste Comte.* Paris: Presses Universitaires de France, 1925.

Commager, Henry Steele. *Jefferson, Nationalism, and the Enlightenment.* New York: G. Braziller, 1975.

Cott, Nancy F. *The Bonds of Womanhood: "Women's Sphere" in New England, 1780–1835.* New Haven: Yale University Press, 1977.

Cott, Nancy F., and Elizabeth H. Pleck, eds. *A Heritage of Her Own: Toward a New Social History of American Women.* New York: Simon and Schuster, 1979.

Countryman, Edward. *A People in Revolution: The American Revolution and Political Society in New York, 1760–1790.* Baltimore: Johns Hopkins University Press, 1981.

Craven, Wayne. *Colonial American Portraiture: The Economic, Religious, Social, Cultural, Philosophical, Scientific, and Aesthetic Foundations.* New York: Cambridge University Press, 1986.

Davis, David B. *The Problem of Slavery in the Age of Revolution, 1770–1823.* Ithaca: Cornell University Press, 1975.

Davis, Joseph L. *Sectionalism in American Politics, 1774–1787.* Madison: University of Wisconsin Press, 1977.

Demos, John. *A Little Commonwealth: Family Life in Plymouth Colony.* New York: Oxford University Press, 1976.

———*Entertaining Satan: Witchcraft and the Culture of Early New England.* New York: Oxford University Press, 1982.

Diggins, John P. *The Lost Soul of American Politics: Virtue, Self-Interest, and the Foundations of Liberalism.* Chicago: University of Chicago Press, 1986.

Fiering, Norman. *Jonathan Edwards's Moral Thought and Its British Context.* Chapel Hill: University of North Carolina Press, 1981.

Flaherty, David. *Privacy in Colonial New England.* Charlottesville: University of Virginia Press, 1972.

Foner, Eric. *The Complete Writings of Tom Paine*. New York: Citadel Press, 1945.

Foner, Philip Sheldon. *Labor and the American Revolution*. Westport, Conn.: Greenwood Press, 1976.

Foster, Stephen. *Their Solitary Way: The Puritan Social Ethic in the First Century of Settlement in New England*. New Haven: Yale University Press, 1971.

Fowler, William M., and Wallace Coyle, eds. *The American Revolution: Changing Perspectives*. Boston: Northeastern University Press, 1981.

Fries, Sylvia Doughty. *The Urban Idea in Colonial America*. Philadelphia: Temple University Press, 1977.

Galenson, David W. *White Servitude in Colonial America: An Economic Analysis*. Cambridge: Cambridge University Press, 1981.

Greene, Jack P. *The Quest for Power: Lower Houses of Assembly in the Southern Royal Colonies, 1689–1776*. Chapel Hill: University of North Carolina Press, 1963.

Greene, Lorenzo J. *The Negro in Colonial New England, 1620–1776*. New York: Columbia University Press, 1963.

Greven, Philip Johannes. *Four Generations: Population, Land, and Family in Colonial Andover*. Ithaca: Cornell University Press, 1970.

————*The Protestant Temperament: Patterns of Child Rearing, Religious Experience, and the Self in Early America*. New York: Knopf, 1977.

Gross, Robert. *The Minutemen and Their World*. New York: Hill and Wang, 1976.

Hall, David. *The Faithful Shepherd: A History of the New England Ministry in the Seventeenth Century*. Chapel Hill: University of North Carolina Press, 1972.

Handlin, David P. *American Architecture*. London: Thames and Hudson, 1985.

Handlin, Oscar and Mary. *The Dimensions of Liberty*. Cambridge, Mass.: Harvard University Press, 1961. Reprint. Boston: Atheneum, 1966.

Hanson, Russell L. *The Democratic Imagination in America: Conversations with Our Past*. Princeton: Princeton University Press, 1985.

Haraszti, Zoltan. *John Adams and the Prophets of Progress*. Cambridge, Mass.: Harvard University Press, 1952.

Hartz, Louis. *The Liberal Tradition in America: An Interpretation of American Political Thought since the Revolution*. New York: Harcourt Brace and World, 1955.

Hatch, Nathan O. *The Sacred Cause of Liberty: Republican Thought on the Millennium in Revolutionary New England*. New Haven: Yale University Press, 1977.

Heimert, Alan. *Religion and the American Mind: From the Great Awakening to the Revolution*. Cambridge, Mass.: Harvard University Press, 1966.

Heimert, Alan, and Perry Miller. *The Great Awakening: Documents Illustrating the Crisis and its Consequences*. Indianapolis: Bobbs-Merrill, 1967.

Henretta, James A. *The Evolution of American Society, 1700–1815: An Interdisciplinary Analysis*. Lexington, Mass.: D. C. Heath, 1973.

Higginbotham, Don. *The War of American Independence: Military Attitudes, Policies, and Practice*. New York: Macmillan, 1971.

Higgins, Robert. *Power, Conflict, and Leadership: Essays in Honor of John Richard Alden*. Raleigh, N.C.: Duke University Press, 1979.

Hirschman, Albert O. *The Passions and the Interests: Political Arguments for Capitalism before Its Triumph*. Princeton: Princeton University Press, 1977.

Hoerder, Dirk. *Crowd Action in Revolutionary Massachusetts, 1765–1780*. New York: Academic Press, 1977.

Hofstadter, Richard. *America in 1750: A Social Portrait*. New York: Knopf, 1971.

Howard, Dick. *Naissance de la pensée politique américaine, 1763–1787*. Paris: Editions Ramsay, 1987.

Innes, Stephen. *Labor in a New Land: Economy and Society in Seventeenth-Century Springfield*. Princeton: Princeton University Press, 1983.

Isaacs, Rhys. *The Transformation of Virginia*. Chapel Hill: University of North Carolina Press, 1982.

Jennings, Francis. *The Invasion of America: Indians, Colonialism, and the Cant of Conquest*. New York: Norton, 1976.

Jones, Douglas Lamar. *Village and Seaport: Migration and Society in Eighteenth-Century Massachusetts*. Hanover, N.H.: University Press of New England, 1981.

Jordan, Winthrop. *White over Black: American Attitudes toward the Negro, 1550–1812*. Chapel Hill: University of North Carolina Press, 1968.

Kammen, Michael Gedaliah. *A Rope of Sand: The Colonial Agents, British Politics, and the American Revolution*. Ithaca: Cornell University Press, 1968.

Kaspi, André, *L'Indépendance américaine, 1763–1789*. Paris: Gallimard, 1976.

Kenyon, Cecilia, ed. *The Anti-Federalists*. Indianapolis: Bobbs-Merrill, 1966.

Kerber, Linda K. *The Federalists in Dissent: Imagery and Ideology in Jeffersonian America*. Ithaca: Cornell University Press, 1970.

Kraus, Michael. *Intercolonial Aspects of American Culture on the Eve of the Revolution, with Special Reference to Northern Towns*. New York: Columbia University Press, 1928.

Kupperman, Karen. *Settling with the Indians: The Meeting of English and Indian Cultures in America, 1580–1640.* Totowa, N.J.: Rowman and Littlefield, 1980.

Labaree, Benjamin Woods. *The Boston Tea Party.* New York: Oxford University Press, 1964.

Lemon, James T. *The Best Poor Man's Country: A Geographical Study of Early Southeastern Pennsylvania.* Baltimore: Johns Hopkins University Press, 1972.

Link, Eugene P. *Democratic-Republican Societies, 1790–1800.* New York: Columbia University Press, 1942.

Lockridge, Kenneth. *A New England Town, the First Hundred Years: Dedham, 1636–1736.* New York: Norton, 1970.

———*Literacy in Colonial New England, 1636–1736: An Enquiry into the Social Context of Literacy in the Early Modern West.* New York: Norton, 1974.

McCoy, Drew. *The Elusive Republic: Political Economy in Jeffersonian America.* Chapel Hill: University of North Carolina Press, 1980.

McDonald, Forrest. *E Pluribus Unum: The Formation of the American Republic, 1776–1790.* Boston: Houghton Mifflin, 1965.

McLoughlin, William G. *Isaac Backus and the American Pietistic Tradition.* Boston: Little, Brown, 1967.

MacWilliams, William Carey. *The Idea of Fraternity in America.* Berkeley: University of California Press, 1973.

Maier, Pauline. *From Resistance to Revolution: Colonial Radicals and the Development of Intercolonial Opposition to Britain, 1765–1776.* New York: Knopf, 1972.

———*The Old Revolutionaries: Political Lives in the Age of Samuel Adams.* New York: Knopf, 1980.

Main, Jackson Turner. *The Anti-Federalists: Critics of the Constitution, 1781–1788.* Chapel Hill: University of North Carolina Press, 1961.

———*Political Parties before the Revolution.* Chapel Hill: University of North Carolina Press, 1973.

Marienstras, Elise. *Les Mythes fondateurs de la nation américaine.* Paris: François Maspéro, 1977.

May, Henry F. *The Enlightenment in America.* New York: Oxford University Press, 1976.

Meinig, D. W. *The Shaping of America: A Geographical Perspective on Five Hundred Years of History,* vol. I, *Atlantic America, 1492–1800.* New Haven: Yale University Press, 1986.

Middelkauf, Robert. *The Glorious Cause: The American Revolution. 1763–1789.* Oxford: Oxford University Press, 1982.

Miller, John Chester. *The Wolf by the Ears: Thomas Jefferson and Slavery.* New York: Free Press, 1977.

Miller, Perry. *The New England Mind: From Colony to Province.* Cambridge, Mass.: Harvard University Press, 1953.

————*The New England Mind: The Seventeenth Century.* Cambridge, Mass.: Harvard University Press, 1954.

————*Errand in the Wilderness.* Cambridge, Mass.: Harvard University Press, 1956.

Morgan, Edmund Sears. *The Puritan Family: Religion and Domestic Relations in Seventeenth-Century New England.* New York: Harper and Row, 1944.

————*The Puritan Dilemma: The Story of John Winthrop.* Boston: Little, Brown, 1958.

————*American Slavery, American Freedom: The Ordeal of Colonial Virginia.* New York: Norton, 1975.

————*The Challenge of the American Revolution.* New York: Norton, 1976.

Morgan, Edmund Sears, and Helen M. Morgan. *The Stamp Act Crisis: Prologue to Revolution.* Chapel Hill: University of North Carolina Press, 1953.

Morris, Richard Brandon. *Government and Labor in Early America.* New York: Columbia University Press, 1946.

————*The American Revolution Reconsidered.* New York: Harper and Row, 1967.

Nash, Gary B. *The Urban Crucible: Social Change, Political Consciousness, and the Origins of the American Revolution.* Cambridge, Mass.: Harvard University Press, 1979.

Norton, Mary Beth. *Liberty's Daughters: The Revolutionary Experience of American Women, 1750–1800.* Boston: Little, Brown, 1980.

Patterson, Stephen E. *Political Parties in Revolutionary Massachusetts.* Madison: University of Wisconsin Press, 1973.

Pencak, William. *America's Burke: The Mind of Thomas Hutchinson.* Washington, D.C.: University Press of America, 1982.

Peterson, Merrill Daniel. *Adams and Jefferson: A Revolutionary Dialogue.* Athens, Ga.: University of Georgia Press, 1976.

Pocock, John Greville Agard. *The Machiavellian Moment: Florentine Political Thought and the Atlantic Republican Tradition.* Princeton: Princeton University Press, 1975.

Pole, Jack Richon. *The Pursuit of Equality in American History.* Berkeley: University of California Press, 1978.

Powell, Sumner Chilton. *Puritan Village: The Formation of a New England Town.* Middletown, Conn.: Wesleyan University Press, 1963.

Rice, Howard Crosby. *Thomas Jefferson's Paris.* Princeton: Princeton University Press, 1976.

Rutman, Darrett Bruce, and Anita H. Rutman. *A Place in Time: Middlesex County, Virginia, 1650–1750.* New York: Norton, 1984.

Ryerson, Alan. *The Revolution Now Begins: The Radical Committees of Philadelphia, 1765–1776*. Philadelphia: University of Pennsylvania Press, 1978.

Schlesinger, Arthur Meir. *The Colonial Merchants and the American Revolution, 1763–1776*. New York: Columbia University Press, 1918.

Shaw, Peter. *The Character of John Adams*. Chapel Hill: University of North Carolina Press, 1976.

———*American Patriots and the Rituals of Revolution*. Cambridge, Mass.: Harvard University Press, 1981.

Shea, Daniel B., Jr. *Spiritual Autobiography in Early America*. Princeton: Princeton University Press, 1968.

Shy, John W. *A People Numerous and Armed: Reflections on the Military Struggle for American Independence*. New York: Oxford University Press, 1976.

Slotkin, Richard. *Regeneration through Violence: The Mythology of the American Frontier, 1600–1860*. Middletown, Conn.: Wesleyan University Press, 1973.

Spurlin, Paul Merrill. *The French Enlightenment in America: Essays on the Times of the Founding Fathers*. Athens, Ga.: University of Georgia Press, 1984.

Stourzh, Gerald. *Alexander Hamilton and the Idea of Republican Government*. Stanford: Stanford University Press, 1970.

Szatmary, David P. *Shays's Rebellion, 1786–1787: The Making of an Agrarian Insurrection*. Amherst: University of Massachusetts Press, 1980.

Thernstrom, Stephen. *A History of the American People*. New York: Harcourt Brace Jovanovich, 1984.

Tolles, Frederick Barnes. *Meeting House and Counting House: The Quaker Merchants of Colonial Philadelphia, 1682–1763*. Chapel Hill: University of North Carolina Press, 1948.

Tyler, Moses Coit. *A History of American Literature*. New York: G. P. Putnam's Sons, 1878. Reprint. Ithaca: Cornell University Press, 1974.

Vincent, Bernard. *Thomas Paine, ou la religion de la liberté*. Paris: Aubier, 1987.

Waters, John J. *The Otis Family in Provincial and Revolutionary Massachusetts*. Chapel Hill: University of North Carolina Press, 1968.

Watkins, Owen C. *The Puritan Experience: Studies in Spiritual Autobiography*. London: Routledge and Kegan Paul, 1972.

Wills, Garry. *Inventing America: Jefferson's Declaration of Independence*. Garden City, N.Y.: Doubleday, 1978.

———*Explaining America: The Federalist*. Garden City, N.Y.: Doubleday, 1981.

Wood, Gordon. *The Creation of the American Republic, 1776–1787*. Chapel Hill: University of North Carolina Press, 1969.

Young, Alfred F. *The Democratic Republicans of New York: The Origins, 1763–1797*. Chapel Hill: University of North Carolina Press, 1967.

Zemsky, Robert. *Merchants, Farmers, and River Gods: An Essay on Eighteenth-Century American Politics*. Boston: Gambit, 1971.

Ziff, Larzer. *Puritanism in America: New Culture in a New World*. New York: Viking Press, 1973.

Zobel, Hiller B. *The Boston Massacre*. New York: Norton, 1970.

Zuckerman, Michael. *Peaceable Kingdoms: New England Towns in the Eighteenth Century*. New York: Knopf, 1970.

———ed. *Friends and Neighbors: Group Life in America's First Plural Society*. Philadelphia: Temple University Press, 1982.

The *William and Mary Quarterly,* with its comprehensive if often acidulous reviews and its excellent articles, is an indispensable tool that has no strict analogue for French history. I have relied on its issues from 1970 to the present, first, for the rich information contained in articles and reviews and, second, for a sense of the work done by scholars in the field of colonial American history during the last two decades.

I am also indebted to the excellent collections of articles which historians of colonial America edit from time to time. These informative essays are of great use in gauging the shifting temper of the field. I have relied especially on the following collections.

Goodman, Paul, ed. *Essays in American Colonial History*. New York: Holt, Rinehart, and Winston, 1967.

Greene, Jack P., and Jack Richon Pole, eds. *Colonial British America*. Baltimore: Johns Hopkins University Press, 1984.

Hall, David D., John M. Murrin, and Thad W. Tate, eds. *Saints and Revolutionaries: Essays on Early American History*. New York: Norton, 1984.

Katz, Stanley N., ed. *Colonial America: Essays in Politics and Social Development*. Boston: Little, Brown, 1971.

Kurtz, Stephen G., and James H. Hutson, eds. *Essays on the American Revolution*. Chapel Hill: University of North Carolina Press, 1973.

Tate, Thad W., and David Ammerman, eds. *The Chesapeake in the Seventeenth Century: Essays on Anglo-American Society and Politics*. Chapel Hill: University of North Carolina Press, 1979.

Vaughan, Alden T. and Francis J. Brenner, eds. *Puritan New England: Essays on Religion, Society, and Culture*. New York: St. Martin's Press, 1977.

Young, Alfred Fabian, ed. *The American Revolution: Explorations in the History of American Radicalism*. De Kalb: Northern Illinois University Press, 1976.

France

Agulhon, M. *Pénitents et francs-maçons de l'ancienne Provence*. Paris: Fayard, 1968.

——*Marianne au combat: l'imagerie et la symbolique républicaine de 1789 à 1780*. Paris: Flammarion, 1979.

Albertini, Rosanna. *Barnave e la Rivoluzione: un sogno dell enthusiasmo?* Pisa: ETS, 1980.

Ariès, Philippe. *Centuries of Childhood: A Social History of Family Life*. Trans. Robert Baldick. New York: Knopf, 1965.

——*L'Homme devant la mort*. Paris, Editions du Seuil, 1977.

Baker, Keith, ed. *The French Revolution and the Origins of Modern Political Culture*. Forthcoming.

Balibar, Renée, and Dominique Laporte. *Le Français national*. Paris: Seuil, 1974.

Barber, Elinor. *The Bourgeoisie in Eighteenth-Century France*. 1955. Princeton: Princeton University Press, 1970.

Bastide, Paul. *Sieyès et sa pensée*. Paris: Hachette, 1939.

Benabou, Erica-Marie. *La prostitution et la police des moeurs au XVIIIe siècle*. Paris: Perrin, 1987.

Bénichou, Paul. *Les Morales du grand siècle*. Paris: Gallimard, 1967.

Bergeron, Louis. *France under Napoleon*. Trans. R. R. Palmer. Princeton: Princeton University Press, 1981.

Berlanstein, Leonard. *The Barristers of Toulouse in the Eighteenth Century, 1740–1793*. Baltimore: Johns Hopkins University Press, 1975.

Bertaud, Paul. *La Révolution armée: les soldats citoyens de la révolution*. Paris: Laffont, 1979.

——*Les Amis du roi: journaux et journalistes royalistes en France de 1789 à 1792*. Paris: Perrin, 1984.

Bien, David D. *The Calas Affair: Persecution, Toleration, and Heresy in Eighteenth-Century Toulouse*. New York: Greenwood, 1979.

Bloch, Marc. *French Rural History: An Essay on Its Basic Characteristics*. Trans. Janet Sondheimer. Berkeley: University of California Press, 1966.

Blum, Carol. *Rousseau and the Republic of Virtue: The Language of Politics during the French Revolution*. Ithaca: Cornell University Press, 1986.

Bois, Paul. *Les Paysans de l'ouest: des structures économiques et sociales aux options politiques depuis l'époque révolutionnaire dans la Sarthe*. Le Mans: Imprimerie Vilaire, 1960.

Bordes, Maurice. *L'Administration provinciale et municipale en France au XVIIIe siècle*. Paris: Editions de l'enseignement supérieur, 1972.

Bouineau, Jacques. *Les Toges du pouvoir, ou la révolution de droit antique, 1789–1799*. Toulouse: Presses de l'Université de Toulouse, 1986.

Brinton, Crane. *The Jacobins: An Essay in the New History*. New York: Macmillan, 1930.

Burstin, Haim. *Le Faubourg Saint Marcel à l'époque révolutionnaire*. Paris: Société de études Robespierristes, 1983.

Carrière, Charles. *Négociants marseillais au XVIIIe siècle: contribution à l'étude des économies maritimes*. 2 vols. Marseilles: Institut historique de Provence, 1973.

Castan, Nicole. *Justice et répression en Languedoc à l'époque des lumières*. Paris: Flammarion, 1980.

Castan, Yves. *Honnêteté et relations sociales en Languedoc, 1715–1780*. Paris: Plon, 1974.

Censer, Jack R. *Prelude to Power: The Parisian Radical Press in France, 1789–1791*. Baltimore: Johns Hopkins University Press, 1976.

Cerati, Marie. *Le Club des citoyennes républicaines révolutionnaires*. Paris: Editions sociales, 1966.

Chartier, Roger. *Lecture et lecteurs dans la France d'ancien régime*. Paris: Seuil, 1987.

Chassagne, Serge. *Oberkampf: un entrepreneur capitaliste au siècle des lumières*. Paris: Aubier, 1980.

Chaussinand-Nogaret, Guy. *La Noblesse au XVIIIe siècle: de la féodalité aux lumières*. Paris: Hachette, 1976.

Chinard, Gilbert. *L'Amérique et le rêve exotique dans la littérature française au XVIIe et XVIIIe siècle*. Paris: Hachette, 1913.

Cobb, Richard. *Les armées révolutionnaires: instrument de la terreur dans les départements, avril 1793–floréal an II*. 2 vols. The Hague: Mouton, 1961, 1963.

———*The Police and the People: French Popular Protest, 1789–1820*. Oxford: Oxford University Press, 1970.

Cobban, Alfred. *The Social Interpretation of the French Revolution*. Cambridge: Cambridge University Press, 1964.

Cochin, Augustin. *L'Esprit du Jacobinisme: une interprétation sociologique de la révolution française*. Paris: Presses Universitaires de France, 1979.

Coornaert, Emile. *Les Compagnonnages en France du moyen age à nos jours*. Paris: Editions ouvrières, 1966.

———*Les Corporations en France avant 1789*. Paris: Editions ouvrières, 1968.

Corvisier, André. *Armées et sociétés en Europe de 1494 à 1789*. Vendôme: Presses Universitaires de France, 1976.

Crow, Thomas. *Painters and Public Life in Eighteenth-Century Paris*. New Haven: Yale University Press, 1984.

Darnton, Robert. *The Literary Underground of the Old Regime*. Cambridge, Mass.: Harvard University Press, 1982

————*The Great Cat Massacre, and Other Episodes in French Cultural History*. New York: Basic Books, 1984.

David, Marcel. *Fraternité et révolution française, 1789–1799*. Paris: Aubier, 1987.

Doyle, William. *The Origins of the French Revolution*. Oxford: Oxford University Press, 1980.

Duby, Georges and Philippe Ariès. *Histoire de la Vie Privée*. Vol. 3, ed. Roger Chartier. Paris: Seuil, 1986.

Duhet, Paule Marie, ed. *Les Femmes et la révolution, 1789–1794*. Paris: Juillard, 1971.

Durand, Yves. *Finances et mécénat: les fermiers généraux au XVIIIe siècle*. Paris: Hachette, 1976.

Echeverria, Durand. *Mirage in the West: A History of the French Image of American Society to 1815*. Princeton: Princeton University Press, 1957.

Egret, Jean. *La Pré-révolution française, 1787–1788*. Paris: Presses Universitaires de France, 1962.

————*Louis XV et l'opposition parlementaire*. Paris: A. Colin, 1970.

Faÿ, Barnard. *L'Esprit révolutionnaire en France et aux Etats Unis à la fin du XVIIIe siècle*. Paris: Champion, 1925.

Ford, Franklin. *Robe and Sword: The Regrouping of the French Aristocracy after Louis XIV*. Cambridge, Mass.: Harvard University Press, 1962.

Forster, Robert. *The Nobility of Toulouse in the Eighteenth Century: A Social and Economic Study*. Baltimore: Johns Hopkins University Press, 1960.

Foucault, Michel. *Histoire de la folie: folie et déraison*. Paris: Gallimard, 1972.

Fox-Genovese, Elizabeth. *The Origins of Physiocracy: Economic Revolution and Social Order in Eighteenth-Century France*. Ithaca: Cornell University Press, 1976.

Furet, François. *Interpreting the French Revolution*. Trans. Elborg Foster. New York: Cambridge University Press, 1981.

————*Marx et la révolution française: textes de Marx présentés, réunis, traduits par Lucien Calvié*. Paris: Flammarion, 1986.

Furet, François, and Jacques Ozouf. *Lire et écrire: l'alphabétisation des française de Calvin à Jules Ferry*. Paris: Editions de Minuit, 1977.

Garaud, Marcel. *La révolution et la famille*. Paris: Presses Universitaires de France, 1978.

Garden, Maurice. *Lyon et les Lyonnais au XVIIIe siècle*. Paris: Flammarion, 1975.

Gay, Peter. *The Party of Humanity: Essays in the French Enlightenment*. New York: Knopf, 1964.

————*The Enlightenment: An Interpretation*. 2 vols. New York: Knopf, 1966, 1969.

Genty, Maurice. *Paris, 1789–1795: l'apprentissage de la citoyenneté*. Paris: Editions sociales, 1987.

Godechot, Jacques. *France and the Atlantic Revolution of the Eighteenth Century, 1770–1799*. Trans. H. H. Rowen. New York: Free Press, 1965.

———*Les Institutions de la France sous la révolution et l'empire*. Paris: Presses Universitaires de France, 1968.

———*The Counter-Revolution: Doctrine and Action, 1789–1804*. Trans. Salvator Attanasio. New York: H. Fertig, 1971.

Goldmann, Lucien. *Jean Racine, dramaturge*. Paris: l'Arche, 1956.

Goodwin, Albert. *The Friends of Liberty: The English Democratic Movement in the Age of the French Revolution*. Cambridge, Mass.: Harvard University Press, 1979.

Goubert, Pierre. *Beauvais et le Beauvaisis de 1600 à 1730: contribution à l'histoire de la France au XVIIe siècle*. Paris: Sevpen, 1960.

Goubert, Pierre, and Daniel Roche. *Les Français et l'ancien régime*. Paris: A. Colin, 1984.

Grange, Henri. *Les Idées de Necker*. Paris: Klincksieck, 1974.

Greenlaw, R. W. *The Social Origins of the French Revolution: The Debate on the Middle Classes*. Lexington, Mass.: D. C. Heath, 1975.

Greer, Donald. *The Incidence of the Terror during the French Revolution*. Cambridge, Mass.: Harvard University Press, 1935.

Groethuysen, Bernard. *Philosophie de la révolution française*. Paris: Gallimard, 1956.

Gruder, Vivian. *The Royal Provincial Intendants: A Governing Elite in Eighteenth-Century France*. Ithaca: Cornell University Press, 1968.

Guérin, Daniel. *Class Struggle in the First French Republic: Bourgeois and Bras Nus, 1793–1795*. Trans. Ian Patterson. London: Pluto Press, 1977.

Guiomar, Jean Yves. *L'Idéologie nationale: nation, représentation, propriété*. Paris: Champs libre, 1974.

Hahn, Roger. *The Anatomy of a Scientific Institution: The Paris Academy of Sciences, 1666–1803*. Berkeley: University of California Press, 1971.

Hampson, Norman. *A Social History of the French Revolution*. London: Routledge, 1963.

———*The Enlightenment: An Evaluation of Its Assumptions, Attitudes, and Values*. London: Penguin, 1982.

———*Will and Circumstance: Montesquieu, Rousseau, and the French Revolution*. Norman: Oklahoma University Press, 1983.

Harris, Robert. *Necker: Reform Statesman of the Ancien Régime*. Berkeley: University of California Press, 1979.

Herbert, Robert L. *David, Voltaire, "Brutus," and the French Revolution: An Essay in Art and Politics*. New York: Viking, 1972.

Hirsch, Jean-Pierre. *La Nuit du quatre août*. Paris: Collection Archives, 1978.

Hirschman, Albert O. *The Passions and the Interests: Political Arguments for Capitalism before Its Triumph*. Princeton: Princeton University Press, 1981.

Hufton, Olwen. *The Poor in Eighteenth-Century France, 1750–1789*. Oxford: Oxford University Press, 1974.

Hunt, Lynn. *Politics, Culture, and Class in the French Revolution*. Berkeley: University of California Press, 1984.

Johnson, Douglas, ed. *French Society and the Revolution*. Cambridge: Cambridge University Press, 1976.

Julia, Dominique. *Les Trois Couleurs du tableau noir: la révolution*. Paris: Belin, 1981.

Kafker, Frank, ed. *The French Revolution: Conflicting Interpretations*. New York: Random House, 1976.

Kaplan, Steven L. *Bread, Politics, and Political Economy in the Reign of Louis XV*. 2 vols. The Hague: M. Nijhoff, 1976.

———*The Famine Plot: Persuasion in Eighteenth-Century France*. Philadelphia: American Philosophical Society. 1982.

———*Provisioning Paris: Merchants and Millers in the Grain and Flour Trade during the Eighteenth Century*. Ithaca: Cornell University Press, 1984.

———*Understanding Popular Culture: Europe from the Middle Ages to the Nineteenth Century*. Berlin: Mouton, 1984.

Kaplow, Jeffrey. *The Names of Kings: The Parisian Laboring Poor in the Eighteenth Century*. New York: Basic Books, 1972.

Kelly, George Armstrong. *Victims, Authority, and Terror: The Parallel Deaths of d'Orléans, Custine, Bailly, and Malhesherbes*. Chapel Hill: University of North Carolina Press, 1982.

Kennedy, Michael L. *The Jacobin Clubs during the French Revolution: The First Years*. Princeton: Princeton University Press, 1982.

Lebrun, François. *La Vie conjugale sous l'ancien régime*. Paris: A. Colin, 1975.

Lefebvre, Georges. *The Great Fear of 1789: Rural Panic in Revolutionary France*. 1932. New York: Vintage, 1973.

———*The Coming of the French Revolution*. 1939. New York: Vintage, 1957.

Leroy-Ladurie, Emmanuel. *Les Paysans de Languedoc*. 2 vols. Paris S.E.V.P.E.N., 1966.

Levy, Darline Gay, Harriet B. Applewhite, and Mary Durham Johnson, eds. and trans. *Women in Revolutionary Paris, 1789–1795: Selected Documents*. Urbana: University of Illinois Press, 1980.

Lichtenberger, A. *Le Socialsime et la révolution française: études sur les idées socialistes en France de 1789 à 1796*. Paris: Alcan, 1899.

Lovejoy, Arthur. *The Great Chain of Being: A Study of the History of an Idea*. Cambridge, Mass.: Harvard University Press, 1936.

Lucas, Colin. *The Structure of the Terror: The Example of Javogues and the Loire*. London: Oxford University Press, 1973.

McManners, John. *The French Revolution and the Church*. London: SPCK Publications, 1969.

———*Death and the Enlightenment: Changing Attitudes to Death among Christians and Unbelievers in Eighteenth-Century France*. Oxford: Oxford University Press, 1981.

Mandrou, Robert. *De la culture populaire au XVIIe et XVIIIe siècles: la bibliothèque bleue de Troyes*. Paris: Stock, 1964.

Manuel, Frank E. *The Eighteenth Century Confronts the Gods*. Cambridge, Mass.: Harvard University Press, 1959.

Marejko, Jan. *Jean-Jacques Rousseau et la dérive totalitaire*. Lausanne: l'Age d'Or, 1984.

Marion, Marcel. *Dictionnaire des institutions de la France aux XVIIe et XVIIIe siècles*. 1923. Reprint. Paris: Picard, 1968.

Martin, Jean Clément. *Blancs et bleus dans la Vendée déchirée*. Paris: Gallimard, 1986.

Mauzi, René. *L'Idée du bonheur au dix-huitième siècle*. Paris: A. Colin, 1960.

Mazauric, Claude. *Jacobinisme et révolution, autour du bicentenaire de Quatre-vingt-neuf*. Paris: Editions sociales, 1984.

Méthivier, Hubert. *L'Ancien Régime*. Vendôme: Presses Universitaires de France, 1979.

Meyer, Jean. *La Noblesse bretonne au XVIIIe siècle*. Paris: Flammarion, 1972.

Michelet, Jules. *Histoire de la révolution*. Paris: Gallimard (Pléiade), 1952.

Moore, Barrington. *Social Origins of Dictatorship and Democracy: Lord and Peasant in the Making of the Modern World*. Boston: Beacon Press, 1966.

Mornet, Daniel. *Les Origines intellectuelles de la révolution française, 1751–1787*. Paris: A. Colin, 1959.

Nicolas, Jean, ed. *Mouvements populaires et consciences sociales, XVIe au XIXe siècles: actes du colloque de Paris, 24–26 mai 1984*. Paris: CNRS, 1985.

Ozouf, Mona. *La Fête révolutionnaire, 1789–1799*. Paris: Gallimard, 1976.

Palmer, Robert Roswell. *Catholics and Unbelievers in Eighteenth-Century France*. Princeton: Princeton University Press, 1939.

———*The Age of Democratic Revolution: A Political History of Europe and America, 1760–1800*. 2 vols. Princeton: Princeton University Press, 1959–1964.

Patrick, Alison. *The Men of the First French Republic: Political Alignments in the National Convention of 1792*. Baltimore: Johns Hopkins University Press, 1972.

Perrot, Claude. *Caen au XVIIIe siècle: Genèse d'une ville moderne*. Paris: Mouton, 1975.

Plongeron, Bernard. *Conscience religieuse en révolution: regards sur l'historiographie religieuse de la révolution française*. Paris: Picard, 1969.

———*Théologie et politique au siècle des lumières, 1770–1820*. Geneva: Droz, 1973.

Popkin, Jeremy. *The Right-Wing Press in France, 1792–1800*. Chapel Hill: University of North Carolina Press, 1980.

Préclin, E. *Les Jansénistes du XVIIIe siècle et la constitution civile du clergé: le développement du richérisme, sa propagation dans le bas clergé, 1713–1791*. Paris: J. Gamber, 1929.

Quéniart, Jean. *Les Hommes, l'église, et dieu dans la France du XVIIIe siècle*. Paris: Hachette, 1978.

Reddy, William. *The Rise of Market Culture: The Textile Trade and French Society, 1750–1900*. Cambridge: Cambridge University Press, 1984.

———*Money and Liberty in Modern Europe: A Critique of Modern Understanding*. Cambridge: Cambridge University Press, 1987.

Reinhard, Marcel. *Le Grand Carnot*. 2 vols. Paris: Hachette, 1950, 1952.

———*Nouvelle histoire de Paris: la révolution, 1778–1799*. Paris: Hachette, 1971.

Richard, Guy. *Noblesse d'affaires au XVIIIe siècle*. Paris: A. Colin, 1974.

Rihs, Charles. *Les philosophes utopistes: le mythe de la cité communautaire en France au XVIIIe siècle*. Paris: Marcel Rivière, 1970.

Roche, Daniel. *Le Siècle des lumières en province: académies et académiciens provinciaux, 1680–1780*. Paris: Mouton, 1978.

———*Le Peuple de Paris: essai sur la culture populaire au XVIIIe siècle*. Paris: Aubier, 1981.

Rosanvalon, Pierre. *Le Capitalisme utopique: critique de l'idéologie economique*. Paris: Seuil, 1979.

Rose, R. B. *The Enragés: Socialists of the French Revolution*. Sydney: Sydney University Press, 1965.

———*Gracchus Babeuf: The First Revolutionary Communist*. Stanford: Stanford University Press, 1978.

———*The Making of the Sans-culottes*. Manchester: Manchester University Press, 1983.

Royot, Daniel, ed. *La France et l'esprit de 1776*. Clermont: Université de Clermont-Ferrand, 1977.

Rudé, Georges. *The Crowd in the French Revolution*. Oxford: Oxford University Press, 1959.

Saint-Jacob, Pierre de. *Les Paysans de la Bourgogne du nord au dernier siècle de l'ancien régime*. Dijon: Imprimerie Bernigaud and Privat, 1960.

Scholem, Gershom. *Du Frankisme au Jacobinisme: la vie de Moses Dobruska, alias Franz Thomas von Schönfeld, alias Junius Frey*. Paris: Gallimard, 1981.

Schwartz, Joel. *The Sexual Politics of Jean-Jacques Rousseau*. Chicago: University of Chicago Press, 1984.

Sewell, William H. *Work and Revolution in France: The Language of Labour from the Old Regime to 1848*. Cambridge: Cambridge University Press, 1980.

Shklar, Judith. *Men and Citizens: A Study of Rousseau's Social Theory*. Cambridge: Cambridge University Press, 1969.

Singer, Brian C. J. *Society, Theory, and the French Revolution: Studies in Revolutionary Imagery.* London: Macmillan, 1986.

Skocpol, Theda. *States and Social Revolutions: A Comparative Analysis of France, Russia, and China.* Cambridge: Cambridge University Press, 1979.

Soboul, Albert. *The Parisian Sans-culottes and the French Revolution, 1793–1796.* Trans. Gwynne Lewis. Oxford: Oxford University Press, 1964.

———ed. *Girondins et Montagnards: actes du colloque, Sorbonne, 14 décembre 1975.* Paris: Société des Etudes Robespierristes, 1980.

Spencer, Samia I., ed. *French Women and the Age of the Enlightenment.* Bloomington: Indiana University Press, 1984.

Starobinski, Jean. *Jean-Jacques Rousseau: la transparence et l'obstacle.* Paris: Gallimard. 1971.

———*1789: les emblèmes de la raison.* Paris: Flammarion, 1973.

Stone, Bailey. *The Parlements of Paris, 1774–1789.* Chapel Hill: University of North Carolina Press, 1981.

Suratteau, J. R. *La République française: certitude et controverses.* Paris: Presses Universitaires de France, 1972.

Sydenham, Michael. *The French Revolution.* New York: Capricorn, 1966.

Tacket, Timothy. *Priest and Parish in Eighteenth-Century France: A Social and Political Study of the Curés in a Diocese of Dauphiné, 1750–1791.* Princeton: Princeton University Press, 1977.

Talmon, Jacob Leib. *The Origins of Totalitarian Democracy.* New York: Praeger, 1960.

Tilly, Charles. *The Vendée.* Cambridge, Mass.: Harvard University Press, 1964.

Tocqueville, Alexis de. *The Old Regime and the French Revolution.* 1856. Garden City, N.Y.: Anchor Books, 1955.

Van Kley, Dale. *The Jansenists and the Expulsion of the Jesuits from France.* New Haven: Yale University Press, 1975.

Venturi, Franco. *Utopia and Reform in the Enlightenment.* Cambridge: Cambridge University Press, 1971.

Verger, Jacques, ed. *Histoire des universités en France.* Toulouse: Privat, 1986.

Vovelle, Michel. *La Mentalité révolutionnaire: société et mentalité sous la révolution française.* Paris: Editions sociales, 1985.

———*Théodore Desorgues, ou la désorganisation: Aix-Paris, 1763–1808.* Paris: Seuil, 1985.

Williams, Gwyn A. *Artisans and Sans-Culottes: Popular Movements in France and Britain during the French Revolution.* New York: Norton, 1969.

Woloch, Isser. *Jacobin Legacy: The Democratic Movement under the Directory.* Princeton: Princeton University Press, 1970.

Woronoff, D. *La République bourgeoise de thermidor à brumaire, 1794–1799.* Paris: Seuil, 1972.

Name Index

Adams, John (1744–1826), 86, 100, 111, 118, 119, 167, 175, 177, 191, 199, 200, 201, 213, 227, 251

Adams, Samuel (1735–1826), 205, 260

Andros, Sir Edmund, Governor (1637–1714), 41

Babeuf, Gracchus (1760–1797): and Babouvism, 6, 128, 186, 190, 218, 268, 269

Bacon, Nathaniel (1647–1676), 25, 41, 87

Bailyn, Bernard, 181, 291

Baltimore, 91, 126

Barère, Bertrand (1755–1841), 2

Barnave, Antoine (1761–1793), 234, 238–240, 247, 259

Beard, Charles, 204, 205

Bercovitch, Sacvan, 21

Bonaparte, Napoleon (1769–1821), 8, 9, 87, 135, 154, 173, 209, 220, 232, 239, 257, 265, 270, 272, 285n3

Bordeaux, 128, 129

Boston, 18, 21, 32, 36, 41, 67, 72, 75, 84, 89, 95, 98, 108, 115, 173, 186, 188

Boullée, Etienne (1728–1799), 135

Bourbons, *see* Louis XIII; Louis XIV; Louis XV; Louis XVI

Bradford, William (1590–1657), 17, 73

Bradstreet, Anne (1612–1672), 30

Brissot, Jacques, called Brissot de Warville (1754–1793), 113, 182, 205, 227, 239, 242, 247, 252

Britain, *see* England; Ireland; Scotland

Burke, Edmund (1729–1797), 179, 229, 271

Calonne, Charles de (1734–1801), 219–220, 222, 233

Calvin, Jean (1509–1564), 28, 92. *See also* Religion: Calvinism

Canada, 16, 88, 118, 122, 127, 153, 171, 193

Carnot, Lazare (1753–1823), 256

Cato (95–45 B.C.), 207

Charrière, Belle de Zuylen de (1746–1805), 162

Chateaubriand, René (1768–1848), 8

Chesapeake, 17, 22–25, 26, 45

Colbert, Jean-Baptiste (1619–1683), 77, 78, 139

Condorcet, Marie Jean Caritat de (1743–1794), 136, 226, 241, 242, 251

Connecticut, 16, 18, 30, 36, 47, 88, 97. *See also* New Haven

Constant, Benjamin (1767–1830), 8, 9, 122

Corday, Charlotte (1768–1793), 253

Corneille, Pierre (1606–1684), 62, 69, 70

Danton, George (1759–1794), 162, 256

David, Louis (1748–1825), 162, 165, 180, 241, 247

Descartes, René (1596–1650), 95

Desmoulins, Camille (1760–1794), 250

Diderot, Denis (1713–1784), 122, 136, 137, 165

Dumouriez, Charles du Périer (1739–1823), 252

Edwards, Jonathan (1703–1758), 15, 87, 92, 94, 100, 108, 118. *See also* Awakening

Subject Index